D0163141

The Affluent Consumer

The Affluent Consumer

Marketing and Selling the Luxury Lifestyle

Ronald D. Michman and Edward M. Mazze

PRAEGER

Westport, Connecticut
London

Library of Congress Cataloging-in-Publication Data

Michman, Ronald D.
The affluent consumer : marketing and selling the luxury lifestyle / Ronald D. Michman and Edward M. Mazze.
p. cm.
Includes bibliographical references and index.
ISBN 0–275–99282–9
1. Affluent consumers—United States. 2. Luxuries—United States—Marketing. 3. Target marketing—United States. I. Mazze, Edward M. II. Title.
HF5415.33.U6M53 2006
658.8'343—dc22 2006021766

British Library Cataloguing in Publication Data is available.

Library of Congress Catalog Card Number: 2006021766
ISBN: 0–275–99282–9

First published in 2006

Praeger Publishers, 88 Post Road West, Westport, CT 06881
An imprint of Greenwood Publishing Group, Inc.
www.praeger.com

Printed in the United States of America

The paper used in this book complies with the Permanent Paper Standard issued by the National Information Standards Organization (Z39.48–1984).

10 9 8 7 6 5 4 3 2 1

With love for Laura, Carol, Marc Ross, Andy, and Maxine and
remembrance for Ruth, Rose and Morris.

Ronald D. Michman

To Sharon, my wife, partner, and friend, and to my
daughter Candace and my son Thomas.

Edward M. Mazze

Contents

Preface

The greatest challenge for business executives is to update themselves with changes in the marketplace. There are new groups of consumers emerging with unique needs and wants. This book deals with the affluent consumer and is about building long-term relationships with this market segment and developing marketing programs to reach them.

Affluent market dynamics have developed an expanded role for marketing strategy. There are few books depicting the affluent market, and those that exist report on research studies of millionaires or advise salespeople on how to sell to the affluent market. A number of articles have focused on broad strategies for marketers to reach this growing market.

Although there have always been affluent consumers, a greater number of households have been attaining this financial status each year. The cause of the greatest increase in the affluent population has been the growth of the female labor force and the dual-income family. The new rich can be segmented by many factors, including lifestyle, age, gender, and ethnic background, in contrast to previous affluent households that consisted primarily of families headed by white Anglo-Saxon men. The new rich represent new challenges and opportunities for retailers, manufacturers of consumer products, and service providers. This market is valued at billions of dollars each year.

This book represents one effort to close some of the gaps in the literature on marketing to the affluent. The book emphasizes a comprehensive perspective on this special market, with a focus on strategic decision making. Past books do not consider cultural forces affecting this market or the psychological and sociological base for purchasing behavior. The economic development of the United States in the past decade has had a profound impact on the nature and structure of the affluent market.

The definition of the affluent market has been limited in the past. This book focuses on the affluent consumer, defined by income and assets, and upscale consumers and others who trade up in their buying of products and services. This new definition establishes a larger mass affluent market and submarkets. Our interdisciplinary approach in writing this book uses materials from economics, psychology, and sociology to explain how the affluent consumer thinks and acts. New research findings illustrate how many companies are developing a competitive differential in dealing with this luxury market.

The first chapter presents an overview of the current status of the affluent market. The second chapter demonstrates the cultural gap between affluent consumers of today and the past, and the third chapter emphasizes the pitfalls of stereotypical thinking when developing strategies to target the affluent market. The fourth and fifth chapters present statistical and demographic information concerning changes over the years in the affluent market. Chapters six, seven, and eight develop comprehensive strategies to segment the affluent market. Chapter nine redefines affluent consumer lifestyles so that marketers can better understand the evolving cultural factors that affect this market. The final chapter focuses on the myths, realities, and future predictions of this market.

This book is directed to business executives and future business executives and can be used as supplementary reading for college and executive training courses in marketing strategy and consumer behavior. To avoid cumbersome references within the text, much of the source materials are listed in the bibliography. Hopefully this book will prevent mistakes and enable marketers to take greater advantage of opportunities as they attempt to reach the affluent market.

Acknowledgments

As in writing any book, a team of hardworking individuals provided research, clerical, and administrative help. Special thanks are given to Kathy Huot and Kathryn Guilbert at the University of Rhode Island who typed the chapters and specifically to Kathy Huot who handled the administrative activities in getting the manuscript ready for publication. We are grateful to the many graduate assistants and graduate students at the University of Rhode Island who supported the authors' research activities by collecting data and asking the right questions. Many companies provided examples to describe how they market to affluent customers.

Ron Michman would like to thank his daughter, Laura Michman Dessel, who contributed insights into affluent consumer behavior in small towns, and his grandson Andy for relating the latest trends in teen purchasing. His grandson Marc Ross provided helpful applications for chapter 4, "Changing Economic Dimensions." Carol Michman offered fresh insights into shopping behavior on the Internet, and special thanks are extended to Maxine Berlin for her perceptions of the affluent. Edward M. Mazze would like to thank his wife, Sharon, who reviewed the entire manuscript as a practitioner who deals with this market, and his colleagues at various academic institutions who provided guidance and encouraged him to continue his scholarly work while serving as dean of the business schools at Seton Hall University, Temple University, the University of North Carolina at Charlotte, and the University of Rhode Island. This book could not have happened without the support of Provost M. Beverly Swan at the University of Rhode Island who provided the climate for him to pursue his scholarly research.

Our family and friends deserve sincere thanks for their support and encouragement. Even with a team effort, any errors or omissions are our responsibility.

CHAPTER 1

Wealth in America

The number of rich Americans is growing. In 2001 over 3 million families filing federal income tax returns reported more than $200,000 in income, as compared to about 1.5 million in 1995. In 2004 there were 8.2 million households with more than $1 million in net worth excluding their primary residence. Marketers attempt to penetrate this market by developing special products and services, building brands through promotional efforts, using prestige pricing, and emphasizing customer service. Today, the affluent consumer can be reached best by emphasizing value in all marketing activities.

Affluent markets have been changing faster than other markets. The affluent market is composed of varying economic, lifestyle, and psychographic market segments, each with their individual values, priorities, and purchasing patterns. The composition of the affluent market has shifted. Previously, marketing efforts were aimed at well-educated, predominantly middle-aged or older white male Caucasians who often inherited their wealth. This segment is now more difficult to define. It includes entrepreneurs, commissioned salespeople, business owners, entertainers, self-employed professionals, highly paid corporate executives, professional athletes, inheritors, members of ethnic groups, retirees, dual-income families, and widows. For example, *Town & Country*, published for over a hundred years, has redefined its coverage in response to a changing affluent population mix. The magazine was once directed to debutantes and *Social Register* types. Now, with advertising revenues dropping 50 percent between 1988 and 1993, audience coverage is more inclusive and encompasses Asians, blacks, and Hispanics, who are in the top income brackets. The age of the average reader in 2003 was 49, down from age 59 in 1994. Circulation has declined from 1994 to 2003; however, advertising pages have more than doubled with a new emphasis on promoting luxury brands. More than 80 percent of the affluent are dual-income families. The size of the affluent market has increased from 11 percent in 1960 to 15 percent in 1980 to 24 percent in 2000.

The composition of students at universities and colleges has changed. Formerly, white males were predominant. Now, enrollment on college campuses throughout the United States is 55 percent females and 45 percent males. As a result, more women enter professions or have careers in management, business, or finance, and their incomes are increasing. The population of ethnic minorities including Hispanics, blacks, and Asians is increasing, and they are entering college at a higher rate. For example, *Savoy Magazine*, launched in February 2001, is aimed at upper-class blacks.

The wealthy of a generation ago were not only rich but knew that they were rich and that they were different. Today's affluent may not feel rich because of the costs of housing, child care and school tuition. They continue with the same buying behavior that they followed in their past lives, which starts at an emotional level. However, the higher their income, the more likely they will shop at prestigious specialty stores—purchasing Armani menswear , Loro Piona knitwear, and Lacoste tennis wear—and at the same time shop at stores like Target and Wal-Mart. They live in wealthy neighborhoods and drive luxury automobiles, such as the Mercedes Benz S Class sedan, the Porsche 911 sports car, and the Ferrari F 355 Spider convertible. Today's affluent consumers are more value conscious and better informed than those of past generations. The pace of change in the affluent market is causing marketers to reconsider their approach to this market, particularly the way they communicate with this type of consumer. Marketers are doing more research. The key questions they must consider include the following: How do you define the affluent market? Should the market be divided into segments? What are the distinctions between affluent and upscale consumers?

AFFLUENT MARKETS ARE PUZZLING

According to *Money Magazine*, people do not believe they are affluent until they have $2.5 million in wealth. There is a denial of affluence even when the minimum income for this group is $75,000, with average total assets of about $665,000.[1]

The Mendelsohn Group has surveyed the affluent for the past 29 years. Frequent revisions in the definition of affluence have taken place based on changes in income and assets. In the 2005 survey, the qualifying definition of affluence changed from a household income of $75,000 or more to $85,000 or more. The annual Mendelsohn Affluent Survey was the first syndicated measurement to concentrate on the affluent U.S. market. Information for the survey is collected by a mail questionnaire using a sample of over 50,000 adults. The survey collects information about the affluent, including their public activities, leisure/athletic activities, travel, investments/assets, ownership of goods, household expenditures, entertainment/alcohol consumption, computer/Internet usage and purchases, demographics, and media consumption. The Mendelsohn Survey's definition includes three categories:

1. Least Affluent
2. Middle Segment
3. Most Affluent[2]

Consumers in the least and middle affluent market segments do not feel they are wealthy. The most important reason is that approximately 80 percent of the affluent market is comprised of dual-income families. The affluent constitute 24 percent of the population. There are also the ultrarich, in the $50 million to $20 billion category. The affluent spend twice the national average and earn half the nation's income. In 2002, the United States had 47 percent of the world's wealthiest people.[3] In 1990, there were 66 billionaires in the United States; in 2004 there were 313. The high end of the market spends as much as $4.5 million to $33 million for Claude Monet paintings and $51,000 to $11 million for John Singer Sargent portraits.

Today, wealth is based on income, occupation, and education rather than birth. There are more than 16 million U.S. households—about 14 percent of the total—with annual incomes of $100,000 and 12 million more with annual incomes between $75,000 and $99,999. The number of households earning $100,000 or more a year has increased every year since 1970. The number of households in the United States in 2003 with at least $1 million in assets, excluding primary residences and retirement accounts, was over 3.8 million; and the number of households with more than $500,000 in net worth, excluding primary residences, was 10.5 million, as compared to 3.3 million in 2002. This represents a market opportunity for almost every consumer goods company. The wealthy have accumulated enough financial resources to maintain their buying capacity in economic downturns. These households together account for $6 trillion in assets. This market responds well to market segmentation strategies such as niche and lifestyle marketing. They spend more on expensive products such as ultraluxury cars that sell at prices of up to $350,000 with options such as armor plating.[4] A few own summer homes in the Hamptons worth millions or more; they pay millions for private airplanes and may even purchase yachts for $75 million or more.

PUZZLING TERMINOLOGY

The affluent market can be defined by income and total net assets. But what is an upscale consumer market? How do you define a market that is not necessarily upscale but trading-up? Should marketers separate the affluent market from the upscale market and from the market that trades up?

The upscale market is designated as relatively prosperous, educated, and stylish. The definition is more psychographic than demographic. The upscale market, in some instances, can be an extension of the affluent market. By contrast, a market that trades up accepts the symbols of more affluent consumers as their own. Sears' customers can purchase the Lands' End brand, or they may spend their money on expensive wines, a Patek Philippe watch, a Gucci handbag, or designer clothing.

Consumers who trade up on occasion tend to be motivated to achieve something. There is a striving for what they perceive as better consumer goods, and this is grounded in their underlying motives and attitudes. Godiva chocolate in the candy industry has attracted not only the affluent and upscale markets but also those who desire, in their perception, to enrich special occasions. Product differentiation strategies used by Godiva and many perfume manufacturers target consumers who are willing to spend more for the convenience, appearance, and prestige of better packaging. Many who comprise this market are aspiring affluents. This group can be identified by their expressed and implied aspirations, not their household incomes. BMW is offering lower-priced models for this market segment.

The affluent market includes the upscale and trade-up markets. A Bergdorf Goodman customer may shop at Sears. This is known as cross-shopping and a manifestation of downscale consumption. Cross-shopping also means a Sears' customer buys a Liz Claiborne blouse at Neiman Marcus. Automobile manufacturers such as Nissan, with Infinity, and Honda, with Acura, have targeted the upscale market. Other retailers have developed store brands for upscale and affluent consumers such as the following:

- Federated, with the Tasso Elba brand of Italian-inspired apparel and the Hotel Collection brand of linens priced as high as $1,350
- Saks, with the Platinum brand of Italian-made separates and the 5/48 brand of women's sportswear

Retailers such as Target and Costco provide customers with upscale brands such as Calphalon cookware, Ralph Lauren apparel, and Waterford crystal. Target has made a strong bid for the patronage of affluent consumers. The use of this strategy helps discounters and upscale department stores compete with specialty stores offering high-quality merchandise. While many upscale consumers desire quality store brands, the retailer assumes the risk and cost of promoting their own private brands without assistance from the manufacturer.

Firms serving the affluent market are also able to target a number of segments through the use of customization. In previous years, manufacturing companies attempted to standardize production, products, and services. Firms developed brands targeted to a mass market to profit from economies of scale. Through new technology, marketers are now able to interact with each customer by customizing products, services, and communications to specific customer groups. Levi's can produce jeans based on an individual's measurements, and Dell Computer can build a personalized computer system within a few days. Through customization, the firm is able to develop a competitive advantage.

An unusual channel for serving the affluent and upscale consumer is the designer resale shop. The National Association of Resale & Thrift Shops estimates that their membership has more than doubled from 1993 to 2003, to about 15,000.[5] Examples of the prices at these shops include Gucci boots (originally priced at $1,050) selling for $500 and a Prada skirt (originally $600) offered at $160.

SOCIAL CLASS MISCONCEPTIONS

Social class is not determined by a single variable but by a combination of factors. Culture, age, family life cycle, and lifestyle influence the purchasing behavior of social classes. Social class, based on lifestyle and income, allows for a corporate executive or a heavyweight-boxing champion to own a Rolls Royce.

Affluent social classes differ in their preferences, activities, interests, opinions, dress, and recreational activities. Here are recent changes in describing social classes.[6]

Upper-Upper (about 1%)—the social elite whose sources of income are inherited wealth, trust funds and real estate. They donate to charity and their children go to the finest private schools. They serve as a reference group for others. Their household income is well over $200,000, and their average total assets are over $3 million. They have a number of homes. They belong to ski resorts like the Yellowstone Club, a 14,000-acre club in Montana with its own golf course and a lodge with three five-star quality restaurants. To belong to this club, members need a minimum net worth of over $3.5 million to afford an initiation fee of $250,000, annual dues of $16,000, and one of the 864 homesites that cost from $1 million to $3 million. They make up the over 30,000 names listed in the *Social Register* and for the most part have the same ethnicity—white Anglo-Saxon—and live in or around major urban areas.

Lower-Upper (about 2%)—those who have attained success through achievement in their profession or industry. They believe work is more important than leisure. Their roots are generally in the middle class. They tend to purchase status symbols such as expensive homes, yachts, and foreign automobiles. They are the new rich. Their household income is from $100,000 to $199,999, and their average total assets are over $1 million. Half of all households in this category are headed by a 45- to 64-year-old.

Upper-Middle (about 12%)—professionals, corporate executives, or those who own their own businesses. Many are dual-income households. Education for their children is important. Members of this group engage in cultural activities. They are civic-minded and are leaders in their community. Expenditures for home decorating and home entertainment are important. Renovated kitchens are popular, with an average makeover running $58,000 in which a granite countertop can cost over $15,000. Household income is from $75,000 to $99,999, with average total assets of about $665,000.

As the ranks of the upper class and the upper middle class have grown in the past 25 years, few consumers identify themselves as affluent based on income alone. According to a *New York Times*/CBS News Poll, over 90 percent of families earning $75,000 a year in 1993 defined themselves as middle class. Inflation means that $75,000 in 1993 is equivalent to $100,000 in 2003.[7]

The American consumer is part of a class system that allows for social mobility. Most Americans do not think about social class but do think about becoming rich. Social class mobility has often been limited to adjacent classes. Education, income, occupation, achievement, and marriage allow upward mobility. The middle class, which consists of the upscale consumer, is adjacent to the lower end of the affluent social class and is composed of executives and professionals, small-business owners, and white-collar and top-level blue-collar skilled workers who live in nice homes in good neighborhoods. The middle class constitutes about 40 percent of the population. Occasionally splurging and treating themselves to the best or premium brands is one method they use to separate themselves from their peers. They are concerned with fashion and recognized brands. Within this class, there is a segment that wants to purchase luxury items in stores such as Nordstrom and Bloomingdales.

Many consumers have turned to a comfortable lifestyle where their attitudes and behavior depends on particular situations rather than overall lifestyle philosophy. The cross-shopping behavior of affluent consumers who make purchases at Neiman Marcus, Bergdorf Goodman, and Target is a manifestation of lifestyle segmentation. Lifestyle segmentation is one way of dividing customers into meaningful buyer groups. Consumers reflect their social class, social position, and status by their behavior and purchases. There is a trend away from social conformity. Individual style and taste is combined with the desire for convenience, material luxuries, physical protection, leisure and a safe and pleasant living environment. These factors should be considered when communicating with this market segment.

The increasing number of families with dual-incomes and the number of women in professional positions in the workplace and with high incomes have impacted social class structure. The number of women earning more than $100,000 a year was 1 out of every 48 working full time in 2001, as compared to 1 out of 143 in 1991. Dual-income families and women in professional positions can withstand inflation and tough economic times. They can purchase in a short time period the products their parents worked for years to acquire.

When targeting affluent consumers, marketers need to carefully define the different segments of the wealthy. The wealthy can be divided into the affluent (early adopters), the Boomers (55+), young professionals, baby boomers (45–55 group), dual-income families, families with children, and Generation Y; they can also be divided by income ranges. Included in this market are the nontraditional affluent consumers, the double-income with no kids segment, and the gay market with college education and employment in professional or managerial positions. Another segment is affluent blacks composed of about 25 percent of the total black market. *Savoy Magazine* targets blacks with advertisements for automobiles such as the Audi A6 and the Lincoln Navigator SUV. Purchases of affluent blacks also extend to expensive apparel and many other product categories.[8] With about 20 percent of the 11 million Hispanic households having digital cable and 25 percent having satellite telecom, the numbers of affluent Hispanics are growing each year. Advertisers like American Airlines, Procter & Gamble, Johnson & Johnson, L'Oreal, PepsiCo, Toyota Motor Corporation, and Home Depot have increased their advertising budgets to reach this affluent market. Asian Americans are the fastest growing group in the affluent market. They account for 5 percent of affluent households, up from less than 1 percent in 2002. The average net worth of affluent Asian Americans was $2.9 million. Many are business owners or members of professions, such as dentists and physicians.

Distinctions may also be used, such as lower middle class, upper middle class and lower upper class. A middle-class family may select wall-to-wall carpeting, while the wealthy family buys oriental rugs. The preferences of social classes can change over the years. Affluent tastes can reflect the ownership of a Ford Explorer, which is considered utilitarian rather than luxurious. The ownership of multiple items indicates an affluent society but not necessarily a wealthy consumer. Families have three or four telephones, a cellular telephone, an extra telephone line for the computer, and a number of televisions sets. Social class has a strong influence on preference in cars, clothing, home furnishings, and leisure activities; and numerous psychological and social pleasures exist in purchasing these products.

Activities, interests, opinions, ownership of assets, age, race, and family structure are also factors used to define an affluent consumer. Occupation, house location by zip codes, educational attainment, and sources of income are other ways. For example, participation in recreational activities is influenced by social class membership. Upper-class consumers attend the theater, operas, and concerts and play squash more than consumers in other classes. The very wealthy are buying ownership shares of professional sports teams for prestige value. Wealthy Americans spend more in nearly all consumer products categories.

The affluent society at the turn of the twentieth century included the upper-upper and lower-upper social classes. The Rockefellers and Vanderbilts were a part of this group, and their heirs had inherited their wealth. Sources of income including real estate and trust funds are characteristic of membership in the upper-upper social classes. The lower-upper social class includes members of the new rich that include business executives.

Today, the new affluent social class is comprised of dual-income families, women, entrepreneurs, and many other groups. Entrepreneurship is easy to understand when small businesses make up more than 99 percent of all employers in the United States. There are 23 million small businesses employing about 50 percent of all private sector workers and creating 75 percent of the net new jobs in the economy. One does not need to be a Rockefeller or a Vanderbilt to be included in the affluent target market. The roots of the changing affluent social class are generally in the middle class. They tend to purchase expensive homes, yachts, and automobiles. They join clubs within their communities. Education for their children is an important consideration, and private school education is sometimes preferred. Members of this group prefer to talk about ideas and engage in cultural activities. They are civic minded. There is a concern with fashion and the ownership of the correct brands. They want prestigious brands at low prices. They will also spend on superpremium items. They are customers of Barneys, Channel, Coach, Dior, Gucci, Polo, Ralph Lauren, Prada, and Tiffany & Co. stores.

David Brooks, in his book *Bobos in Paradise*, describes the conflict between the materialism of the bourgeoisie and the culture of the bohemians in the formation of a new upper social class. This new upper social class, composed of those who have their roots in the bourgeoisie and the bohemian ways of life, can now get together at a Pottery Barn, a Starbucks, a museum shop, a Nature Company, or any other institution that targets educated affluents. The rituals of acquisition and consumption include spending on necessities, such as the improvement of a bathroom or kitchen, but not spending a great sum on a sound system or a wide-screen television. It is also acceptable to spend $50 for a hoe in a "gourmet" gardening store but not $9 for an ordinary hoe. The $50 hoe is perceived as a so-called professional tool. Educated elites spend huge sums for items that were once cheap, such as coffee at $5 a cup, a T-shirt for $75, or even beach sandals for $100. There is a new code of correctness as some items have been elevated to demonstrate an uplifting experience and self-expression.

Social class is an important variable in the selection of retail stores for shopping. Nordstrom has targeted affluent and upscale consumers. Other consumers would likely patronize a store like Nordstrom only to make a special purchase. Once upon a time, social class lines were distinct. The poor shopped at discount stores, and the wealthy shopped on North Michigan Avenue in Chicago, Fifth Avenue in New York, and Rodeo Drive in Los Angeles. Today, easy credit, the Internet, designer brand extensions, and counterfeits have merged social class distinction. A new mass affluent social class has been created as all social classes shop at Costco and Sam's Club. The Internet has made it possible for marketers to profit from significant market niches. Cross-shopping has become characteristic of the twenty-first century.

A HUGE AND GROWING MARKET

In previous generations, the size of the affluent market was relatively stable. Since 1970 the number of households earning $100,000 or more a year has increased every year. The affluent market is likely to respond well to market segmentation strategies such as niche and lifestyle marketing. From an income perspective, affluent and upscale consumers spend more than the general population on luxury products. They control more than half the wealth in the United States.

Affluent households are concentrated in the Northeast, in the Mid-Atlantic States, and on the West Coast. The largest metropolitan areas include the largest concentrations of people earning $100,000 to $199,999 a year. The affluent market buys jewelry, antiques, homes, vacations, and services such as financial planning, insurance, personal training and child care. For example, the number of certified financial planners grew from 23,350 in 1991 to 45,000 in 2003, according to the Certified Financial Planners Board.

This market is inclined to dress conservatively since most of the affluent are between 45 and 64 years old. Lifestyles are focused heavily on careers, private clubs, social causes, and the arts. Today, by using information technology, marketers can determine the purchasing patterns of the affluent in order to find the best way to reach them. The affluent also shop by catalog and the Internet, and they use private shopping services at specialty and department stores.

Fashion appeals to the affluent. Retailers attract the affluent consumer for the $1000 leather jacket or handbag. Product categories that are highly visible or that serve as symbols of social class, such as jewelry, clothing and automobile ownership, are important to them. Leisure activities include the theater and membership in social and athletic clubs. The lower end of the affluent social class and upscale consumers view prosperity as being college educated, being more sophisticated, being more discerning in their activities, living in fine homes, driving expensive automobiles, and being well traveled.

Many in the upper-middle class prospered during the 1990s by accumulating wealth as investments rose to record levels. This lower end of the affluent social class has a propensity to express confidence in their behavior. They are concerned about the ability of their children to maintain their lifestyle. They register their children for private schools years in advance. Education is an important goal. Charitable work is also important.

To reach these customers, the best strategies include the following:

- Recognition and isolation of specific group members
- Identifying psychological differences that influence purchasing
- Recognition of consumption patterns that define identity
- Discerning consumption tastes and preferences
- Recognizing mobility/stability dimensions that help to understand lifestyle
- Realizing that social class influence for some items may not be as persuasive as previously thought, without the use of other variables like lifestyle

A SELF-IMAGE MIRROR

Marketers can affect consumers' buying behavior by influencing the degree to which consumers perceive a product or service to be self-relevant. Therefore, marketers develop broad images that match the target market's self-image.

Consumers endeavor to maintain a favorable self-image by accepting experiences that promote their self-image and by rejecting experiences that tarnish it. Self-image affects the choice of lifestyles and consequently influences the consumer's purchase decision process.

Although his or her self-concept may change over time, the consumer gains identity which will provide for consistent and coherent behavior through an indeterminate time span depending on the individual.[9] Self-image has four components. First, there is the real self, or the way individuals actually are. Second, there is the way that others perceive the individual. Frequently, this is referred to as the "looking-glass self." Third, there is the way the individual would like to be. This goal may or may not be viewed realistically and is called the ideal self. Fourth, the way the individual sees himself or herself is referred to as the self-image. It is a combination of the real self and the ideal self. Self-concept has its limitations. For example, which self will the consumer try to satisfy in selecting a brand?

When viewing the actual self-image, the affluent consumer will say, "I have achieved much in life." When viewing the ideal self-image, the affluent consumer will say, "I have made it." Marketing strategies will be more effective if the target market's self-images are matched or enhanced. Marketers could appeal to the affluent consumer in the following ways:

- Offering a unique product
- Charging a relatively high price
- Distributing through an exclusive outlet
- Having special events
- Providing special services

These strategies are directed toward achievement. The Lenox Company has used these strategies in marketing fine china, and Lenox has extended its product line to crystal candles, silver-plated hollowware, and jewelry.

LIFESTYLE MARKETS ARE MORE ACCURATE

Marketers who appeal to the affluent market must keep up with changes in their market and how their customers think. The perceptions of consumers change and will frequently vary with age or geographic region. American culture emphasizes achievement. The symbols of achievement change over time. Visual cues are often important as status symbols, such as wearing apparel designed by Gucci. In some geographical regions, wearing expensive cowboy boots is a desired status symbol. Affluent status symbols vary over the life cycle of the individual. A desirable status symbol for a young affluent couple may be a sailboat; for a middle-aged consumer, a custom-built home in a prestigious neighborhood; and for a senior citizen, a luxurious condominium in a resort community.

Lifestyle can reveal a more accurate picture of consumer motivation than affluence alone. For example, a dentist earning $500,000 per year with assets of $3 million who is interested in purchasing a bicycle might be a fitness buff; a recreational rider; a nature lover; or an individual who desires to jog, swim, and cycle. Lifestyle marketing strategies should be combined in order to reach affluent markets. Lifestyle market segmentation strategies will enhance target marketing and make niche strategies possible. For example, lifestyle encompasses such activities as sailing and skiing and such interests as the collection of art objects and antiques.

Affluent consumers who are dual-income couples are prone to performing one or more activities at the same time. They will also pay others to perform work because time is more important than money. Companies aiming to serve a time-conscious affluent market target convenient services for this group.

Lifestyle fragmentation is most noticeable among affluent consumers as they increasingly emphasize style and taste. Cross-shopping is apparent as affluent consumers purchase pillows and sheets at Target, housewares at Pier 1, and shoes from Allen-Edmunds or Balley's. Affluent and upscale consumers select products and services that best express their desire for uniqueness.

As more dual-income families enter into affluence, they adopt a component lifestyle whereby attitude and buyer behavior depend on specific situations rather than on overall lifestyle philosophy. Examples of component lifestyles include a couple taking their children on a tour of the Grand Canyon as a vacation to express family values; a husband, wife, and children sharing household tasks and thus blurring gender roles; and the whole family dining out because of time pressures.

TOMORROW'S AFFLUENT CONSUMER

With the increase in consumer wealth, there has been a shift in consumer purchasing behavior in the middle market for upscale products and services. It is now possible for middle-class families to have the kind of life only the rich could afford 20 years ago. Consumer purchasing behavior has also been extended to trading up for products and services for specific products and on special occasions. Many consumers have migrated toward the high-end of the purchasing continuum, namely, buying luxury products. Luxury products are defined as goods in each category exceeding a given price threshold, such as a man's suit priced at $750. Although wealthy men can afford this suit, there are also less wealthy men buying it. This change in buyer's behavior has been initiated by baby boomers whose lifestyles have changed as a result of empty-nest status. There are a growing number of baby boomers who believe middle class status is a starting point not a goal. Thus, the candy industry has attracted less-affluent consumers by successfully marketing a 20-piece box of Grenache Chocolates for $37 and a 28-piece box of Jubilee Chocolates for $32.50. Lifestyle items seem to correlate with product usage. Tiffany & Co. has been able to combine affluent and upscale markets in the sale of diamond engagement rings.

Each decade demonstrates how certain products represented success: early 1900s, Model T Fords, pianos, radios, and hand-cranked Victrolas; from 1910–1919, fur hats, fountain pens, a Cadillac, Kodak cameras, and transatlantic travel. In the 1920s, fur coats, vacuum cleaners, and electric washing machines. In the Depression era of the 1930s, status symbols included sporting events and other forms of entertainment. The World War II era of the 1940s featured television, air travel, and electric refrigerators. In the 1950s and 1960s, status symbols were color televisions, credit cards, convertibles and Porsches, stereo sound systems, and Andy Warhol lithographs. From the 1970s to the 1990s, designer jeans, VCRs, solar-heated homes, BMW cars, computers, and vacation homes became symbols of success. From the 1990s to the present, status symbols include having a personal banker, owning an airplane, having a media room in the house, and taking adventurous vacations.

Nonaffluent consumers purchased what they deemed to be upscale products and for specific products on special occasions traded up. Many upscale product brands are now available to nonaffluent consumers, for example, the Mercedes-Benz C for $27,000 is competitive with lower-priced automobiles. To reach tomorrow's affluent consumers, marketers must do the following:

- Identify clusters of consumers who perceive the market in a similar manner.
- Recognize the set of needs satisfied by each group of products or a specific product.
- Ascertain distinguishable preference data used with group characteristics that may determine the consumer product "ideal."
- Adopt relationship marketing strategies.

A WEALTHIER GRAYING MARKET

Although many athletes, actors, and actresses who are young are wealthy, the affluent market segment is mostly made up of baby boomers and individuals over 55. The senior market within this segment has discretionary income. They often do not have a mortgage. The average age of the luxury automobile buyer is 65. Many seniors join health clubs to enjoy socialization with other people. Seniors are better off due to Social Security, Medicare, their companies' pension plans, and an increase in the value of their homes. The children's products industry does well when it targets this market to purchase apparel, toys, games, and sports equipment for their grandchildren. Sixty-five million grandparents account for more than 25 percent of the toys purchased. Many in this segment own vacation or second homes. They tend to exhibit brand loyalty for products they grew up with like Campbell's soup and Heinz ketchup, which have been top brands for more than 50 years. Value is a critical factor for this group when making purchasing decisions. They expect to be rewarded for loyalty with special services such as presale notices and special shopping hours. They spend more money on travel, reading, and medical care.

They want goods and services tailored to their needs. Older Americans have over 70 percent of all the wealth and represent 50 percent of all discretionary spending. They control four-fifths of the money invested in savings and loan associations and own two-thirds of all the shares on the stock market. They are defined as empty nesters, the retirees and the rehires. This market buys luxury automobiles. Favorite sports include golf and tennis. They purchase the Ping Golf irons, the Tear Drop putters, and the Wilson Carbon tennis rackets. They prefer vacations in Aspen, Nantucket, and Miami. However, only a small percentage of the wealthy spend thousands of dollars a year on apparel, belong to two or more country clubs, and own more than one residence. But, an increasing number of those who are retiring are purchasing $1 million homes with spas, swimming pools, exercise rooms, and home theaters.

Census data in 2000 showed that 3.5 percent of households in the age 55 to 64 category earn more than $200,000 annually. The 2000 U.S. Census reported that almost 35 million people were 65 years of age or older, about 1 in 8. The number of people in this age group will double in size by the year 2030. This group of customers is more likely to buy products and services, remember an advertisement, or shop at a store or on the Internet when they can relate their purchases to situations they already know through their own experiences. Purchasing behavior is particularly age-related in clothes, furniture, and recreation. Marketers need to monitor changing life circumstances—divorce, widowhood, and remarriage—and their impact on consumption as seniors go through transformations from empty nest to solitary survivor.

THE NEW EDUCATIONAL ELITE

The market for certain consumer products is influenced by education. With an increasing number of people attaining undergraduate and graduate degrees, there are changes in product preferences. College graduates, according to the U.S. Census Bureau, have increased from 21.3 percent in 1990 to 27.3 percent in 2003. Buyers have more discriminatory tastes. The trend toward white-collar and service occupations is continuing. Another important change is the increase in females graduating from college. Educated consumers want more information and demand better quality products and services and engage in comparison shopping. This market is more likely to purchase books, newspapers, listen to radio, view television, and read upscale magazines.

The children of the affluent are enrolled in private schools where students not only study a traditional curriculum but also learn the social graces. They attend summer camps where equestrian skills, tennis, and other activities are learned. A college education can lead to affluence for middle-class families. Harvard receives about 20,000 applications for 1,600 freshman seats. Amherst gets 5,200 applications for 400 freshman openings.

The student population at Ivy League colleges is changing. For example, at Harvard University one-third of the students are from a minority background,

7 percent of the students are international, and close to 60 percent graduate with debt. Yale University is composed of approximately 30 percent minority students and 7 percent from foreign countries, and more than half graduate with debt. Vassar, formerly a college only for women, is now composed of 60 percent females and 40 percent males, with 60 percent graduating with debt. Mount Holyoke College remains at 99 percent female, with 20 percent from minority backgrounds and 12 percent with international backgrounds. Over 70 percent graduate with some debt. The student population mix of years ago, primarily white and male dominated, no longer exists. The ratio of minority, female, and international students has dramatically increased. The female to male ratio at the University of North Carolina, Boston University, and New York University is 60–40. Overseas study has become a priority in the strategic plan of an increasing number of colleges. In the past five years, from 1997–2002, the University of Texas sent over 16,000 students to 66 different countries; and New York University sent over 1,700 students, which was three times as many as in 1997. The University of Chicago has introduced a dozen new overseas programs, and the University of New Hampshire has increased the number of students studying abroad by 32 percent from five years ago.

Cultural organizations such as museums, operas, ballets, and theaters have broadened their appeal to new market segments. As education levels increase, a customer emerges who is interested in products such as fine wines, second homes, and luxury automobiles. Services such as financial planning are important since income can be converted into future wealth.

Since the changing educational scene has impacted affluent customers, new strategies need to be devised to reach these customers. The importance of the female market cannot be ignored and neither can the emerging ethnic markets. Marketers can reach these markets by using the following strategies:

1. Product positioning
2. Internet selling
3. Positive atmospherics in retail outlets

To illustrate, Rolex watches are positioned as expensive, sold at a limited number of dealers, and promoted with an exclusiveness of brand and status. Consumers go out of their way to obtain this brand due to loyalty. Red Envelope has used strategies like Internet selling as a niche medium and selling gifts by occasion, such as birthdays. Saving time is the paramount motivation to use the Web for purchasing. Tiffany & Co., known for its ambience, sells a restricted range of products that are high-status quality.

RELATIONSHIP MARKETING

Relationship marketing is the process of developing strong customer loyalty. Competition has intensified between companies, making customer retention critical. The variables of consumer overall satisfaction, trust, and commitment are an integral part of relationship marketing. Relationship marketing recognizes that the purchase transaction does not terminate when the sale is made. Relationship management preserves an intangible asset referred to as goodwill and is not easy to accomplish.

A stronger basis for strengthening a customer retention program is to offer financial and social benefits and to develop structural ties. Frequently, marketing programs offered by hotels and airlines provide financial rewards. Some companies such as Fidelity Investments, contact their customers with suggestions about improved portfolio performance or new funds that have been opened. Companies such as Merrill-Lynch manage customer accounts creating a strong structural relationship. Other companies, such as Harley-Davidson have established club membership programs. Members receive *Hog Tales*, a magazine; a touring handbook; emergency road service; a theft reward service; and discount hotel rates.

MANAGING CHANGE

Social and cultural patterns in the United States have changed. Many of these changes are reflected in the affluent market. Repositioning marketing strategies are important as potential affluent markets such as senior's, dual-income families, women, and various ethnic groups grow larger in size. Niche strategies will be advantageous in targeting the affluent. Customers categorized as affluent have a distinct set of needs and pay a premium price to satisfy these needs. Williams-Sonoma, the Bombay Company, Wright Shoes, and Allen-Edmunds have effectively targeted various segments of this market. Williams-Sonoma estimated that 70 percent of its customers are in the top two income brackets.

The affluent consumer is more knowledgeable and is more concerned with maximizing value for the purchase. Value is meant primarily as a combination of quality, service, and price. Value increases with product quality and service. Marketers can increase value primarily by raising real and perceived benefits. Positive relationships with the customer can easily be built through demonstrating personal recognition and gratitude for the business. Customer service is an important part of the purchasing decision. The quality of information can also increase the value experienced by the consumer. Information that stresses how a brand may reinforce the affluent or upscale consumer's feeling of individuality is especially appealing. This striving for a feeling of uniqueness motivates the affluent and upscale buyer to be more willing than typical consumers to try unknown brands. Disdain for the average has polarized the marketplace. The fastest growing retailers sell image-oriented merchandise like Victoria's Secret or offer low prices such as Wal-Mart.

Yesterday's upscale customers who purchased radios, Kodak cameras, electric washing machines, and color television sets over computers are now part of the affluent market. Organic food is the latest luxury product to be introduced as Kroger, Safeway, Albertson's, and Stop & Shop rush to compete by offering their own private brands similar to those specialty brands sold at health food and gourmet stores. Companies will continue to target wealthy individuals by developing new products or by modifying existing products to reach this market. Segmenting by investible assets is discretionary based on the marketer's objectives. Segmenting by household income allows marketers to define market segmentation categories such as the super rich ($200,000 plus), affluent ($100,000 to $199,000), near affluent ($75,000 to $99,000) and those consumers who trade up and are described as the aspiring affluent. The problem with defining precise market segments for the purchase of specific goods and services is that there is an overlap that becomes blurred in the actual purchase situation.

The vast majority of families have experienced a rapid growth in income and wealth over the past few decades. According to the U.S. Census Bureau the percentage of families earning more than $75,000 a year has tripled from 1967 to 2004, from 9 percent to 27 percent. The middle class is getting richer. Social mobility into the upper-middle-class is made possible since family income has accelerated. Most families are achieving levels of wealth and income that far surpass those of their parents. An affluent society has become more widespread. A concern with class consciousness is the extent to which social status is desired by the individual. Class consciousness is low for an inner-directed individual who is more concerned with product operation and reliability and not with social mobility. An outer-directed person is interested in social mobility and reference group approval and is attracted by products with social visibility.

Financial institutions such as Merrill Lynch and Morgan Stanley are targeting wealthy clients by developing tiers of service aimed at top-level, middle-level and lower-level clients, according to their liquid assets. Although financial institutions are cultivating the superwealthy, they are also endeavoring to reach the new rich, or those with at least $100,000 in investible assets. The new rich market has grown rapidly in recent years and is highly profitable since these customers pay high fees for services, and the superwealthy often use their assets as leverage to obtain better terms. Merrill Lynch provides those with $100 million to invest with trust and estate planning, advice on philanthropy, bill paying, and tax and accounting advice. For their clients with $10 million or more to invest, Merrill Lynch offers wealth management advice and a special loan program. Clients with $100,000 to $10 million receive a management plan and financial planning advice, including asset allocation. Morgan Stanley serves clients with $20 million or more with advice on portfolios of alternative investments, philanthropy, and transgenerational planning and tax strategies. Wealthy people with $1 million to $10 million receive access to professionally managed portfolios, alternative investments, financial planning, and special services for small-business owners and corporate executives. Lower-level clients are divided into two groups: the affluent and mass affluent. The affluent who have $250,000 to $1 million to invest obtain wealth accumulation, preservation, and financial planning strategies. The mass affluent with less than $250,000 to invest receive financial planning assistance and advice in a broad spectrum of investment products. Other financial institutions provide the new rich who have a minimum $100,000 to invest with offerings that include retirement planning, life insurance, and asset allocation services.

Thomas Stanley, chairman of the Affluent Market Institute in Atlanta and author of the book *The Millionaire Next Door: The Surprising Secrets of America's Wealthy*, says a typical wealthy person is likely to be a small-business owner who has lived his entire adult life in one city and who married once and stayed married. He's likely to live in a middle-class neighborhood next door to people much less wealthy. He probably spends no more than $400 for a new suit and does not own an expensive watch, while the higher income, lower net-worth individual drives an expensive luxury car! The "typical" millionaire tends to shower his or her children and family with gifts, the children often end up less affluent than their millionaire parents. A survey from Northern Trust Corporation reveals that the new millionaire is just as concerned about rising health care costs diminishing their savings as typical income individuals.

There are a growing number of consumers who drive their BMWs to Costco. The new luxury, which involves substituting luxury brands for mass brands, has been growing rapidly in recent years. Trading up means finding goods that are chic or cool. Marketers will need to convince consumers that a luxury brand item, such as a Viking gas stove, is worth more than the standard Kenmore range. There is no real average affluent consumer, but a whole group of consumers that includes dual-income households, seniors, women, entrepreneurs, athletes, ethnic minorities, celebrities, and senior executives.

CHAPTER 2

Bridging the Gap

There is a large gap between the values, ideas, attitudes, and symbols that shaped the previous generation of wealthy people as compared to the present one. The consumption patterns and aspirations of the previous generation reflect a different time in history. This behavior has now changed because of technology, entrepreneurship, and education. The impact of these changes is fragmentation of the market into micromarkets such as the affluent market. The affluent market can be subdivided and differentiated by age, gender, lifestyle, and other characteristics.

Companies wanting to bridge the gap between the values and attitudes of yesterday and today need to do a better job of satisfying customer expectations. Customers who are stereotyped by marketing strategists don't buy! Today's customers are harder to please since they are better educated, more demanding, more time and price conscious, and less forgiving. There are companies that have better hamburgers than McDonald's, but McDonald's is still number one in the industry because of quality, service, cleanliness, and value. These characteristics add up to customer satisfaction. Today's customers are value maximizers.

The previous affluent consumer is an endangered species. No longer is there an affluent group that can be easily identified by their common goals, motivations, and values. Instead, a huge and growing market of affluent consumers has emerged, and marketers will need to focus more and more on specific market niches. The power of the affluent consumer is demonstrated by the number of affluent consumers more than doubling from 1980 to 2000. Spending on luxury items is not necessarily confined to the affluent but also includes those consumers who trade up in their purchases. This market is projected to amount to $1 trillion by 2010.[1] There is a new, powerful affluent consumer (depicted in Figure 2.1) with diverse goals, motivations, and values. For example, there is a trend toward older motherhood that may benefit the luxury toy market. In 1990, 30 percent of women gave birth over the age of 30; in 2002 that percentage increased to 38 percent of all births. FAO Schwartz has reopened in New York, and manufacturers are targeting the affluent market. Mattel's American Girl collection doll set sells for $189, the Adventurers' Tropical Tree House sells for $119, and a Kettler Tricycle is priced at $189.

Marketers need to narrow the gap that has developed as more and more affluent and upscale consumers shift their expectations and preferences in the infants and young children's market. Parental demand for luxury baby and children's merchandise is attracting new interest from marketers. Even Wal-Mart has entered this premium market by introducing a line of organic cotton clothing from Carter's Inc. Fisher-Price is increasing sales by marketing educational toys for infants and preschoolers, while Mattel is experiencing decreasing sales on their line of traditional toys. Parents and grandparents support educational learning, and children over 5 prefer video and computer games as the demand for traditional toys, such as building blocks and stuffed animals, is shrinking.

Demographic characteristics are frequently used alone or in combination with behavioral characteristics and qualitative dimensions to segment markets. Qualitative dimensions such as product usage, brand loyalty, brand attitudes, and purchasing intentions need to be constantly adjusted and viewed with flexibility in developing market niches. For instance, luxury cruises have allowed passengers to visit different ports and try new foods. Travelers are also introduced to goods such as clothing and furniture that they have not seen previously. There is not a mass affluent market for yachts or rare books. In contrast, there is a much broader market for luxury automobiles among affluent and upscale consumers. The design of marketing strategies is primarily a function of the market to be served. An understanding of the new affluent consumer begins with knowledge of buyer characteristics and the purchasing process. Accelerated changes in the affluent market caused primarily by increases in income and education force marketers to reconsider strategy development.

The growth rate for Internet use in the United States has increased from about 4.5 million users in 1992 to over 160 million in 2002. The Internet has become important as a communication vehicle for marketers and has been valuable for promoting brand awareness, advertising, distribution, and pricing strategies. The Internet adds a new set of meaningful and significant values to develop a competitive differential. Christian Dior and Louis Vuitton once believed that fashion merchandise could only be sold through specialty shops; today, these fashion houses have not only developed their own Web sites, but have also made their merchandise available through department stores.

The new luxury reflected by consumers who are affluent, who are upscale buyers, and who trade up in their purchasing behavior, is driven by an increase in disposable income among people who earn from about $50,000 to $200,000. The variables contributing to this new consumer purchasing behavior are later marriages, the impact of increasing real estate values, and low interest rates. There is also a new attitude among female purchasers that it is all right to indulge in affordable luxuries. New luxury products involve an emotional sentiment. Louis Vuitton and Hermès, therefore, have for some years broadened the definition of luxury to include scarcity. Banana Republic, with over 450 stores, limited quantities in their Café Society collection, making it available to only 30 stores and through their Web site. J. Crew has offered items that can be produced in limited quantities, such as $600 crocodile shoes.

There are other trends that give new meaning to Figure 2.1. African American, Hispanic, and female heads of household earning more than $100,000 a year have increased by 154 percent, 126 percent, and 197 percent, respectively, from 1991 to 2000. The affluent consumer has grown younger and wants to be assured of style and quality. These younger affluent consumers are not afraid of the unfamiliar or the exotic. The new emerging rich, ages 28 to 44, known as Generation X, have earned their wealth quickly and have not grown up with luxury products and services. This generation is fast becoming a significant segment of the affluent market.

Figure 2.1 shows that affluent consumers tend to be motivated by psychological factors when making purchasing decisions. The affluent today do not desire to keep up with the Jones' but to be different. Tension is present in their daily lives, and they are willing to pay for the highest level of expertise and the best professional services. They tend to trust their own judgment to define value in products and services but at varying times will consult those who are more knowledgeable.

Figure 2.1
The Affluent Consumer

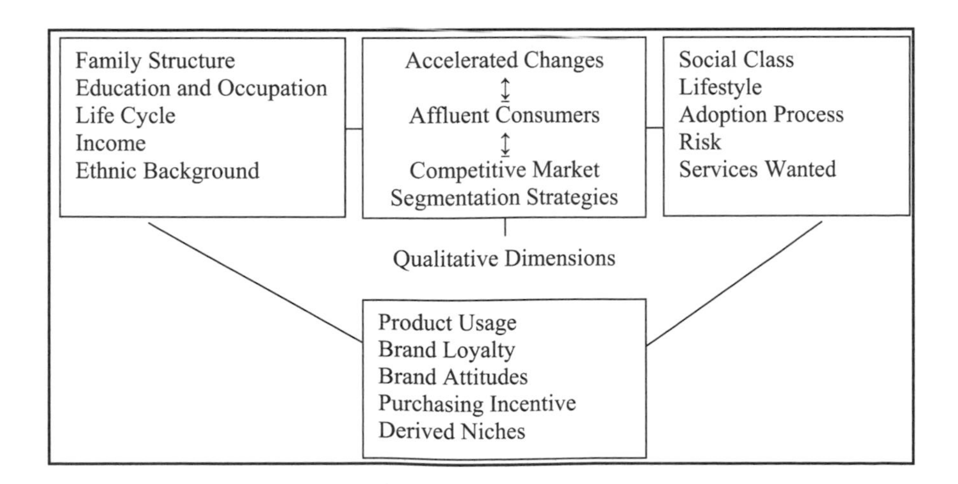

The most important change occurring today is the shifting view of the role of women and marriage partners. Shared tasks, nontraditional relationships, and more people living alone are among significant cultural changes. Marketers need to address these shifting activities, interests, and opinions to generate ideas for new products. There is a gap between available products and unsatisfied consumer needs. Need-gap intensity can be tested against purchase intention levels. A marketing strategy would then need to be developed based on potential market size, market structure, and buyer behavior. Affluent consumers have a propensity to select some products, such as perfume, automobiles, and clothing, not just for functional value but because these products project an image for them. These products have high identity value for affluent consumers.

Market segmentation groups potential buyers by demographic characteristics such as geographical area, age, gender, income, occupation, and other factors. These factors are then combined with behavioral, lifestyle, ethnic, and other variables to develop strategies. Market segmentation strategies are sometimes combined with product differentiation strategies that alter the products' physical characteristics like branding, packaging, pricing or other components.

CASTLES: OLD AND NEW

The gap between generations of wealthy individuals is demonstrated in their homes, their willingness to take purchasing risks, their readiness to purchase new products, their purchasing participation in the fashion cycle, and the products they own and the services they use.

There is an old axiom "There's no place like home." Home to the wealthy affluent of the nineteenth and early twentieth century meant something far different than to the affluent majority at the beginning of the twenty-first century. The ostentatious symbols of yesterday are now hidden, and the wealthy symbols of today are far more subtle, such as built-in bars and appliances, hand-carved staircases and railings, and stained-glass windows in the bathrooms. Stoves and refrigerators are concealed to make the kitchen resemble an ordinary room. The standards for evaluating wealth and social class have evolved over the years. For example, in the days of Jane Austen—author of *Pride and Prejudice*, *Emma*, and other books—success was measured by the carriage, which required a stable, horses, a coachman, grooms, and the vehicle itself. Superrich meant an individual with an income of 10,000 pounds a year, in contrast to an income of only 4,000 or 5,000 pounds a year that defined the rich. Today, the superrich generally own a Van Gogh or a similar painting.

The mansions and summer cottages of the late 1800s and early 1900s reflect the symbols of an affluent society. The Vanderbilt mansions of 1898 exemplify the nineteenth century architecture of the Gilded Age. One of their mansions in New York City had 137 rooms, which made it the largest house ever built in New York City; their Biltmore Castle in North Carolina contained 250 rooms. The French and Italian furnishings were imported. French tapestries and oriental rugs gave a rich opulence to the Hyde Park, New York, mansion. The Henry Flagler home in Palm Beach, Florida, also displays wealth. Flagler was a railroad magnate whose 55-room mansion, constructed in 1902, earned the title "Taj Mahal of North America." The mansion includes a Louis XIV music room, a Louis XV ballroom, and an elaborate entrance hall. The epitome of opulence is the Hearst Castle in San Simeon, California, constructed by newspaper magnate William Randolph Hearst in 1919. The Hearst Castle took 30 years to complete. There are 115 rooms and three huge cottages surrounded by pools, gardens, and statues from ancient Greece and Spain. The castle has 41 fireplaces, 61 bathrooms, and a subterranean Neptune pool the size of a football field. Many of these structures have been donated to charities because the cost of upkeep was too high.

Homes of the affluent are concentrated in metropolitan and coastal areas that are in close proximity to work since many hours are spent at work and in vacation areas such as Vail and Aspen, Colorado, and Park City, Utah. An indoor gym with treadmills, a swimming pool, and tennis courts are typical. Bathrooms are spacious, numerous, and may be designed for "his" and "her." Kitchens are well equipped with the latest technology and a chef, and maintenance people such as gardeners may be employed. Tapestries decorate the walls, but the feeling of opulence compared to the Vanderbilt, Flagler, and Hearst mansions is not present. These homes have eight or nine rooms with seven or eight bathrooms.

A recent trend targeting the wealthy is million-dollar recreational vehicles and pricey RV resorts in upscale locales. These new mansions are on wheels. Newell and Prevost Corporation dominate the industry and charge from $1 million to $2 million for these coaches. A few years ago, a RV lot in Naples, Florida, cost $84,000; in 2005 it was worth more than $200,000. As these mansions on wheels become more prevalent, more executives and professional people will be buyers. Private owners are typically new retirees who are partial to country music, boating, and horse shows and who have made their money the hard way. Another trend is that co-op developers are prepackaging condos with brand-oriented design furnishings. For example, the Caribbean in Miami Beach sells units from $1 million to $7.5 million that have private wine lockers and humidors. The Legacy at Millennium Park in Chicago sells from $300,000 to more than $3 million with sky gardens and lounges, and the Museum Residence in Denver, with units selling from $340,000 to $1.1 million, will offer a rooftop garden measuring about one-third of an acre. Famous designer names such as French designer Phillippe Starck, Barbara Barry, and Jodi Jagger are among the furnishings offered by condo developers.

The top four states in per capita income in 2002 were Connecticut, New Jersey, Maryland, and New York. The largest gains according to the 2000

Census were Teton, Wyoming; Summit, Utah; Greene, Georgia; Somerset, New Jersey; and a number of counties in California, including Santa Clara, Marin, and San Mateo.[2] The ten wealthiest counties in terms of median household income appear in Table 2.1. Promotional campaigns using highly regionalized strategies can be aimed at local markets.

Geo-demographics used in multiattribute segmentation have a rating index by zip code markets created by Claritas Inc., the Potential Rating Index by Zip Market (PRIZM). The index includes 39 factors in five broad categories: (1) education and affluence, (2) family life cycle, (3) urbanization, (4) race and ethnicity, and (5) mobility. For example, one PRIZM group, called Cashmere and Country Club, includes aging baby boomers who live in the suburbs, are likely to buy a Mercedes, have a propensity to subscribe to *Golf Digest*, use salt substitutes, enjoy European getaways, and buy high-end television sets. Median income adjusted for inflation would be about $100,000.[3] Zip codes have been used to identify the highest-median homes sales markers.

The top five zip codes in average annual family income in 2003 according to the U.S. Census Bureau were the following:

94027	Atherton, CA	$410,734
19035	Gladwyne, PA	$388,904
22067	Greenway, VA	$381,518
60043	Kenilworth, IL	$362,469
94028	Portola Valley, CA	$358,422

Marketers using the above information can match products such as home furnishings, automobiles, media subscriptions, and lifestyle activities to consumers in those zip codes.

Table 2.1
Median Household Income: Ten Wealthiest U.S. Counties

Rank	County	Median Income ($s)
1	Somerset County, NJ	89,289
2	Howard County, MD	88,555
3	Prince William County, VA	82,926
4	Morris County, NJ	82,025
5	Fairfax County, VA	80,753
6	Nassau County, NY	80,647
7	Santa Clara County, CA	76,544
8	Montgomery County, MD	76,439
9	Rockland County, NY	72,276
10	Collin County, TX	71,458

Source: U.S. Census Bureau, *2003 American Community Survey*.

The geographic area of residence affects social interactions and is an indicator of social class membership. The location of residency by zip code can demonstrate affluence. The neighborhood by itself is not the sole measure but an important variable in conjunction with occupation or income. Since 1993 the American Lines Migration database has generated the names of 38 million people who have moved. Family mobility data can tell us how a neighborhood is changing and where promotional strategies should be directed. Migration data can also be an aid to real-estate developers, banks and retail institutions in their expansion plans. The long-distance mobile market is generally composed of well-educated, professional, or managerial families earning good incomes and with children at home. To reach this market, strategies should include persuading mobile families about the value of adjusting their patronage patterns to the new geographical area.

There is a link between geographic preference and economic opportunity. There is a strong link between the geographical movement of the affluent, purchasing behavior, and also philanthropy. Affluent individuals value their involvement with the communities in which they live. They tend to give their financial support and volunteer time if they believe their efforts will support their community. Geographic location has long been considered useful as a basis for market segmentation strategies. For example, Hilton Hotels in the Northeast are sleeker and more cosmopolitan, and in the Southwest more rustic. Each area is formed by population dispersion and cultural development, resulting in particular behavioral patterns. This may mean that a firm will decide to operate only in specific regions or make variations in its product depending on regional consumer demographics and preferences.

Economic opportunity presently has taken the form of decorating and demonstrating distinctive characteristics for each room. For example, chandeliers with frogs, colored light bulbs used to brighten bedrooms, kitchens, bathrooms and walk-in closets. A halogen 12-light chandelier in brushed nickel with snakelike arms and handblown ornaments costs about $2,000, and an Artemis Rock Crystal that is made from rock crystal with hand-cut quartz costs about $10,000. Moreover, furniture marketers design formal children's rooms with a Venice bed for about $8,000 and an Out of Africa collection of twin bedding in mixed faux furs for $500. The master suite can include a fireplace, a marble bath, a Jacuzzi, and a wine cellar. The focus of the new luxury home is the kitchen. When adjusted for inflation, the average kitchen remodeling job cost about $9,000 in the 1950s. Today, the average cost of remodeling a kitchen is approximately $58,000. The design of the kitchen has become a symbol of a successful life.

AFFLUENT CONSUMERS AND THE UNKNOWN

Although affluent consumers because of their resources have more choices than average consumers, all consumers attempt to decrease their risk when making a purchase by modifying, postponing, or avoiding the purchase decision. The degree of perceived risk varies with the amount of money in question, the amount of product-attribute uncertainty, and consumer self-confidence. Affluent consumers are aware that perceived risk can be reduced by decreasing the probability of failure. For example, product reviews in *Consumer Reports* and restaurant reviews in Zagat guides can be used to reduce risk. One type of perceived risk can be shifted to another to diminish the impact of error or to postpone the decision. And, of course, the purchase can be made and the risk absorbed. Perceived risk is a function of uncertainty and positive and negative consequences and is an unknown before the purchase is completed. Perceived risk tends to be higher when there is little information about the product, when the product is new, when the price is high, when understanding the operation of the product is technologically complex, when the buyer is inexperienced with the product, when there are substantial quality distinctions among brands, and when peer opinion is considered important. Affluent consumers have more access to information than the typical buyer, but all consumers develop their own approach for reducing risk, such as information gathering from friends, buying a known brand, and obtaining warranties and guarantees.

Perceived risk includes time loss, hazard loss, ego loss and money loss. Time loss involves merchandise adjustments in quantities or styles. Hazard loss has a direct relationship to either the loss of health or safety to the buyer. Ego loss occurs if the product does not work properly and the buyer perceives the purchase as a foolish expenditure or an error in judgment. Money loss is a loss due to the improper operation of the product or due to the overexpectation of potential results. Each perceived loss can vary in intensity, and shifts from one type of risk to another can occur.

The method of reducing risk depends on the situation. Endorsements or testimonials from trusted individuals are used as a risk reliever, provided the buyer can relate to the individual who gives the product endorsement. Some buyers purchase only well-known brands since they rely on their brand's reputation. Brand or store loyalty can be generated when the product has been used previously and has been found satisfactory. Depending on the type of product and its cost, some buyers rely on testing organizations like Consumers Union, or the government to evaluate a product. Educated consumers will often rely on a well-known brand name with a reputation of long-standing quality as an effective way to reduce risk.

The consumer values sources of information in the purchase of new products. Affluent consumers will spend time searching before buying a product. When making financial decisions or purchasing complex products and services, the affluent consumer can hire an advisor. The affluent consumer has a disproportionately larger share of discretionary income to use for this effort.

Time loss for the affluent is an important consideration and is generally related to the economic cost of carrying out an activity. It is often not economically feasible for affluent individuals to perform their own tasks. The income earning level may determine such activities as doing one's own tax return or mowing the lawn instead of hiring an individual. There are psychological variables such as enjoying gardening, which may preclude hiring someone else to do it even though the cost is less.

Affluent consumers frequently rely on word-of-mouth referrals to reduce risk. A key element in a word-of-mouth transmission is the role of opinion leaders. These individuals are regarded as having expertise and knowledge on a particular subject and can influence others to purchase a product. Word-of-mouth strategy has been important to the success of the Nordstrom department store and Amazon.com. Nordstrom is known for its personal service but does not advertise its services. Amazon.com focuses on customer service and depends on word-of-mouth for customer referrals.

THE POWER OF VISION

Although consumers differ in their readiness to try new products, many affluent buyers may be more eager than average buyers because they are more willing to assume the risk. Affluent buyers are equipped with a power of vision due to a wider access of information and superior financial resources. This power of vision focuses on consumption pioneers. These people are the first to adopt new clothing fashions and new appliances and to take advantage of new technology. New product adopters are risk takers. A comparative profile between early adopters and later adopters would point to more social integration, more group memberships, higher incomes, higher occupational status, and more social and occupational mobility. Early adopters are willing to assume higher risks and pay high prices in order to satisfy a need for status, convenience, and luxury. The adoption of new products can be a slow process. The home computer was launched in 1977 but only two percent of the population owned a home computer by 1981. Marketers must motivate the innovators and early adopters through promotion and communication techniques to lead the way for the rest of the population.

The adoption process is a behavioral process that describes how a consumer purchases a product not previously used. The adoption process includes awareness, interest, evaluation trial, and adoption. In the awareness stage, the consumer becomes aware of the new product but lacks information about it. The interest stage reflects the stimulation needed for the consumer to search for information about the new product. The evaluation stage is when the consumer assesses the new product against established goals and financial resources. A decision is then made whether or not to try the new product. The consumer tries the new product in the trial stage. Sampling in small quantities may be used. The adoption stage occurs when the consumer decides to make regular use of the new product. Sources of information have an impact on the adoption process, and different sources have varying degrees of credibility.

The process by which totally new products are adopted is called the diffusion process. Some people will buy a new product right after it has been introduced, while others will delay acceptance or may never buy it. Researchers have pinpointed five categories of consumers based on a time dimension of adoption in the diffusion process. Innovators are the first group to adopt a new product, followed by early adopters, early majority, late majority, and laggard consumer market segments. The socio-demographic variables most closely correlated with early adoption are education, income, and standard of living. A strong attitudinal variable in conjunction with early adoption includes the willingness to accept change. The intensity of these variables varies from individual to individual, but it is likely that the affluent consumer would be a potential market for new products depending on the product and its benefits. Some doctors are among the first in their profession to prescribe new drugs, and some farmers are among the first to use new farm machinery. Some consumers who are fashion conscious are among the first to adopt a new fashion. Marketers need to identify those consumers who are interested in particular items and who are likely to be among the first to purchase a new product. Information technology is now available to establish a significant database.

Everett Rogers categorized about 2.5 percent of the population as innovators, 13.5 percent as early adopters, 34 percent as the early majority, 34 percent as the late majority, and 16 percent as laggards.[4]

Adopter groups differ in their value orientations. Innovators are venturesome and are eager to try new ideas and products. They generally are better educated than the average consumer, are financially secure, and have social status. They tend to have high incomes and a great deal of self-confidence. Innovators rely more on impersonal sources of information rather than on salespeople or other word-of-mouth sources. Early adopters are perceived as opinion leaders. Early adopters have many of the same characteristics as innovators—self-confidence, income, and good education—but are a part of the social system in their communities. The early adopter is an important link to the mass market of the early and late majority segments because their group popularizes the products accepted by the innovator group. The early majority tends to be slightly more educated and better off financially than those in the late majority. Although they are rarely leaders, they adopt new ideas and products before the average person. The late majority are skeptical about new product ideas and may adopt products because of social pressure or because the purchase risk has been diminished. Laggards are a tradition-bound group with a resistance to change.

The speed of adoption may be affected by the relative advantage of the new product. This relative benefit may be lower cost or superior quality. The degree to which the new product or idea may be sampled on some limited basis may also affect the adoption rate. Another factor would be whether the consumer could observe a change in a situation as a result of immediate use of the product. Naturally, there are people who never adopt new products or ideas, and these people are simply referred to as nonadopters. The adoption process is the decision-making activity of the individual, whereas the diffusion process is the procedure in which the innovation is transmitted within the social system. There may be a link between the affluent market and innovators and early adopter groups.

For new luxury products, marketers need to develop a strategy that includes (1) the identification of the segment of affluent consumers who are likely to try a new product before others, (2) understand the time required for the adoption of the product, (3) recognize the degree of resistance that will be encountered, and (4) promote the benefits of being among the first to own the new product. Moreover, a product-augmentation strategy is frequently used. Consumers buying luxury goods are usually willing to pay extra costs. Augmented benefits are in the form of packaging, services, customer advice, financing, or delivery arrangements that customers value and that exceed their expectations.

THE TRICKLE-DOWN THEORY

There is evidence that fashion trickles down from higher to lower social class levels and even across at the same time to different social classes. With the advent of rap music and clothing associated with this movement, some styles trickle up. The significance of fashion has not been limited to clothing and accessories but has been extended to eyeglasses, telephones and furniture. Perceived product quality is intertwined with aesthetic design and fashion, and marketers need to know how fashion and other product characteristics influence perceived product quality.

How affluent consumers perceive fashion is rooted in sociological and psychological variables. Affluent consumers are basically conformists and are concerned about social acceptance while trying to look and act a little different from their friends. Fashion serves as an instrument that reflects their concept of good taste, and self-image and that provides them with the opportunity for self-expression.

The risks associated with selling fashion apparel come with the uncertainty of the consumers' degree of acceptance and the duration of this acceptance as a fashion. Fashion shows are a good strategy to reach affluent consumers. Many stores such as Saks Fifth Avenue and Neiman Marcus conduct fashion shows that feature the latest fashions advertised in such periodicals as *Vogue*. Some of the fashion shows also serve to raise funds for charitable organizations.

Many fashion styles come from Paris, Rome, New York, and Los Angeles. The fashion cycle—introduction, accelerated development, and decline—provides opportunities for manufacturers and retailers planning to cultivate the affluent market. Fashions pass through three stages. First, a small number of consumers, usually the wealthy, become interested in something new to set them apart. Second, other consumers, including some of the upscale market, desire to emulate the fashion leaders. And third, the fashion becomes popular and is introduced to the mass market, and over time it eventually declines. Fashion is also a reflection of taste and self-image. Some consumers have a strong preference for clothing that has detailed designs, while others prefer design simplicity.

The fashion cycle usually moves downward through socioeconomic classes, which is referred to as the trickle-down theory. Allen-Edmunds and Bally's are known for stylish shoes; they both have their own retail outlets and sell to specialty stores. Their shoe styles are then copied, and the styles trickle down to Lord and Taylor and Wal-Mart. The beginning of the fall season has new fashion dresses sold in small, exclusive dress shops or boutiques attracting affluent consumers. These designs are then sold in large department stores appealing to the middle class and also in discount stores targeting the general market. The early purchasers are opinion leaders or innovators within each social class. Early adopters and a large segment of early and late majority consumers then purchase the new style.

The trickle-up theory has historical roots. Levi Strauss introduced the rugged, thigh-fitting blue jeans that date back to the 1848 California gold rush days. The blue jeans were first sold to miners who needed durable clothing in their work. The product gained acceptance in the United States among lower- and middle-class teenagers since it symbolized rebellion against the establishment, which represents the trickle-up model. The wearing of jeans spread to upper-class youths. Jeans evolved with the introduction of designer labels such as Calvin Klein in the 1970s, thereby reversing the trickle-up model. Yves St. Laurent and Calvin Klein now design T-shirts.

The trickle-across theory projects itself horizontally and simultaneously in a number of social classes. A style with different levels of price and quality is launched at the same time in exclusive high-priced specialty boutiques, medium-priced specialty and department stores, and discount stores. Although price and quality vary, the style is basically the same. The trickle-across theory is best applied for fashion, which originates with big-name designers.

EBay, an Internet company using an auction method of selling, has established a nontraditional channel of distribution in the fashion industry. The marketing of the apparel, shoes, and accessories category ranks among the top five fastest-growing products sold by eBay. Products like Hermès handbags sell for $10,000. EBay's users do not have to wait months to obtain their spring orders. EBay receives items immediately from some designers.

EBay is an alternative to shopping in department stores and boutique specialty shops because it saves time and offers convenience to its customers. Marketers wanting to reach this market need to broaden their product line, develop a positioning strategy and product offerings that are different from their competitors, and sell their products through the Internet.

DANGERS OF POSTPURCHASE COMPLACENCY

Affluent consumers spend more for items such as furniture, automobiles, housing, premium wines, boats, cigars, and jewelry. Consumers generally experience a level of satisfaction after the purchase, and usually the higher the item price, the higher the degree of satisfaction or dissatisfaction. Affluent consumers with large families who were frequent shoppers had a greater propensity to report dissatisfaction with purchases than typical consumers. The average age of these consumers was in their 40s, and gender did not make a difference.[5] The marketer's job is not over once the product is purchased. Marketers must be especially careful in monitoring affluent consumer postpurchase satisfaction and responses. There may be a gap between the buyer's expectations and the product's perceived performance. It is the marketer's job to close this gap so that the consumer is not disappointed and has a favorable reaction regarding the purchase.

The gulf between contented customers and completely contented customers allows neutral customers to be lured away by competitors. Company objectives should be to treat customers exceptionally well when something is wrong. Companies need a program to track neutral customers and turn these customers into loyalists. The United States auto industry has suffered the consequences of not listening to their customers, and new foreign competitors entered the market. It is not sufficient to treat customers well when basically everything is going right.

After the purchase is made, the consumer's satisfaction or dissatisfaction with the product will influence subsequent behavior. The purchase of a Cartier watch can lead to the purchase of other jewelry items. Positive word-of-mouth communication with friends and relatives can influence the affluent consumer's purchasing behavior. Follow-up telephone calls and mail communications may increase satisfaction for the purchaser, particularly in the electronics industry. The sale of computers often needs a high level of after service. Electronic retailers would do well to offer interactive demonstrations. A high level of customer service can be maintained if manufacturers provide information that helps the consumer use the product properly. Marketers make a great mistake by allowing complacency to manifest after the purchase. For example, a major challenge of the furniture industry is to service the needs of consumers. Affluent consumers may grow discontented since furniture delivery may take months. A furniture retailer with the ability to solve this problem as well as effectively deal with damaged or incompletely assembled furniture gets repeat business. The growth of IKEA and the Bombay Company, with the strategy of flat packing and the sale of ready-to-assemble furniture, are examples of this phenomenon.

The manufacturer or the retailer can minimize customer discontent by summarizing the product benefits in their literature. After the purchase, customers can be reassured by repeating why the product is better than alternatives not selected in their advertising. Follow-up contact is needed to ensure that no problems occur in delivery, financing, installation, routine maintenance, and other areas important to customer satisfaction.

MANAGING CHANGE

Over 28 million households represent the affluent market today, and as time goes by, even more households will join these ranks. There is a widening gap between affluent and non-affluent households. For instance, at the University of California, San Francisco, Medical Center members are charged $1,500 a year to get same-day appointments, invitations to lectures, and the private cell-phone number of the chief of cardiology. The Cooper Clinic in Dallas charges $3,000 for an eight-hour physical exam, and its client base has grown 45 percent in the last four years. The opportunity for marketers is to bridge this gap by identifying the needs and wants of this market, since luxury spending is growing rapidly. This market can be elusive since many households are trading up in their purchases. The degree of perceived risk in making the purchase, and the willingness to purchase new products and unknown brands are intangible factors to be considered with demographic and behavioral factors.

The media used for reaching affluent households has changed over the years from television and magazine to the Internet, in-home shopping by catalog, and direct marketing. Affluent consumers rely on the Internet to gather information and purchases. The Internet is now used by all customers. More than half of all online shoppers are women over 40 years old who are married and college educated. The Internet as the number one source for influencing buyer behavior of affluent families grows each day as time has become the ultimate luxury. Internet purchasing has far-reaching implications and will change the shape of purchasing in the future. Other technology-driven channels include call centers, ATMs, kiosks, and interactive technology.

As the new rich encountered the old rich in Nantucket they were unconcerned about social acceptance. If the new rich cannot join an exclusive country club, they establish their own, such as the Carnegie Abbey Club in Rhode Island. The hyperrich want to be with other successful people. They are willing to strike out and develop their own traditions apart from wealthy people who have inherited money.

There is a conflict in Palm Beach, Florida, as the new rich clash with the older elite who largely derived their money from inherited wealth. About half the people in the richest 1 percent by net worth in 2001 were not included in the list in 1989. The number of superwealthy has surged with 430,000, households worth more than $10 million, up from 65,000 in 1989. For the richest 1 percent, only 9 percent inherited their wealth in 2001, down from 23 percent in 1989. Bentley GTs and Rolls Royce Phantoms have replaced the Volvos favored by the older elite. Many of the old historic mansions have been sold to the new superrich. New values and symbols are now apparent in Palm Beach.

DeBeers plans to introduce a luxury jewelry retail chain that will place its brand in direct competition with such high-end retailers as Tiffany, Cartier, and Harry Winston. A liaison will be formed with Louis Vuitton of Paris to form a joint venture. The first DeBeers store on New York's Fifth Avenue opened in June 2005. The strategy will also include the low end of the luxury market by selling items priced as low as several hundred dollars up to $200,000 and higher.

The purchasing behavior of the affluent is not as simple as it was 30 years ago. Affluent consumers have higher expectations and desire more value for their money. When making a purchase, customers desire ease of information and do not have the patience for poor customer service, poor follow-up, poor quality products and services, and not having their needs satisfied.

The key to generating high customer loyalty and retention is to deliver value. Volvo has changed its promotional appeal from just a safe car to encompass a longer-lasting car, excellent service, and a long warranty period. The value expected by customers represents a total experience. Saturn has changed the buyer relationship by offering a fixed price, a 30-day guarantee or money returned, and salespeople on salary not commission. This change in marketing has given Saturn a customer loyalty rate in the 60 percent range compared to the industry average of below 40 percent. Amtrak has begun changing its image by upgrading long distance trains with carpeting, quality food, and superior overnight sleep accommodations to target the affluent.

Chapter 3

When Good Is Not Good Enough

Marketers find it difficult to understand how customers behave. There is no set of universal motives. Each purchasing situation requires its own analysis. The purchasing motives of both affluent and nonaffluent consumers may converge at times and in other situations be separate and distinct. Although marketers are increasing their knowledge of buyer motivation, precision in targeting specific markets does not always happen. People apply both emotional and rational calculations to purchasing decisions. Naturally, purchasing decisions do not actually work this way. Anger, fear, greed, altruism, and other motives are present in purchasing behavior.

Individual buyer behavior is influenced by underlying motivations, perceptions, attitudes, beliefs, and previous learning. Involvement in the purchasing decision is either of low involvement or high involvement. Low involvement decisions are either of a routine or limited process associated with the purchase of such goods as toilet tissue, cookies, paper clips, or light bulbs. Purchases important to the consumer, whether expensive or not, are high-involvement purchases. When the product reflects self-image, like some clothing or jewelry items, motivations, perceptions, and attitudes are influencing factors. Some purchases require complex decision making, such as the purchase of a mutual fund or an automobile, whereas other decisions are by brand loyalty. Consumer thinking in the decision process involves such phases as problem recognition, information search, available options, the actual purchase selection, and the outcomes from the choice. Rational decision making is not always present, and therefore many emotional criteria may be used. Marketers need to develop strategies that assist the buyer in learning about a product's attributes and benefits that are superior to competing products.

Two developments have made the need for marketing information about the affluent consumer greater now than in the past. First, the size and potential of a growing market, and second, the trend toward nonprice and other forms of competition. The development of strategies directed to this market requires information. Building a customer database is the process of learning more about the customer and establishing a customer profile. A precise customer profile influences the development of products and leads companies like Porsche to market only upscale sports cars.

Information is needed to satisfy the needs of a changing affluent market. Information is not an unstructured activity; it is a disciplined and multifunctional activity that combines creativity with analysis. Information, in many instances, is an outcome of analysis and marketing intelligence. Figure 3.1 depicts the functions needed to improve marketing performance. Many marketing functions are increasingly fragmented as a result of information technology and can be codified and placed into software. Much of marketing research is replaced by daily transaction data analysis, forecasting is now replaced by computer simulations from a market transaction database, and market segmentation is aided greatly by data mining. Marketing functions help to develop a sound strategic marketing plan, but an outstanding plan means little if not implemented properly. Strategy addresses the what and why of marketing functions, but implementation directs itself to other questions such as who, where, when, and how. Implementation involves budgeting, organizing, and motivating personnel. Strong systems and personal execution of tactical plans help marketers to cope with internal and external crises. For example, a prestige goods strategy enables a marketer to satisfy an unmet need by offering a product of a little higher quality and price. Mercedes responded to a market need and increased market share over Cadillac by slightly increasing their price to show exclusiveness, introducing automobiles ranging in price from $27,000 to $452,000, including sedans, wagons, convertibles, coupes, roadsters, and light trucks.

The affluent market can be lucrative to many, but the tracking of costs is needed to determine the overall payoff of both entering and maintaining a position in this market. Measuring growth allows a firm to learn from past successes and failures. The management of implementing a program designed to cultivate the affluent market requires the ability to mobilize members of the entire organization to participate in the marketing program. Many firms desire to develop a differential advantage that consists of a company's unique features in a marketing program to attract consumer patronage away from its competitors. After evaluation of feedback, the firm needs to engage in adaptation to fine-tune its marketing program to capitalize on its differential advantage. Avoiding marketing myopia is necessary for continued success in marketing programs.

The analysis of marketing intelligence varies from one company to another. Neiman Marcus has been building a strong Web presence for

Figure 3.1
Improving Performance

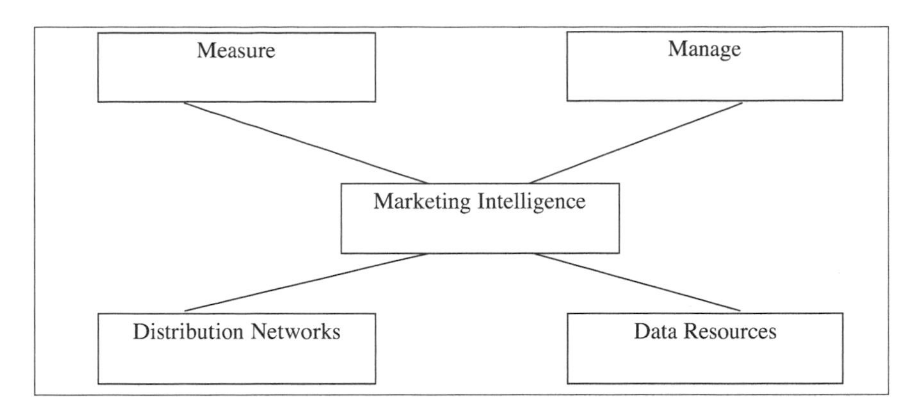

several years. Banana Republic and Eddie Bauer have also established Web sites. But many other retailers declined to sell online because they believed that their customers would not make expensive purchases without examining the merchandise. The use of the Web is critical for collecting information about customers. Marketing intelligence is dependent on data sources. The Internet has a destination Web site of a PC equipped with a Web browser. If companies want to reach the affluent market, the Web site should be ubiquitous, and wireless telephones, kiosks, and interactive TV should be used. Retailers such as Bloomingdale's, Diane von Furstenberg, Elie Tahari, BCBG, Max Azria, and Milly have also found that selling on the Internet has pitfalls. Clothing pictures are poorly presented, merchandise may be delivered late, and packaging may result in damaged products. Competition from online retailers like Bluefly Inc. and Net-A-Porter Ltd., with quality selections and minimum shipping and packaging problems, emphasize that good is not always good enough.

Much of the conventional wisdom about customer loyalty is being challenged. Marketing intelligence could disclose whether or not it costs less to serve loyal customers. Many affluent consumers demand a wide range of services that may make this market unprofitable. Word-of-mouth is an important factor but difficult to measure.

Affluent customers want more choices. Dell Computers developed a new business model by allowing customers to select which features and functions they want to be placed into their computers. The concept of personal computers has been changed to personalized computers. There are children, teenagers, and adults who customize their own levels in video games and prepare their own Web pages. Affluent consumers are knowledgeable and make purchases after researching available options. These consumers value firms that provide information useful for making purchasing decisions.

MOTIVATION SHIFTS

Motivation is an internal state of purchasing behavior. While consumer behavior is observable, motives are psychological constructs that are inferred. Many of an individual's specific needs are dormant or latent much of the time. The arousal of any set of needs may be related to the individual's physiological condition, they can emanate from the emotional or cognitive processes, or they may be a reaction to stimuli in the external environment. The diversity of motives among consumers makes it difficult to activate motives that are satisfying to a specific group of consumers. Purchasing decisions require deliberation and planning over extended time periods. Learning what motivates consumer-purchasing behavior is not easy. But if the concepts of buyer behavior are meaningfully translated they can help to understand what motivates people to buy. It is possible to identify groups with common motives and goals. There are many theories of consumer motivation. However, Maslow's hierarchy, even with its limitations, is still one of the most comprehensive.

Abraham Maslow divided human needs into five categories: physiological, safety, social, esteem, and self-actualization.[1] Maslow arranged human needs in a hierarchy from the most important to the least important. Physiological needs include hunger, thirst, and sex. After these needs are satisfied, safety needs ranging from security to protection are addressed. Next, social needs that cover affection and a sense of belonging become important. The next need is esteem, which includes recognition, status, and self-esteem. Finally, self-actualization needs for self-development and realization become the focus. Maslow's theory helps marketers understand how products are considered in the plans and lives of consumers. Maslow's theory also reinforces underlying social-class aspirations of desiring to purchase goods and services purchased by adjacent social classes that are upwards in the social hierarchy. The affluent market can be pictured as striving to achieve esteem and self-actualization needs.

There are limitations to Maslow's hierarchy. First, the hierarchy cannot be tested empirically. Second, lower needs in the hierarchy are never completely satisfied and consequently are replaced by psychologically equivalent needs that are qualitatively or quantitatively more demanding. And finally, the satisfaction of higher-order needs does not necessarily await the satisfaction of lower-order needs. Although Maslow's theory is useful for studying purchasing behavior, new theories have emerged that include the following:

- Motives are not permanent. Motives change throughout a person's life cycle.
- Aspirations tend to grow with achievement and decline with failure.
- Motivation is influenced by the performance of other members of a group to which a person belongs, namely, the reference group.
- Consumers are actively learning and acquiring new wants.

There has been a shift in consumer-purchasing behavior for upscale products and services. While many affluent consumers survive economic events and the stock market's downturn, half of the wealthy worry about money all the time.[2] Many are in debt and wish they had more financial security, yet dual-income households still purchase luxury products. Tiffany & Co. attracts all economic classes of consumers by pricing diamond engagement rings from $850 to $850,000, while the average sells for $7,000 to $8,000.

Shopping and purchasing motives occur outside of the home and include communications with others, peer group attraction, status and authority, and pleasure of bargaining. These variables change from individual to individual. There are personal motives for shopping, like role-playing; diversion; self-gratification; learning about new trends; physical activity, such as leaving the house; and sensory stimulation, such as recreation.[3] Shopping motives can be based on impulse and the distance or the time traveled to the mall, shopping center, or stores—which are convenience factors. Purchasing motives may also be complex based on a combination of rational, emotional, and patronage variables.

Goods once perceived as luxury are now commonplace. Consumers purchase more and better products and services as their income increases. Many consumers in the early 1980s viewed the purchases of central air-conditioning systems, dishwashers, and home computers as luxuries. Families today consider these necessities. Crown molding, two and three car garages, fireplaces, outdoor grills, and modern kitchens are common today. Cell phones are now owned by everybody. The term *luxury* has become largely subjective. Aesthetics have played an important role in marketing such brands as Montblanc pens and Godiva chocolate.

The middle-class is a major market for boats, golf clubs, mountain bikes, and other recreational equipment that only the rich were once able to afford. The new status symbols are Black Berry pagers, flat-screen plasma televisions, and designer accessories for pets. At the same time, if you are selling very expensive luxury brand products, such as a $100,000 automobile, you need to target a subset of the affluent market that makes more than $500,000 a year, since many of the affluent are paying high taxes, school tuition, mortgage, and other payments and could not afford this type of automobile.

Personality traits are a moderating variable for understanding motivation shifts in purchasing behavior and must be used in conjunction with other variables. *Money Magazine* has analyzed six affluent personality types. Important factors in distinguishing personality types are approach to money management and satisfaction with present financial affairs. The personality type known as *controllers* are the wealthiest segment and pride themselves in their ability to administer both their personal finances and their investments. They are older than other personality segments and about half are empty nesters. This personality group likes skiing, fishing, bicycling, and is not interested in spending a lot of money for luxuries.

The *contented spenders* are the second-wealthiest group and are high wage earners. This personality type is a self-disciplined, careful shopper. Money is for them an instrument to make their lives more pleasurable. Time is precious for them and the contented spender is more likely than any other personality type to pay for services that will save time. They frequently consult financial professionals and believe they need help in conducting their daily personal financial affairs.

The *wealth accumulators* are the only group to use investment to gain wealth. Most benefited from the economic boom of the late 1990s. This group is reluctant to spend money but will spend a lot to have a good time.

The *altruists* give their money to social and charitable causes. Otherwise, their focus is spending money on their home and their children. More than half have children under the age of 18. Vacation and family time is important to their personality segment.

Security seekers never seem to believe that they have enough money. Security seekers are always looking to increase their wealth. This group is constantly trying to achieve the affluent lifestyle, but it appears beyond their grasp.

The *aspirers* are younger than the other personality groups and have the least financial assets. They love success and are risk takers. Many are hard workers and participate in activities such as sailing, gambling, and accumulating collectibles. This group is motivated by the rewards that money can buy. The aspirers are not especially knowledgeable about investing and are not actively seeking professional advice, even though they assess themselves as only fair to poor money managers.

Each individual has a distinct personality that has an impact on buying behavior. A strong relationship exists between certain personality types and product and brand choices. Self-concept fundamentals have a mixed record of success in predicting consumer responses to brand images.

PATRONAGE MOTIVES

The reasons why consumers shop at certain retail stores or click onto a retailer's Web page are known as *patronage motives*. Shopping is a socially visible activity. Patronage motives include value, merchandise selection, purchasing convenience, location, store services, personal service, merchandise quality, and store reputation and status. In-store shopping behavior is affected by sales personnel, displays, store décor, and merchandise breadth and depth. Web page visitors to luxury store Web sites look for ease in ordering, variety of merchandise available, and quick delivery. Online retailers offer their customers concierge and personal-shopper services. Luxuryfinder.com features a portal of links to thousands of preselected sites and a calendar listing charity and art events while selling products such as a $1,000 Nepalese cashmere shawl. Online luxury retailers include among others Tiffany & Co., Thomas Pink, and Nieman Marcus. Art, jewelry, designer clothing, rare wines, and automobiles are being purchased online. Among luxury product Web sites are the following:

Epicurious.com
Nordstrom.com

Ashford.com
Omahasteaks.com
Tavolo.com
Redenvelope.com
Wine.com
Chefscatalog.com
Adiamondisforever.com
Williams-Sonoma.com
Firstjewelry.com
Bloomingdales.com

Retailers tailor the design of the store to the lifestyles of specific market segments. Retailers such as Brooks Brothers, Neiman Marcus, Nordstrom, and Tiffany use atmospherics, such as a lounging area with upscale magazines and beverage services.

The choice of a retail store can be either high involvement or low involvement. At times, the decision may be highly important, and at other times, especially with convenience items, the decision may be of low importance. For example, products such as automobiles and a component stereo or home-theater system have high relevance because of their price, complex features, large difference among alternatives, and perceived risk of making a wrong decision. For these purchases, the consumer desires more personalization in their shopping experience. There is little risk if one brand is bought over another.

Store loyalty is a basis for market segmentation. Store loyalty allows the consumer to minimize risk. Purchasing motivation, brand choice decisions, store choice decisions, and lifestyle consumer characteristics are intertwined.

Store image is the perception that consumers have about a retail store as it relates to their expectations. Opening a gift box from Tiffany has a different feeling than a J.C. Penney box. Consumer perceptions of a store vary greatly. Usually a particular retailer is most attractive to certain customers belonging to the same social class or lifestyle group. The personality of the store is built on location, personal services, merchandise assortment, ambience, personal sales efforts, and promotion and communications. Some stores even have personal shoppers or personnel online to help customers who do not have the time or experience to make special purchases. These factors all help to create a favorable store image that will attract the right consumers. The better the retailer addresses the most desired needs of its target market, the more likely it is to gain store loyalty. Stores targeting the affluent market must be situated in the right location. Upscale malls should do well in the future, but there will be a shakeout of regional malls anchored by stores targeting the middle of the market. Freestanding stores such as Home Depot will do well. It is also important that the retailer provides the right location, merchandising, personal services, and promotions that recognize the needs of their affluent customers.

Marketers and retailers develop brand loyalty and repeat purchase behavior through product quality and service. Brand image is another variable that can stimulate repeat purchasing, especially among those who have a favorable image of the brand. Even manufacturers who change packaging find brand loyalty a critical component in purchasing decisions. Godiva packages it products in a distinctive manner and has been a leader in upscale marketing. Godiva symbolizes high-quality chocolates sold through selected specialty stores. Godiva chocolates appear in boxes that convey status and prestige.

MOTIVATION AND THE UPSCALE CONSUMER

The upscale consumer has similar achievement, motivation, and aspiration levels as do affluent consumers. Upscale consumers strive toward accomplishment, higher incomes, better future jobs, and a higher standard of living. Upscale consumers attach importance to upward mobility and the ownership of automobiles like the Porsche and household appliances like the Sub-Zero refrigerator, a $10,000 gas grill, and an in-home movie theater. People who are upscale consumers are likely to purchase imported cars, bank through a home computer, and wear designer jeans.

The affluent consumer is defined by income and total assets. The upscale consumer may fall into the income categories but does not have the accumulated assets of the affluent consumer. For instance, two recently married college graduates might have a total household income of $80,000, which is over the $75,000 minimum for the low end of the affluent market, but not possess total assets of $665,000. Another example would be the young doctor with a household income of $150,000 a year, with few assets and large debts from college tuition and from medical equipment purchases. Current income is an indication of wealth, and asset value is another measure.

There are many affluent consumers who have the household income and total assets but do not feel affluent. A dual-income family with a household income of $100,000 and an inheritance of $700,000 but also a large mortgage, a number of automobiles, high college costs for their children—all while trying to save for their future retirement—do not feel wealthy. Another family may have a household income of $150,000, with average total assets of $700,000, a high mortgage, and high tuition to private schools and country club membership, feels that they are just getting along. There are upscale consumers who receive gifts from family members that help them feel affluent. Upscale consumers have desires and aspirations above their immediate financial circumstances and wish to indulge themselves on special occasions. For example, gift wrap has gone upscale as sales have increased 5.1 percent in 2003 to about $10 billion, while the growth rate for the past few years was approximately 4.7 percent. Style-conscious upscale consumers desire gift wrap decorated with pearls, silk, and chenille. Demand for luxury wrap has motivated the development of niche stores such as Papyrus and Kate's Papeire, which has four stores in Manhattan and one in Greenwich, Connecticut.

Many retailers have developed upscale store brands to satisfy customers who may also be cross shoppers, such as the following:

- Sears with Lands' End
- Marshall's and T. J. Maxx with Ralph Lauren
- Target with Isaac Mizrahi

SERVICES AND MOTIVATION

The affluent demand more and higher-quality services. Services, unlike physical products, are intangible and are not seen before purchased. The consumer getting advice must envision the outcome. For example, Pinnacle Care International of Baltimore charges members between $5,000 and $25,000 a year to maintain medical records, coordinate health care, and obtain speedy appointments with overbooked specialists. Since services are intangible, consumers try to discern evidence of quality in order to reduce risk.

Services are often inseparable from their providers, whether the providers are people or machines. For example, dentists create and disperse their services at the same time and require the presence of the individual for performance. Consequently, the reputation of the dentist is paramount.

Services can be variable. Hotels such as the Four Seasons, the Fairmount, and the Ritz-Carlton strive to provide consistent services to customers so the customers want to return to the hotel again.

Services are perishable, and therefore special promotional efforts are important. Service marketers try to offset this limitation with visual images and tangible reminders of their services by offering packaged products with their names. Services cannot be stored. Empty seats on an airplane or in a concert hall are sales lost forever. The market for some services has a fluctuating demand that varies by season, day of the week, and hour of the day. For example, airlines use pricing strategies that adjust to holiday and weekend travel since consumers are willing to pay for convenience and demand preferences.

Marketers of services need to take advantage of market opportunities as they become available. More than 50 percent of affluent households are online. They use the Web to visit financial sites, buy airline tickets, and make hotel reservations. Therefore, marketers of banking, hotels, and insurance services need to use the Internet to reach this market. The Marriott Corporation, with its hotel, resort, restaurant and food services, broadened its market to include senior citizens by establishing upscale assisted-living and retirement communities across the United States.

The development of service marketing strategies requires five steps:

1. Identify service opportunities.
2. Define the target market.
3. Position the service.
4. Develop a service marketing mix: promotion, product, and price and place strategies.
5. Evaluate and control service performance.

This is the way it would work for financial institutions. The first step in developing a service marketing strategy for a financial institution is to identify market opportunities that require monitoring customers, competing firms, and the marketing environment. Multi-income families have become much more of the norm, and the challenge has been how to serve this market. More dual-income households means more affluence. Previously, these financial institutions served clients with a million or more dollars in liquid assets.

The second step is to define the target market before developing a new service strategy or modifying existing ones. Some financial institutions have broadened their definitions of the low end of the affluent market. Bank of America has designated its clients with $100,000 to invest as a minimum account, and Fidelity has designated $250,000 for private banking customers.

Positioning a service because of its intangible benefits is more difficult than product positioning of tangible advantages. Since Bank of America and Fidelity desired to appeal to the low end of the affluent market, these firms had to demonstrate that the high end of the market was already receiving acceptable financial services. Targeted were those low-end affluent consumers who would be willing to try these new investment services.

The fourth step is to develop a service mix designated to deliver a service to the target market similar to the same mix as for a product. Promotion could be directed to customers who already maintained smaller accounts by direct mail. Perhaps a separate account name could be designated for such accounts, developing brand identity. A distribution strategy would be to provide special telephone numbers to reach representatives. Price could be determined based on investment size and a comparison made of competing firms.

The evaluation function is more difficult than product performance because of the variability in service performance. One method is to obtain feedback from customers as to their satisfaction with the services provided.

LIFESTYLE MARKETING AND MOTIVATION

The theory of social class was introduced before the new role of women emerged and higher education became widespread. In the past, women married into a social class and had limited access to education or careers. Today, women bring educational, financial, and occupational status to the household. This market segment has discovered that particular types of lifestyle activity give identity and that both lifestyle and identity can be merged together in determining the purchase of items that reflect a desired lifestyle. The status value of the purchase preoccupies many consumers who desire to create a personal identity through consumption. Traditional status symbols included the ownership of a Bentley automobile, fashion clothes, furniture, Cartier jewelry, the Rolex Submariner watch, and other items. Spending behavior of the affluent is based on lifestyle and personal identity. Veblen emphasized the importance of the purchase and coined the term "conspicuous consumption."[4] One aspect of conspicuous consumption is that the individual achieves status not only in the eyes of others but also in his or her own eyes, and it is reinforced by a desired lifestyle.

A second aspect of lifestyle marketing is the selection of a target market. As a result of declining sales, Spiegel changed its marketing strategies and selected a different target market. The new target market was the upscale consumer, particularly women engaged in the workforce or in activities outside the home who wanted fashion and quality and who were brand conscious. Spiegel aimed to target a younger, better-educated customer employed in a managerial or professional position with higher income than other catalog users. Spiegel's repositioning meant replacing its merchandise assortment with high-fashion home furnishings and apparel. Spiegel has also gone after segments of the target market such as plus-sized women because of competition from L. L. Bean and Neiman Marcus.

A third aspect of targeting is to take advantage of lifestyle trends. The lifestyle trend of voluntary simplicity contributed in part to L. L. Bean's growth. Consumers who adopt this lifestyle seek material simplicity, strive for self-actualization, and adopt an ecological ethic. Voluntary simplicity is marked by a balance between inner and outer development and growth. It is a return to frugality and puritanical self-reliance. Outdoor activities such as camping, rafting, and mountain climbing reflect this lifestyle. Ecological awareness becomes paramount and so does the interconnection between people and natural resources. This new consciousness is concerned with the reduction of environmental pollution and is receptive to new products that preserve and maintain the natural environment. Knowing the lifestyle of the target market will help in segmenting those members who will respond to a consumption identity that enforces good environmental behavior.

LIFESTYLE MARKET SEGMENTATION STRATEGIES

Marketing strategy includes segmenting, targeting, and positioning. Within segments there are different needs and tastes that lead consumers to spend differently. The determination of a segment that leads to the definition of a target market is important in developing a marketing strategy. A marketer can use mass-marketing strategies to target one or more segments, such as the senior citizen market. Affluent seniors, instead of all seniors, could be targeted for a credit card company. Credit cards for affluent seniors may be used as a convenience, while other seniors use them as a basis for installment purchases.

Positioning strategy is linked to lifestyle market segmentation. Positioning is the process of distinguishing a company or product from competitors along such dimensions as product characteristics or values that are meaningful to consumers. Dior is positioned as a French designer, and the Rolex is positioned as a watch of prestige and quality. Harley-Davidson has successfully identified and dominated the upscale-user market. The typical Harley-Davidson buyer is 46 years old with a household income of approximately $75,000. Positioning strategy aids customers in evaluating product attributes that are of significance or value to them.

Many marketing opportunities can be developed from lifestyle analysis. The manufacturer of Lexus automobiles targets those people considered achievers with high personal and professional goals. Brooks Brothers used a lifestyle-based marketing strategy to convey conservatism and good taste for over 100 years. Price-skimming strategies can be used to attract the affluent consumer by using high prices, since this segment is more concerned with product quality, uniqueness, or status than price. Nonprice strategy can be used to target the upscale market by minimizing the role of price as a variable through promotion, packaging, delivery, customer services, or other marketing features.

PRECISION TARGETING

The challenge in satisfying the affluent market is the realization that there are a series of ongoing opportunities and threats. Marketers must understand how the affluent market views itself, others, organizations, and society. The following checklist should be devised for precision targeting this market:

- Affluent market segments can be identified by the products and services they currently use or need. The affluent market segment has characteristics that distinguish itself from the overall market, such as the need for financial services.
- The affluent target market must also be measurable. This means that the market potential should be of significant size. The market segment must possess sufficient purchasing power to make the marketing effort worthwhile.
- Once the affluent market segment has been pinpointed and measured, the next step is to learn whether or not it is accessible. Reaching the market segment must be possible through distribution or promotion techniques. This means that certain types of retail stores are present where the target market shops or an alternative distribution channel is available for purchasing these product or services.

- Finally, the market segment should favorably respond to marketing strategies tailored to their specialized needs. For example, J.P. Morgan has designated $250,000 for private banking customers. Once this market was the domain of clients willing to invest $1 million or more.

The affluent market can be reached effectively through magazine advertising. There are any number of magazines for a niche audience. The messages in the past have tended to be the same in all magazines, but in the future, marketers will be developing customized messages for different kinds of magazines. For example, an advertisement by Allstate insurance placed in *Modern Bride* showed a white car and a black van parked next to each other outside a church, and the copy reads, "Your policies could have a blissful union too."

Market opportunities in the mass affluent market abound. Total paid magazine circulation growth leaders in 2003 were *Bicycling*, *Weight Watchers*, *National Geographic for Kids*, *Golf for Women*, *Latina*, and *Organic Style*. These magazines segment the health and fitness market, the women's and children's market, and the Hispanic market.

MANAGING CHANGE

The changing social structure reflects four current trends that have had an impact on consumer behavior. First, marketers are increasingly aware that dual-income families are joining the ranks of the affluent-and upscale-consumer market. Some of the outcomes of increased discretionary purchasing power are two-car families becoming three-car families and one-computer households becoming two- and three-computer households. Although family size is smaller than 25 years ago, housing purchases include homes with more square footage. Second, the professional woman has become a major market for products and services ranging from financial services to art objects to trips to exotic travel locations. Third, men are taking more interest in fashion, gourmet cooking, expensive hobbies, and other products and services as they become more affluent. For example, the men's clothing industry is shortening their product cycle as Brooks Brothers and Banana Republic change their inventories more frequently. The affluent market is also growing older. The first baby-boomers born between 1946 and 1964 will turn 60 and half will be over 50 in 2006, and they will comprise a significant segment of the affluent market in the future. The *Consumer Expenditure Survey, 2003* reported that baby boomers from age 45–54 have the highest household income ($68,028) and the highest household spending ($50,101) of any age group. Consumers over the age of 50 account for half of automobile sales. Eighty percent of people over age 65 own their own homes, and only 21 percent have mortgages.

The following strategies may help marketers target and motivate the affluent market:

- Product positioning
- Positive shopping atmosphere
- Internet selling
- Promoting new and unique products
- Developing strong store and brand images
- Appealing to cross-shopping behavior
- Developing a high level of customer service

Each individual has distinct motives for purchasing that change over time. Consumers often combine rational and emotional motives when making a purchase. Marketers can generate positive consumer motivation by identifying and appealing to a consumer's buying motives. This is not an easy task since the profile of a consumer involves personality, attitudes, perceived risk, innovativeness, class consciousness, and the importance of the purchase. For example, over time affluent consumer values and lifestyles have been altered. Wine consumption peaked in the mid-1980s and more expensive wines were purchased in the 1990s. Products targeted to the affluent market should reflect core and secondary values and address changing needs.

Component lifestyles are most noticeable among affluent consumers and reflect consumer attitudes and behavior that will vary by situation. For example, an individual may own a Mercedes but go to Wendy's for lunch and buy a good wine for dinner. Cross shopping is a manifestation of component life styles. The new rich seek social status and prestige but are less constrained by social custom. There is a desire for self-expression, but also a desire for convenience.

The purchase of new luxury products involves obtaining a low price on a 24-pack of bottled water but also desiring a $500 handbag or a $50,000 piece of jewelry. Luxury retailers think of Rodeo Drive in Los Angeles and North Michigan Avenue in Chicago. Mall developers want their same glamorous appeal and locate luxury malls where warranted by demographics. A new way of thinking is necessary to serve affluent consumers. Wal-Mart is testing an upscale store in Texas by selling gourmet food, vintage wines, and trendy clothing to determine if affluent consumers will shop at a retailer known for dealing exclusively with the mass market.

The growth of the service economy has occurred in part to serve a more affluent consumer. Affluent consumers spend more on services than on products. The main reason for this has to do with demographic changes. There are increasing numbers of career women, single-person households, senior citizens, and dual-income households. The massive time crunch of many dual-income families, smaller families, and more singles has created opportunities to allow consumers to purchase more services. Expenditures for services related to travel, entertainment, hotels, restaurants, health care, and fitness have soared. Manufacturers and retailers have used the Internet and catalogs to make shopping easier. As consumers become more affluent, new services are needed to satisfy their needs.

Chapter 4

Changing Economic Dimensions

There has been a greater polarization of income in the United States since the end of World War II. The market for goods and services has divided itself, with affluent consumers purchasing expensive items and working-class people shopping at discount stores. Marketers selling medium-price goods have been the most vulnerable during this period. Retailers selling to the affluent, like Neiman Marcus and Nordstrom, have profited. Wal-Mart and Target, two discounters, have grown tremendously. Brands such as BMW in automobiles, Viking Range in kitchen appliances, Coach in leather goods, Sam Adams in beer, and Victoria's Secret in lingerie have made new inroads into the affluent market.

The increasing number of dual-income families has been an important reason for the growth of the affluent market. These families include those who do not necessarily satisfy income and financial capacity guidelines but who nonetheless desire to trade up in their purchasing. The belief is maintained that since they work hard they are entitled to a comfortable lifestyle. Purchasing behavior in many instances manifests itself with a visible luxurious lifestyle. As incomes increase, a greater proportion is expended on intangibles such as health clubs. The new rich seem to enjoy doing activities rather than acquiring goods. An experience is valued. For example, people enjoy different cuisines in pleasant environments—the experience the restaurant provides—rather than eating out just to avoid cooking. Products and services that distinguish themselves through aesthetics, adding emotional value, are desired.

The affluent market has a larger share of discretionary income than typical consumer markets; therefore marketers will benefit from selling higher-quality, high-priced goods and services. Goods and services in demand will include the following:

- Goods that save time and ease household maintenance and drudgery
- Goods that are durable, such as quality furniture, fixtures, appliances, and those goods and services that improve housing and are related to household services
- Goods and services that enhance the physical self and maintain and restore youthfulness
- Goods and services that are of a psychological nature, such as education, counseling, and stress management and physical fitness
- Goods and services that support mobility and gratification, such as cell telephones, laptop computers, instant photography, and 24/7 services
- Goods and services that allow improvement of self-image and express a lifestyle, like gourmet foods, wines, decorating, and top-designer products and services

As consumers' incomes have increased significantly in recent years, marketers can anticipate pronounced shifts in the relative demand for different categories of goods and services. Purchasing power is an important consideration for buyer behavior. Household income trends are especially important since the household is the primary economic unit of consumption. For example, the singles market has doubled since 1980, and together with increased educational and income levels, this market offers lucrative potential to marketers. The singles market has shown a steady growth of interest in such activities as opera, ballet, theater, symphony orchestras, travel, and various sports events. Moreover, the gay market has emerged as an important part of the singles group.

Table 4.1 compares the percent of expenditures at different income levels. Those people earning $70,000 or more comprise the affluent market. It is obvious that the affluent market compared to other household markets is exceptionally lucrative for purchasing housing items, transportation, clothing, entertainment, and insurance. Many affluent people own a second residence; purchase quality apparel; possess two or more automobiles; and attend concerts, the theater, and other forms of high-priced entertainment. Charitable contributions are significant, and insurance for multiple cars, houses, jewelry, art objects, household goods, and life insurance is considerable. Their lifestyle is heavy in discretionary income and travel and allocating expenditures for recreation. The education of children is paramount, and expenditures for private preparatory schools and then college are significant. Home security has become an increasing problem, and elaborate systems have been sold to affluent consumers to protect their residences from theft. Usually, as family income increases, the percentage

Table 4.1
Consumer Spending at Different Income Levels: Percent of Spending at Different Levels

Expenditures	$10,000–15,000	$20,000–30,000	$30,000–40,000	$70,000 and Over
Food	16.5	15.7	14.3	11.9
Housing	26.5	24.7	23.6	26.0
Utilities	9.7	8.6	7.5	5.0
Clothing	4.2	3.7	4.6	4.6
Transportation	17.1	19.7	21.3	18.2
Health Care	8.7	7.3	6.2	3.8
Entertainment	3.8	4.1	4.6	5.2
Contributions	2.9	3.1	3.0	3.6
Insurance	3.4	6.2	8.5	15.2

Source: Consumer Expenditure Survey, 2001, U.S. Department of Labor, Bureau of Labor Statistics www.bls.gov/cex/cxann01.pdf. (accessed April 2003).

spent for necessities decreases and the percentage spent on luxuries or savings increases.

The cost of enjoying affluence continues to increase over time. In 2004 the price of a natural Russian sable coat at Bloomingdale's was $160,000; a case of Dom Perignon from Sherry-Gebmann in New York City was $1,439; a concert grand Steinway piano was $96,000; and two James Purday & Sons shotguns sold for $167,000, at Griffin and Howe in Bernardsville, New Jersey. For those who wish their children to be educated at Harvard, the cost was $39,880 a year for an undergraduate education. Naturally, income and financial resources, credit and debt will influence the new rich consumer in making these purchases.

Initially, the concept of conspicuous consumption was used to convey the buyer behavior of rich individuals. For instance, the mansions of Vanderbilt in 1898, the Henry Flagler home in Palm Beach, Florida, and the Hearst Castle in San Simeon, California, showcased opulence. Conspicuous consumption is the acquisition and visible display of luxury goods and services. Visibility communicates to others wealth and power.

A more modern perspective related to conspicuous consumption is that individuals desire to "keep up with the Joneses"—meaning friends, relatives, and neighbors. Vacationing in Vail or Aspen, Colorado, is a method to communicate to others that the individual or family has achieved a desired status. Frequently, individuals are evaluated based on the clothing they wear, and a specific style and sophistication is desired. The ownership of a Mercedes will likely be viewed as a possession of an affluent and upper-class individual, and the purchase may be made to impress neighbors and friends. Others make purchases in expensive stores because the labels and packages show the name of the store.

Product and service symbols are important for self-image. Many members of the affluent market and those who trade up in their purchasing behavior are endeavoring to achieve and display a certain lifestyle. This lifestyle is important to their self-perception and also how others may envision them. Conspicuous consumption has a new meaning of self-expression, individual identity, and desiring meaningful experiences.

ECONOMIC ASSUMPTIONS

Much of the conceptual, theoretical, and empirical studies related to consumer behavior have evolved from many behavioral sciences including economics, psychology, sociology, social psychology, and anthropology. Although all of these disciplines are useful in explaining buyer behavior, their methods and units of analysis vary. Economics was the first discipline to develop a theory of buyer behavior, and marketers relied heavily on this theoretical foundation. But economic theory related to consumption behavior was largely based on rational and economic calculations, and this was to prove inadequate for marketers.

Consumers do not necessarily make purchasing decisions on a rational basis. Consumers are not aware of all product alternatives and are not always capable of ranking all possible purchasing alternatives. Complete knowledge of alternatives in terms of product benefits and disadvantages is not present. Frequently, consumers have incomplete information and in many instances lack the motivation to make perfect decisions. People are limited by their existing values and goals and the degree of their knowledge.

The consumer does not always act in an objective manner. Theoretical economics depicts a world of perfect competition and rational rather than subjective decision making. This theoretical economic model can be criticized as too idealistic and overly simplistic. For instance, if a family of four decides to eat out at Burger King, it may cost $20 compared to $10 to eat the same meal at home. Therefore, the economic model suggests that this family will make a rational decision and eat at home. This perspective ignores the pleasurable aspects and the utilities of eating out. Another view expressed by the model is that a price reduction of a product increases the value of the goods in buyers' minds and leads to increased sales. However, some individuals may believe that the quality of the product has declined or that status value has been diminished. Obviously, economic factors alone do not explain this purchasing situation.

There are some economic assumptions that stem from economic theory that are much more defensible. For example, a consumers' primary objective in purchasing goods and services is to maximize satisfaction. Consumer satisfaction would be increased if products that are desired were produced, and this premise leads to the conclusion that human wants are infinite. Furthermore, the lower the price of particular products and services, the higher the sales;

and the higher the consumer's real income, the higher the sales—provided the products reflects quality and value.

PURCHASING POWER

Economic conditions are the forces in the economy that have an impact on the business organization's ability to compete and consumers' willingness to purchase goods and services. Paramount to marketers are consumer perceptions of the economy. For example, if consumers believe that economic trends are favorable, they may increase spending, but if consumers believe the opposite, spending may be reduced. Williams-Sonoma, a retailer of $400 toasters and other gadgets, may find its organization vulnerable to recessions even of a temporary nature. Markets need purchasing power as well as people who have the ability to buy goods and services. Purchasing power depends on income and resources, prices, credit, and debt. Estimating the market potential for specific goods and services means monitoring major trends in income and consumer-spending patterns. Increasing interest rates generally represent increases in inflation, which erodes the purchasing power of fixed incomes over time.

Since there are differences in abilities, educational levels, occupations, and wealth, income is not equally distributed. Consumer income should be viewed from three different perspectives: (1) disposable income that is money remaining for spending or savings after paying taxes; (2) discretionary income that is disposable income after paying taxes and making essential personal and household expenditures such as food, clothing, and shelter; and (3) real income, which is earnings adjusted for inflation. The affluent market will have the most discretionary income of all consumer markets.

Consumer buying power reflects individuals' resources and includes income, ability to obtain credit, and wealth. Economic conditions have an impact on buying power. Consumers will have less buying power during inflationary periods since prices are rising and those who are upscale buyers will become more dependent on credit to finance the purchase of luxury items. The ability to obtain credit from banks and their sources allows for the purchase of goods and services that might not otherwise be possible. Consumers may postpone purchase of expensive items when interest rates are high and make those purchases when interest rates are relatively low. The accumulation of past income such as savings and financial resources like real estate, stocks, bonds, jewelry, art objects, and antiques is referred to as wealth. It is possible for an individual or a family to have a high income and very little wealth, and the reverse is also true but not likely.

Marketers are able to assess the general state of the economy by observing the Gross Domestic Product (GDP), which reflects economic growth. The GDP is now the standard measure of growth since it is the appropriate measure for much of short-term analysis of the economy and was first used in 1991. The Gross National Product (GNP) is larger than the GDP. For instance, if General Motors produces a car in Mexico, it is counted for GNP but not for GDP. Changes in growth rates will represent threats or opportunities for some marketers. Consumers may increase or decrease their consumption of luxury goods and services based on their perception of the economy. The GDP and its rate of growth is one of the most important variables influencing consumers and business organizations.

Table 4.2 lists sources for estimating market potential, which are frequently generated from social and economic variables linked to aggregate demand. The main sources for forecasting consumer buying power can be gathered from the Survey Research Center, the F. W. Dodge Corporation, the Standard Industrial Classification System, and the Survey of Buying Power.

Table 4.2
Sources of Market Data

- *Survey Research Center*: Attitudes reflect the decision whether to purchase a product or service and the choice of a specific brand. The Survey Research Center at the University of Michigan is one of the best-known approaches to relating attitudes to buyer behavior. Consumer spending interests for large durable goods are analyzed. For instance, consumers are asked if they have a definite intention to buy, a probable intention to buy, an indefinite intention to buy, or a definite intention not to buy a new automobile, home, or major appliance over a definite period of time. The results are interpreted for short-run demand for consumer goods expenditures.
- *F. W. Dodge Corporation*: Compiles data on new home construction. The demand for household appliances, carpeting, furniture, and insurance among other items could be partially ascertained from new housing starts.
- *North American Industral Classification System*: The NAICS classifies all manufacturing into 20 major industry groups. For example, number 25 is designated furniture and fixtures. Each major group is further broken down into about 150 groups with three-digit codes such as 251 for household furniture and 252 for office furniture. This guide is useful for discerning area market potentials and promotes uniformity and comparability of information.
- *Survey of Buying Power*: Published annually by Sales and Marketing Management. Data is presented for geographic areas, including states, countries, and cities. Provides estimates of population, income, and retail sales for all standard metropolitan statistical areas in the United States. Retail sales are further subdivided by various categories, such as food, automotive, and apparel. Two indicators are used when comparing the buying power of one region with another. The first is the Effective Buying Income Index, which includes salaries, wages, dividends, and other sources of income less taxes. The second is a weighted index referred to as the BPI or the Buying Power Index, which consists of population, effective buying income, and retail sales data. The BPI should be used only as a market potential yardstick. Although consumers may have the buying power to make purchases, this does not necessarily mean the purchasing power will be used for specific goods and services.

When analyzing the economic environment, many uncertainties exist. The impact of declining birth rates after the baby boom years, a maturing population, a changing American family, the increase of nontraditional households, geographic shifts in population, increasing educational attainment, consumer expenditures, and ecological perspectives must be monitored. How will such factors as inflation, prosperity, recession, and ecology affect affluent market spending? Assumptions about the new rich will not always be correct, and the results of incorrect forecasting can be staggering.

The status of the dollar is still another aspect of uncertainty. The dollar had declined to a 12 year low against the British pound at the end of 2004. British tourists visiting the United States found that an Apple iPod retailing for $426 in London could be purchased for $299 in New York City, and a Gap reversible faux-fur vest selling for $132 in London would retail for $68 in New York City. Travel from European countries to the United States increased 25 percent in 2004, and the luxury market has benefited. As the dollar declined, many Europeans found that for many luxury goods, purchasing in the United States accounted for practically a half-off sale. However, a weak dollar would also increase prices for luxury imports in the United States. For example, the French apparel firm Hermès has raised its silk twill scarves by as much as 7 percent to $315. Louis Vuitton Pegase luggage, Anichini Giova domestic linens, and Niami Allae loudspeakers have all experienced significant price increases because of the falling dollar.

Consumption patterns are influenced by occupation and economic trends. Occupation may be a more significant variable than income in some circumstances. An electrician may earn as much as a young business executive, but purchasing behavior is different because of education, attitudes, interests, and other lifestyle factors. An electrician will purchase work clothes, work shoes, and lunch boxes. A young business executive will buy suits, an attaché case, and a country club membership. Education has been associated with the purchase of books, health foods, recreation, and travel. Education also influences decision making. Educated consumers desire more information and demand products that reflect value. Since there is a link between education and occupation, these variables should be considered together when segmenting markets. For example, general dentists earned $166,460 in 2000; general internal medicine doctors, $164,000; psychiatrists, $145,700; family practice physicians, $144,700; and pediatricians, $137,800. The spouse's income was not provided but if taken into account would probably increase family income considerably. Product choice is reflected by disposable income, savings and monetary resources, debts, credit availability, and attitudes toward spending versus saving.

ECOLOGY AND THE NATURAL ENVIRONMENT

Ecological awareness has become important to the affluent consumer. This new consciousness is concerned with the reduction of environmental pollution and is receptive to new products that preserve and maintain the natural environment. Consumer values on the issue of ecology have changed over the years and are still evolving. A growing concern about the impact of environmental factors on product development, labeling, and other strategies has emerged as a result of increased public awareness. Consumer organizations have increasingly focused their attention on ecology.

The problem of ecology is holistic in nature and affects not just affluent consumers but all consumers no matter where they live. The interfaces between marketing and ecology have become important as problems of air, water, and noise pollution; overburdened travel arteries; decaying cities; overpopulation; and poverty have received increased scrutiny.

Environmental groups have taken a stand against aerosol-spray cans because of their potential damage to the atmosphere's ozone layer. Nonreturnable or throwaway containers have been the subject of public referendums in some localities. The conservation of natural resources is sometimes counter to economic growth policies. Finally, scarcities of oil and the potential depletion of other natural resources have caused many firms to invest heavily in research and development to find other energy alternatives.

The movement promoting ecological awareness has been spearheaded by many educated, highly concerned citizens who are likely to be innovators and early adoptees in their purchasing behavior. Consumer organizations have motivated public concern over ecological problems that include a variety of dimensions. Environmental parameters include such factors as population, economic development, and urbanization. Resources such as energy, solid wastes, and recycling have received increased attention. Control over air pollution, water pollution, radiation, pesticides, noise, and toxic substances has increased costs for some industries but has created opportunities for other industries. Finally, the concern for quality of life underlies environmentalists' policies on housing, transportation, aesthetics, occupational environment, and recreation.

The new millennium will witness the continuing emergence of green marketing, whereby environmental ramifications for society are considered as goods and services are sold. Many consumers are willing to pay higher prices to purchase "green" products. There are additional costs involved for recycling centers and landfill systems. The consumer environment has pressured McDonald's and Burger King to eliminate their polystyrene cartons and use recyclable paper wrappings and paper napkins. The Clean Air Act Amendment of 1977 strengthened emission standards for automobiles, thereby increasing prices for consumers. Business organizations like DuPont, Amway, AT&T, 3M, and Procter & Gamble have all developed products and packages that are less harmful to the environment.

CHANGING FAMILY CONSUMPTION ECONOMICS

There is no longer a common American family. The profile of the American family has changed dramatically as the proportion of nontraditional families has increased. The most notable changes in the past two decades have been delayed marriage, dual careers, divorce, and singles living alone. Couples have postponed marriage to achieve success in careers and are more financially secure and sophisticated in the consumer decision process than in the past. A high divorce rate usually means that children play a greater role in purchasing decisions. Since there are fewer children in marriages, more money can be spent on their clothing, toys, and other products, including education. The changing roles of men and women manifests itself in purchasing behavior. The traditional stereotype of the husband as the primary wage earner with a nonworking wife and two children at home has vanished from the American scene.

Changes in household structure, such as single parents with children and extended families, increased cohabitation, and the more openness of gay couples, are becoming increasingly important for marketers to monitor. Age plays an important role in the consumption behavior of family members and in particular the age compression of children as they act older and grow up faster than in previous generations. These nontraditional family patterns will change many of the expenditures made by household members.

The traditional roles of men and women are not as distinct as in past generations. Products formerly marketed to men are now marketed to women. And products that traditionally were marketed only to women are also marketed to men. Because of the blurring of gender roles, new trends are emerging in family decision making. Instead of appealing to the same old stereotypes, alert marketers must adapt quickly to these changing roles.

TRENDS BROADENING AFFLUENT-FAMILY BUYER BEHAVIOR

Several factors have altered the basic structure and characteristics of affluent households and will reshape markets. These include (1) the purchase of conspicuous goods and services, (2) the income of ethnic groups, (3) the changing singles market, (4) age compression and its impact on selected industries, and (5) dual-career families. Although the profile of the affluent American family has radically changed, the household is still the more important unit of analysis for consumer behavior.

CONSPICUOUS GOODS AND SERVICES

The wealthy are competing in the market of luxury consumption. The ability to pay high prices has become an indicator of social standing. The most expensive Mercedes in the late 1990s was the CL600, which cost about $100,000. The Maybach 62 was introduced in 2003 and was sold for $350,000. Plans have been made by Mercedes to launch the SLR, which is priced over $450,000.

Patek Phillippe, Rolex, and Brequet are selling watches that are priced at more than $200,000. Limited edition watches are priced in the millions.

These high prices command a growing market. The number of millionaires has increased from about 360,000 in 1989 to about 650,000 in 1998 and 1,200,000 in 2001.

The market for luxury yachts has more than tripled since 1997. The size of a megayacht has grown from about a typical length of 80 to 110 feet in the mid-1990s to over 150 feet by 2004. Prices can now cost over $100 million.

The latest in luxury is the development of six-star hotels. The Setai in Miami is offering rooms with rates starting at $900 a night. The Ocean Club in the Bahamas has rooms starting at $725 with a garden view. Some luxury hotels focus on highly individualized services such as personal butlers, chefs, drivers, and concierges. The Amangani in Jackson Hole, Wyoming, prices suites $700 and upward and provides dog-sledding or horse-drawn carriage sleigh rides. The Park Hyatt hotels, the luxury tier of the Hyatt chains, are able to charge rates 35 percent higher in 2004 than in 2003. Luxury hotels and their services are perceived as an expanding industry for the future.

INCOME OF ETHNIC GROUPS

Income distribution in the past was shaped like a pyramid, with the highest incomes at the top. More recently, the picture is more rectangular in shape, with large increases in the number and proportion of affluent households. There has been a spectacular rise in black and Hispanic households occupying the affluent segment. According to the Census Bureau, black households earning over $75,000 increased from 6 percent in 1980 to 12.4 percent by 1998, and the affluent of Hispanic origin increased from 6.7 percent in 1980 to 10.7 percent in 1998. The median income of Asians showed the greatest increase from 1990 to 1998. Before 1990 complete data of Asian income is not available.[1]

Merrill Lynch is aggressively endeavoring to target affluent Hispanics since excellent opportunities exist. There are 3.7 million affluent Hispanics in the United States with combined buying power of close to $300 billion. Hispanic households earning more than $100,000 grew 126 percent, compared to 77 percent for the general population, from 1990 to 2000. More than two-thirds of affluent Hispanic households are concentrated in California, Texas, and New York, with a growing potential in Florida and Chicago. Many of these affluent Hispanics are small-business owners, and they tend to spend the same or more in such sectors as apparel, housing, food, telephone services, TV/radio and other equipment, and transportation. Hispanics are the fastest-growing ethnic group in the United States, and business organizations are trying to learn more about serving this market. The Census Bureau projects that by 2010 Hispanics will outnumber blacks in the United States. Since affluent Hispanics are geographically concentrated, this market should be relatively easy to reach using various types of media.

The proportion of the population of Asians, blacks, and Hispanics aged 40 and over is growing. Compared to the white population, they tend to be younger; but the highest-earning years are over the age of 40, so this segment of the affluent market can be expected to increase in the future. As children are educated and leave the household, more ethnic families will enter their most affluent stage. Already, Asian children in particular, and blacks and Hispanics are increasing their educational attainment by completing college. All of this is promising for marketers of luxury goods and services. There will be growth opportunities for marketers of travel, recreational, and leisure products; items that enhance personal growth and appearance; and products and services that offer convenience.

The United States ski industry experienced phenomenal growth during the 1970s, but growth has been flat for the past 20 years. The ski industry, seeking growth, is now targeting minorities. The data is indeed impressive, with 70 percent of the U.S. minority population under the age of 18 (either black or Hispanic) and in many metropolitan areas such as Denver, Los Angeles, and Philadelphia outnumbering whites. Minority participation for skiing is currently less than 8 percent. The ski industry needs to change its image as a sport not just for the wealthiest Americans. Southern California is targeting minority youth, and in 2003 about 40 percent of the skiers were African American, Hispanic, or Asian. Meanwhile, plans have been made to penetrate the New Hampshire, Vermont, and Massachusetts ski areas. Ski operators in Utah, New Mexico, Oregon, and Washington are also interested in cultivating this minority market.[2]

THE CHANGING SINGLES MARKET

The Census Bureau's *Current Population Survey* reveals that the age at which individuals marry for the first time increased in 2000 to 27.1 for men and 25.3 for women, up from 23.3 for men and 20.8 for women in 1970. This is further evidence that young people are postponing marriage to concentrate on careers and education before beginning families. One-third of the men and nearly one-quarter of the women between the ages of 30 and 34 have remained single, nearly four times the number in 1970. The rate of never-married men increased from 9 percent, and for women from 6 percent, since 1970.

Individuals who delay marriage have greater discretionary income to purchase high quality furniture, infant apparel, and home-maintenance services. Older parents are in a better position to spend more money on child care, housing, and transportation. Since marriages are at a later age, there are usually fewer children, and more money can be expended on toys, vacations, and recreation.

Important segments of the affluent singles market are gays and lesbians. Marketers in recent years have directed advertising and promotional materials to gays and lesbians as a direct consumer group. Estimates range to a population size of 18.5 million and spending power of over $500 billion.[3] According to Ketchum Global Research, gays and lesbians are highly geographically concentrated in urban areas and easy to reach. Gays and lesbians show a high brand consciousness and loyalty if the brand is perceived as friendly to their sexual status. They constitute between 6 and 7 percent of the total population.

The gay and lesbian market can be reached by such media as Shocking Gray, Olivia Records and Travel, and RSVP Travel Productions. Research studies endeavoring to discern differences in tastes between the gay and lesbian market in contrast to the predominant culture are still in the beginning experimental stages. Early research does suggest that different appearance aesthetics may be present for homosexual and heterosexual men and may suggest the importance of appearance in socialization. More studies are needed on needs, motivation, attitudes, lifestyles, and psychographic characteristics for marketers to deliver satisfactory products and services to the market.

Since research studies indicate that the gay and lesbian market is more brand-loyal than the typical consumer, marketers believe that the estimated buying power presents numerous opportunities. Business organizations are increasingly taking exhibit space or decorating a float in a pride parade for gays and lesbians. For example, San Francisco, Chicago, and Tampa have annual pride parades. Wells Fargo & Company, a San Francisco–based bank, contributed $2.1 million in corporate funding to many nonprofit companies that serve this market. The gay/lesbian Consumer Online Census in conjunction with Syracuse University reported in their survey that 27 percent of respondents had income in excess of $100,000. These statistics have motivated more firms to participate in gay pride events. Bank One and J. P. Morgan Chase have been sponsoring floats in the Chicago Gay Pride Parade for the past few years. Bank One has also paid between $2,000 and $5,000 for sponsorships in Columbus, Ohio, and Indianapolis, Indiana. These also included educational workshops designed for same-sex couples.

The singles market includes everyone from carefree youths in their early 20s to elderly individuals. A broadened definition might not only include same-sex couples who spend much like singles but also those who cohabit in residences and even elderly couples. Spending is similar for travel, recreation, and other types of activities. Naturally, a further market segmentation breakdown would be necessary to target submarkets within the singles groups. The singles segment is widely dispersed geographically, although they cluster in large cities throughout the United States. The singles market has evolved from one in which there is dating with a search for a mate and marriage preparation to a market concerned with personal growth, the development of individual identity, and the accumulation of experiences.

AGE COMPRESSION

According to the 2000 U.S. Census, 25.7 percent of the population—72.3 million people—is under the age of 18. That represents a growth of 13.7 percent over 1990. *Age compression* is a term that means children are growing up more quickly than they did a generation ago or even a decade ago. The tweens are between the ages of 9 and 12 and are replacing Barbie and Lincoln Logs with video games, clothes, and cosmetics. Children no longer have to play dress up since they can wear children's versions of their parents' clothes from stores like Gap and Laura Ashley. This acceleration process is primarily a result of access to influences and information. The children, tweens, teens, and the college market represent enormous potential for marketers, and the trend of age compression will have great impact on such selected industries as toys, apparel, cosmetics, shoes, and jewelry.

An illustration of age compression is the toy industry. Mattel is producing computers, computer accessories, and interactive software aimed at extending their former toy lines. An alliance between Mattel and Hewlett Packard allowed these firms to build Barbie and Hot Wheels printers and imaging software. Tweens are more technology friendly and are familiar with e-mail, cell phones, and beepers. The shift in age compression has benefited the electronics industry. Many children under the age of 12 desire electronic gadgets costing hundreds of dollars instead of toys. These children desire a cell phone, an iPod, a laptop computer, CD and DVD players, and digital cameras.

Apparel is another industry that will be greatly affected by the trend of age compression. Evidence of age compression is found in fashion. Dollhouses holiday line of tween fashions includes dark denim jackets. Moreover, retailers who once offered childish smock dresses for 10-year-olds now carry sophisticated designs, such as beaded-silk Capri pant suits, reflecting a more mature taste. Tweens learn about fashion trends by surfing the Web and reading magazines like *Cosmo Girl*. Designers such as Tommy Hilfiger and Ralph Lauren aim their advertisements to this market.

Recently, cultural variables have reflected changes in lifestyle market segmentation strategies. Age compression has been an important challenge confronting marketers in the past two decades. Although dependency has been extended because of the educational process, children, tweens, teens, and college-bound youths are assuming older roles and behavioral patterns. Young people have altered their appearance to reflect older ages much more than previously.

DUAL-CAREER FAMILIES

The image of the woman employed as a secretary, typist, cashier, bookkeeper, or telephone operator has changed. Women outnumber men on college campuses 55 percent to 45 percent and enter professional positions. In the past, a woman who desired a professional career became a teacher, a nurse, or a social worker. Today, women are lawyers, judges, government officials, medical doctors, veterinarians, psychologists, college professors, editors, accountants, and pharmacists. In past decades, it was difficult for women to obtain these jobs. Consumption habits of these professional families can range from the purchase of joint life-insurance policies to art objects to trips to exotic travel locations. A whole new world of financial advisors and personal trainers and interior decorators has developed to serve the needs of career families. These families shop at stores such as Bloomingdale's, Nordstrom, Neiman-Marcus, or Tiffany. The professional career woman will not have time to casually browse. The professional man married to a career woman will devote more time for shopping to purchase his apparel needs. Teenage children of these families, in particular, will have more impact on purchasing decisions as spending habits of these families are altered.

The *National Study of the Changing Workforce*, which has traced the characteristics of American workers for over 25 years, has reported that 39 percent of women were in managerial or professional jobs in 2002, compared to 36 percent in 1997 and 24 percent in 1977. The study also reports that there is declining prejudice against mothers working outside the home.

Dual-career families in which the woman is concerned about career advancement and personal fulfillment have had a dramatic impact on consumption behavior. These households represent a new contemporary and progressive unit of the affluent market. Dual-career families have more discretionary income and spend more on restaurants, child care, and services. Since the demands of two careers leaves less time for household tasks such as cooking, housekeeping, and shopping, products and services that save time are especially valued.

The Internet and the use of catalogs fulfill the need to save time. The career wife is responsible for earning more of the family's financial resources and therefore has greater influence when it comes to purchasing expensive and luxury items such as housing, automobiles, and vacations. In the interest of saving time, more household responsibilities are shared and also delegated to the husband, including grocery shopping.

THE NEW MILLIONAIRE

The *2004 World Wealth Report*, compiled by Merrill Lynch, indicates a financial resurgence among millionaires in the United States. Households with at least $1 million in financial or liquid assets increased to 2.27 million in 2003 from 2 million in 2002. Approximately half of millionaires were self-made millionaires. Those who inherited their wealth represented less than 20 percent of the high-net-worth individuals in 2002. The increase of new millionaires is anticipated to increase by 7 percent a year for the next few years.[4] Another survey conducted by TNS Financial Services found a record 8.2 million households in mid-2004 emerged, among millionaires, from the previous year.

Homes costing more than $1 million have become common in some cities. Census data reveals that such high priced homes constituted 11.6 percent in Cambridge, MA, 7 percent in San Francisco, 4.7 percent in Pasadena, CA, 3.8 percent in Los Angeles, 3.3 percent in Fort Lauderdale, FL, 3.2 percent in Berkeley, CA, 2.7 percent in Stamford, CT and 2.6 percent in Honolulu, Atlanta and Fremont, CA. The total percent of million dollar homes in the

United States cited by the U.S. Census 2000 was 0.6 percent. According to Thomas Stanley, author of *The Millionaire Mind*, approximately 97 percent of millionaires are homeowners and purchased their homes 12 years ago. Few millionaires have homes constructed for them, and they prefer to spend their time in their businesses or professions. The majority of millionaires have not moved in the past 10 years and live in homes built 40 years ago. Mortgage balances tend to be small despite the high value of the homes.

The picture of the millionaire is a picture of stability. The majority have been married to the same spouse for more than 25 years and are in their 50s. These millionaires are exceedingly careful in handling money and are conscious of home appreciation, investments, and total net worth.[5] Those millionaires included in the Thomas Stanley survey had an average net worth of $4.3 million. The typical millionaire in the survey had never spent more than $41,000 for an automobile or $4,500 for an engagement ring. The majority of millionaires included in the survey had acquired their wealth without obtaining any inheritance, financial gifts, or deriving income from an estate or trust.

Furthermore, the typical wealthy person is likely to be a small-business owner who has lived his adult life in one city and probably lives in a middle-class neighborhood next door to people much less wealthy. The typical millionaire has spent no more than $400 for a new suit and does not own an expensive watch. In contrast, a high-income, lower–net worth individual who is an upscale buyer frequently drives an expensive luxury car.[6]

The new millionaires have a propensity to live a comfortable yet not extravagant lifestyle. Their homes are situated in upper-middle-class neighborhoods, and they have little or no debt. Very few new millionaires have Phi Beta Kappa keys and most are devoted to their selected vocations. The majority play either golf or tennis, spend considerable time planning investments, and are active in raising funds for charitable causes. Many new millionaires would prefer to visit a museum or attend a grandchild's or son's or daughter's sporting event or just play bridge with friends than visit a casino. There is an allocation of expenditures for antiques, original art, vacationing overseas, and attending a major-league sporting event.

In recent years, the superrich who are at the top of America's pyramid have pulled ahead of the rest of the population. The average income for the top 1 percent was $3 million in 2002, the latest year for which averages are available. No other segment has grown that rapidly. There are 5 times as many households worth more than $10 million, even adjusting for inflation, than two decades ago.

CHANGING TECHNOLOGY SHAPES NEW MARKETS

The most dramatic force in modifying and altering consumer markets is changing technology. The affluent consumer, in many instances, is in the forefront acquiring the goods and services associated with advances in technology. Only a few decades ago, such products as CB radios, microwave ovens, no-cholesterol egg substitutes, videotape machines for home use, electronic pocket calculators, and a list of other products so commonly accepted today were completely unknown.

The development of new products may mean the destruction of existing markets for established products. To illustrate, the development of the auto industry diminished the industry for horse-drawn carriages, and the transistor hurt the vacuum-tube industry. Presently, DVD players are replacing VCRs. Flat-screen TVs are altering the television industry. Changing technology may greatly alter the practice of many industries. The extension of credit cards in retailing was substantially facilitated by bank credit cards such as Visa and MasterCard. The continuing advance of electronic data processing and the electronic transfer of funds have made possible the introduction of debit cards.

Among the new products that will reshape markets will be the digital camera. Eastman Kodak will offer a digital camera that can connect wirelessly to the Internet. Consumers will be able to instantly send their pictures to friends for the approximate price of $600. Another innovation is offered by Sharut Furniture. Their new Sierra product is able to hide a megaplasma television screen for about $3,000 and provides a handsome storage unit. Moreover, Havier, a Chinese appliance manufacturer, has developed a cell phone that is the size of a pen and has a clip to fit in a shirt pocket. The cell phone will be able to make calls, take pictures, and download ring tones with a price from about $400 to $500. Although many new product innovations will not reshape an industry, such as DVD players replacing VCRs, nonetheless present markets will be altered in many respects.

Technology will continue to advance, particularly in the fields of electronics and communication. Technology is already making possible a cashless society. In-house shipping will become more prevalent. Affluent people are increasingly pressured by time constraints and are especially receptive to time-saving devices. Consumer markets will be better serviced because of point-of-purchase terminals that monitor inventory levels. Electronic developments have allowed mass promotion via television and telephone, and satellite communications have brought world markets closer. More rapid technology has accelerated product obsolescence that will reshape existing markets and open new markets.

MANAGING CHANGE

The multi-income family, the growth of the baby boomers, and the nontraditional family households are all changing family structure and consumption habits. The successful marketers of the future will be those who anticipate and adapt to these environmental changes. The most obvious change in the population mix is that it is growing older. An expected change has been the growth of nontraditional markets and the growth of affluent ethnic markets. Such changes mean a shift in consumption patterns and a corresponding change in culture as well as social attitudes. Many marketers are overlooking these important shifts and therefore are not penetrating new and important markets.

As income increases in the United States, especially as more households become dual-income families, the new rich will possess a broader choice over their wants and needs. The fulfillment of psychological needs in an affluent society becomes much more important than the satisfaction of physiological needs. A larger share of income will become available for discretionary consumption, and some durable goods industries, such as the electronics industry, will be the chief beneficiaries of their discretionary income. Consumption patterns will show a decrease in the percentage expended for food and clothing and will increase for consumer durables and services. Moreover, affluent consumers especially desire the services of financial service companies. Phoenix Marketing International, an independent marketing services firm, surveyed households with at least $250,000 in investible assets or annual income over $150,000 and found that the respondents rated highly such firms as USAA, TIAA-CREF, Vanguard, A.G. Edwards, Wachovia, and Edward Jones. These firms received high consumer satisfaction ratings based on financial planning and personal services rendered.

The new rich will be even more knowledgeable in the purchasing process. Although consumers will be more sophisticated, a wider product choice in the future will make the buyers' selection problem more difficult. Consequently, affluent consumers will require more product knowledge and a better awareness of purchasing alternatives. This will increase demands for better and more reliable product grading and labeling. Consumers will also demand that the level of product performance be raised. Many of the new rich households will be composed of professional and career women, and this will influence not only food consumption habits but expenditures on other items as well. Scarcity-of-time pressures will modify purchasing behavior patterns of the new rich in the future.

Final consumer demand, through the accelerator principle, has a profound impact on manufacturers, wholesalers, and retailers. Should affluent consumers desire higher-priced quality cars, there will be increased automobile makers' demand for steel and other raw materials and steel workers' demand for iron ore. Anticipated demand for final consumers by organizational consumers will impact the economy.

Goods and services demanded in the future will reflect an environment of showmanship and a valued experience. The hybrid automobile will attract those who are early adopters, environmentalists, and those who value a new experience. Spas and face-lifts will enhance the physical self, and the luxurious spa will also provide a place of sociability. The new rich will desire personal trainers to ease stress and to make certain that fitness training is correct. The digital camera will provide gratification, and video telephones will provide 24/7 psychological support. The services of interior decorators will create a new self-image so that the new rich can redefine themselves.

E-business is changing the structure of the economy. The use of the Internet has increased the capability of organizations to conduct their operations faster, more accurately, at reduced costs with the ability to customize and personalize customer offerings. Countless companies have established Web sites. Many retailers, such as the Bombay Company, Circuit City, and Victoria's Secret have adapted to Internet selling with products once considered unlikely to be marketed over the Internet, such as furniture, appliances, and intimate apparel. Opportunities appear unlimited; for example, companies can design specialized software for occupational groups like teachers, accountants, and computer professionals.

A new economy has been established, created by technological advances. This new economy makes better use of directing business practices in organizing by customer segments, some by focusing on lifetime value and customer retention. Technology has made it more feasible to build a customer database and conduct data mining to discern trends, profitable segments, and satisfy individual needs.

CHAPTER 5

The Affluent All-American Consumer

No study of the magnitude of the *Mendelsohn Affluent Survey* has ever been undertaken by any other business organization in relation to the habits of the wealthy. Studies have been conducted for specific products or services by companies. The *Mendelsohn Affluent Survey* revises its guidelines for affluence when the affluent category increases to about 25 percent of all adults in the United States. During the first eight years of the survey, $40,000 and above was used to define the wealthy. While income and total economic resources are important dimensions, occupation and other variables are also important for understanding the affluent market.

The affluent market is described on the basis of social, psychological, and lifestyle factors. Many variables are often combined to define the affluent market. For example, social class and stage in the family life cycle is used by the hotel industry. The Fairmount Hotel chain attracts families with children by offering supervised activities for children while parents enjoy other activities. Products like Michelin Tires and Calvin Klein clothes are aimed toward the upper-end market for consumers who desire the highest quality and are not concerned about price. Affluent consumer spending in many instances is driven by desire, not need.

The upscale market is defined as relatively prosperous, educated, and stylish. The upscale market is a subset of the affluent market. Both markets share one or more characteristics. They are interested in the arts and culture. They buy one-of-a-kind products and services. They purchase homes with four to six garages; have custom wine cellars, in-home movie theaters, and home spas. They own Humvees, mountain bikes, and climbing equipment. They purchase getaway "toys" such as light jet aircraft, adventure vacations, and stays at luxury hotels. Pet owners have transferred their tastes to their pets by purchasing gourmet foods and clothes; their pets are often treated like family members.

Targeting the upscale market is not new. Sears targeted electric refrigerators to the wealthy in the 1930s. Recently, Sears has been targeting the upscale market with products from Lands' End. Brands such as Bold Spirit, Crossroads, and Trader Bay have been replaced by Covington and Lands' End. Sears has changed its focus and is now targeting customers with incomes from $50,000 to $100,000. The problem now is to understand how customers will react to the Lands' End brand when the customers are Hispanic or black since Lands' End customers have been primarily white baby boomers.

The importance of the affluent market is growing each year. Table 5.1 shows the increase in income of the affluent market from 1993 to 2003. Income segmentation is a standard strategy used for such product and service categories as automobiles, boots, apparel, cosmetics, recreation, and travel. Expensive cars may be purchased by the upper level of each social class. Some companies, such as the Gap and Walt Disney, are targeting both the high- and low-end markets. The Gap has Banana Republic to target the upscale market and Old Navy to target the low-end market. Walt Disney presents Winnie-the-Pooh on fine china, pewter spoons, and expensive children's stationery in stores like Nordstrom and also a cartoonlike Pooh adorns polyester bed sheets in stores like Wal-Mart.

Table 5.1
Affluent Household Income
(number of households)

Year	Over $75,000	Over $100,000
1993	12,114,000	
1994	13,521,000	
1995	7,678,000	7,114,000
1996	8,235,000	8,293,000
1997	9,186,000	9,661,000
1998	9,935,000	10,926,000
1999	10,258,000	14,116,000
2000	11,050,000	14,262,000
2001	11,837,000	15,124,000
2002	12,230,000	15,696,000
2003	12,313,000	16,945,000

Source: Statistical Abstract of the United States, U.S. Census Bureau, www.census.gov.

Establishing strategies to reach the affluent market has advanced rapidly in recent years via home shopping, the personal shopper, the Internet, direct and telephone marketing, and the use of auctions. These distribution channels are challenging the traditional ways of reaching this market by specialty shops and department stores.

Table 5.2, Average Affluent Household Expenditures in 2004, shows the amount of affluent household money expended annually on selected goods. These consumer-spending patterns range from the lower to middle to high end of the affluent consumer market. Table 5.2 also shows the markets where the most money is allocated for selected items. These items include home furnishing, laptops and desktop computers, home improvement materials, artwork and collectibles, women's apparel, and matching jewelry.

Home furnishings are the largest expenditure made in Table 5.2. IKEA, a furniture retailer, has recognized this market opportunity and has targeted the upscale and affluent market. IKEA operates a limited-menu restaurant in each store, offers child-care service while parents shop, and features a comprehensive catalog. These services are of high quality and differentiate IKEA from competitors as a store offering good quality furniture at affordable prices.

Table 5.2 indicates average affluent household expenditures in 2004, but it would be a mistake to believe that the percentage of all expenditures would remain constant or grow in the future. For example, future predictions are that apparel as a percentage of household expenditures will continue to decline as consumers have shifted their purchasing preferences to insurance, retirement, home furnishings, home improvement, and other activities such as physical fitness. The total dollar sales of apparel in 2004 was 1.7 percentage points less than in 2000. Manufacturers are concentrating on selling apparel at higher profit margins. Calvin Klein, Tommy Hilfiger, and Ralph Lauren are reducing their midprice collections, and stores like Lord & Taylor and Saks Fifth Avenue are closing some units. But the high end of the affluent market exemplified by Neiman Marcus is still doing well.

Product demand obviously reflects the consumer's ability and willingness to purchase. Packaging, pricing, promotion, personal selling, and distribution are all important factors in demand patterns. Marketers need to understand the demand for a product at each possible price point. Consumer demand is also based on wants and needs and shifts in response to economic factors. Periods of shortages, inflation, or recession are components of changing demand patterns. However, it would be a mistake to believe that the purchase of new luxury goods is a function that includes only a strong economy, consumer confidence, and an increase of home equity. Economic conditions do not necessarily have a strong impact on the purchase of new luxury goods, even in a downturn. Purchasing behavior of luxury goods has an emotional base meaningful to the individual. A shift in consumer desire over time may take place in the categories of luxury goods that are associated with an emotional appeal that displays genuine product and service differences.

Table 5.2
Average Affluent Household Expenditures

Category	❖	➢	•
Home Furnishings	$2,352	$3,357	$7,069
Personal Computers (Laptop or Desktop)	$1,469	$1,716	$2,617
Home Improvement Materials/Equipment/ Windows	$1,995	$2,592	$4,141
Artwork and Collectibles	$671	$1,127	$3,194
Women's Apparel	$796	$1,249	$2,284
Watches and Jewelry	$798	$1,296	$2,297

Household Income Key

- ❖ $ 75,000 – $99,999
- ➢ $100,000 – $199,999
- • $200,000+

Source: Mendelsohn Affluent Survey, 2004.

Table 5.3 shows the actual size of selected markets in 2004. Market potential will vary during periods of recession and prosperity. Bloomingdale's and Tiffany have used different services levels with different assorted product breadths to serve the large apparel market cited in Table 5.3. Bloomingdale's uses a strategy that features a broad product assortment while cultivating an exclusive image. Tiffany uses a narrow product assortment that cultivates an exclusive image.

A product-related segmentation strategy could be used in markets for watches and jewelry or entertainment appliances. This strategy is based on consumer behavioral characteristics related to the product. Two strategies would be benefit segmentation and product usage rate segmentation. Benefit segmentation divides the market into groups according to the different benefits that consumers desire from the product. A consumer's attitudes, values, lifestyle, and

Table 5.3
Market Size for Selected Items

	In Billions
Apparel	
Women's	$32
Men's	$21
Children's	$ 6
Home Furnishings	$83
Home Improvement	$54
Computers	$35
Watches and Jewelry	$23
Entertainment Appliances	$26
Mail Order/Telephone	$11

Source: Mendelsohn Affluent Survey, 2004.

past purchasing habits have a great impact on the benefits sought in specific purchasing circumstances. For example, in segmenting the affluent market for entertainment appliances, benefits such as recreation, education, and rest and relaxation could be emphasized.

Another product-related basis for market segmentation is product usage. The market for watches and jewelry could be divided into categories for non-users, light users, medium users, and heavy users. Usually, marketers are most interested in targeting the heavy product users. The 50 percent of consumers who are designated heavy product users buy over 80 percent of the product. Usage patterns have a tendency to remain constant over long periods of time. There are instances when marketers try to move medium or light users to a higher category.

Marketers rely on experience to present a picture of the spending patterns of affluent customers. Some conclusions include the following:

1. There is remarkable homogeneity.
2. The desire to own and consume goods can lead to credit and loan debt.
3. There may be some regional differences, but these are not significant across income divisions.
4. Suburban living may include more funds spent for pet food and sports.
5. The presence of children is a significant variable.
6. Education and private schools represent large expenditures.

The most significant impact on the increases of the affluent market in the past two decades has been the emergence of the professional woman. Table 5.4 demonstrates the growth of women in such occupations as accountants, computer professionals, physicians, lawyers, and psychologists. To attract professional women, designers such as Donna Karan, Calvin Klein, and Liz Claiborne have developed their own line of designer jeans usually sold for over $100. Their apparel can be purchased by mail or on the Internet. Professional women generally have personal computers to facilitate in-home shopping. As a group, female professionals tend to be more style conscious and convenience oriented. Many professional women are concerned with self-identity through the purchase of goods and therefore want a broader product assortment than most retail stores can display. Professional women generally use the Internet for in-home shopping.

Women constituted about one-third of executive, administrative, and managerial occupations in 1983 and more than one-half in 2004. In approximately 30 percent of dual-income households, wives earned more than their husbands. Households with husbands who do not work are still a minority, or about 5 or 6 percent. The educational attainment of career women and their rapidly increasing income has far-reaching implications for future spending growth as well as for advertisers. Increasing income will change what career women buy and how frequently they buy luxury goods. This trend is an important factor in the rising preference for more healthful or organic food, more natural ingredients in cosmetics, and more environmentally friendly products.

Table 5.4
Women in Professions (in thousands)

Profession	1983	1998	2004
Accountants and Auditors	427	940	1,042
Mathematical and Computer Professionals	137	506	848
Chemists and Material Scientists	22	43	46
Physicians and Surgeons	82	196	244
Teachers (College and University)	219	388	541
Lawyers	93	260	280
Editors and Reporters	52	74	88
Psychologists	51	96	123

Source: Bureau of Labor and Statistics, ftp://ftp.bls.gov/pub/special.requests/1f/aat11.txt.

Another change has been the trend in delayed marriages. These couples typically are in a better financial position to spend more on their house, services, and children. Children of affluent couples are targeted with a variety of activities and enticements. As a result, children learn to be discriminating consumers at an earlier age. Resorts such as Club Med and the Westin, in St. John, Virgin Islands, have added teen programs that include in-line skating, free diving lessons, and golf. Hotels such as the Ritz-Carlton in Naples, Florida, and the Mark Hopkins in San Francisco have kids' lounges with video libraries to attract a younger, wealthy clientele group. Since women with higher incomes usually marry men with high incomes, the result is increased concentration of household spending power in higher-income categories.

The price of satisfying dreams can be expensive. Golf equipment ranges from $750 to $2,500 for clubs, shoes, and apparel. The annual cost to play on various courses ranges from $2,600 to $5,000, with association and tournament fees of $1,500 to $2,000 and coaching fees of $1,000 to $6,500. Tennis equipment can cost from $500 to $1,200 for rackets, shoes, apparel, and balls. Fees for tournaments, association dues, and membership at the local tennis club are $1,100 to $1,600. Coaching fees range from $2,600 to $6,000. Figure-skating costs are from $1,500 to $4,000, and travel associated with the sport costs from $1,200 to $6,000. Fees including ice time are $4,000 to $7,000, and coaching fees are about $8,000.[1] The affluent encourage their children to compete and become part of upward mobility through sports associations.

Grandparents, in an effort to ease the pressure on the career family, give career couples time to themselves by spending more time with grandchildren. A $30 billion industry has evolved that targets grandparents and grandchildren and allows grandparents to bond with their grandchildren at summer camps and on travel tours. Grandkids and Me Camp offers canoeing, hiking, and dog-sledding, while Archeological Tours offers visits to pyramids and the Sphinx and a Nile cruise.

The buying behavior of career women is changing. Time for shopping is limited, and convenience is desired. Some retail stores offer personal-shopping services that select appropriate merchandise for customers who telephone in their needs and then come at their convenience to make a selection from the offered merchandise. A database of size, tastes, and apparel needs is maintained by these retailers. Manufacturers presell the customer, particularly by direct mail, national advertising, and coordinated promotions with retailers. Career women make quick decisions and demand presentations aimed at their needs that are concise and relevant. They use the Internet more. Frequent online consumer purchases include books, music, air tickets, clothing, videos, flowers, and wines.

The affluent customer has been a traditional target market for direct marketers. This customer is also a target for selective shopping and has discriminating tastes. The rise in affluence may decrease price sensitivity for those who value convenience from Internet shopping. Many career women are concerned with self-identity though the purchase of goods and therefore want a broader product assortment than most retail stores can offer.

Women earn more than half of the bachelor's and master's degrees in the United States. The spending behavior of affluent women is dominant in every state and racial and ethnic group. There is a strong relationship between education and social-class membership. The gap between female and male attainment of the M.D. and Ph.D. degrees has closed. Females make up almost the majority of law students. Financial services firms such as Merrill Lynch & Company and Citigroup Inc. are recruiting more female advisers to serve their increasing number of female clients. These female financial advisers are relationship driven and build long-term relationships.

Marketers interested in reaching the affluent market should:

- Use a proactive rather than a reactive approach.
- Use value approach strategies.
- Position image and product offerings to distinguish offerings.
- Survey clientele to determine what they want.
- Sponsor a charity that has a national presence.

THE VOICE OF THE AFFLUENT

The *Mendelsohn Affluent Survey* has traced the interests of the affluent household in three different income categories in activities such as travel, cultural events, and sports.

The affluent consumer seeks life-enriching experiences and is stimulated by new and different situations. They want to be recognized as worldly with a social conscience. This has brought about a renaissance in the arts. Sports and the arts are now waging a competitive battle for leisure-time expenditures. This change has been accelerated by educated baby boomers and an arts-loving generation. Increased interest in the arts, poetry, dance, music, and theater has spread from large cities like New York, Boston, Chicago, and Los Angeles to cities such as San Diego, Charlotte, Cincinnati, and Houston and to rural areas like Orono, Maine; Ashland, Oregon; and North Adams, Massachusetts. A 1,600-seat concert hall opened in Orono, and the world's largest museum of contemporary art was established in North Adams. The Mendelsohn survey found that the favorite cultural events among those earning more than $200,000 were opera, art auctions and galleries, dance performances, museums, theater, antique shows, concerts, boat shows, sporting events, and auto shows.

Even with the arts becoming an integral part of affluent consumers' activities, sports activities, both professional and for recreational and health purposes, remain important. There is a strong interest in professional basketball, tennis, football, and baseball. The number of individuals purchasing high-priced tickets and boxes to these events has grown steadily since the 1990s. College football teams such as the University of Michigan attract over 100,000 people per game, while alumni of Notre Dame, Penn State, and other Big Ten college teams remain fiercely loyal.[2] These consumers join health, golf, and tennis clubs and own a four-wheel drive pickup, a Humvee, a mountain bike, or climbing equipment. Many combine their business and social activities together. They play squash, tennis, golf, and racquetball.

Marketing opportunities resulting from educational achievement include the following:

- New ways to deliver education at all levels while college enrollment rates increase.
- Older people tend to read more and participate in more cultural activities. New book superstores with coffee shops sponsor discussion groups. Affluent seniors have more disposable income to spend on cultural activities.
- The growing dual-income market.
- The quest for self-fulfillment—this lifestyle suggests an individualistic orientation. Hobbies can include photography and playing musical instruments.

As individuals acquire more education and greater discretionary income, their choice of goods and services become more selective than those persons with less education and discretionary income. Although targeting the affluent consumer is now more widespread, there is historical precedence for going after this market. For example, Pullman in 1864 developed a railroad car for the wealthy to travel in. Continuous upgrades were made, and by 1883, Pullman became fashionable for those families referred to as the so-called elite. Today, the Pullman railroad car is displayed as a part of American history in the Henry Ford Museum in Dearborn, Michigan.

The new voice of affluence reflects the changing tastes and culture of American society. There is a growing audience for travel, books, museums, theater, and dance companies. These activities give a new meaning to daily living.

Marketers have learned that new methods of distribution are required to reach the affluent educated market as convenience and time constraints become more important influences in consumer decision making. Books are ordered from Amazon.com and Barnes & Noble because it is easier to order out-of-print books, hard-to-find books, and books by lesser-known publishers. Amazon.com and others have rapidly moved into the sale of products such as CDs, videotapes, and audiotapes through the Internet. Home improvement stores such as Home Depot and furniture stores such as Ethan Allen use Internet selling. Best Buy and Tandy are selling electronic products on their Web sites.

Baby boomers have adopted healthy lifestyles where they strive for lifelong fitness—the ability to remain active, alert, and independent, even as aging advances. Affluent boomers hire personal trainers, eat more health-oriented foods, and desire cleaner air. Many boomers hold memberships at athletic clubs and choose healthful activities such as walking, jogging, and swimming. For many people, golf is a rewarding activity. Chrysler is seeking to attract an upscale market by appealing to golfers. Golfers have a very high average income, are usually multiple car owners, and are much more likely to purchase a new automobile than the average household. Consequently, Chrysler sponsors the Greensboro Scramble Golf Tournament. Nearly 60 percent of older baby boomers are professional, managerial, or other white-collar workers; and those over 50 are among the best-educated men in America.

Many affluent consumers have found travel an enriching experience. Consumers aged 55 to 64 spend over $17 billion a year on travel-related goods and services. Affluent consumers travel by air approximately 7 times a year. Tour organizations such as Touch Tones designate special dates on the itineraries to the Grand Canyon, Yellowstone Park, and other destinations for the entire family. They include guest lecturers with a background in music, literature, and other fields to provide educational experiences. Cruise lines provide financial experts to talk about the direction of the economy and investments.

Table 5.5 shows the travel variations of the affluent consumer. Lifestyle analysis in conjunction with this data is useful in understanding different segments of the affluent market. Cruise travel in recent years has become almost as important as air travel in the tourist market. Travel both within the United States and abroad has introduced consumers to a variety of ethnic foods, which has created a growing market for producers and marketers of ethnic food products.

Favorite destinations of the most affluent were Europe, Hawaii, Australia/New Zealand/Orient/South Pacific, the Caribbean, Nantucket, Vail, Aspen, Palm Beach, and Lake Tahoe. The favorite destinations of the middle affluent

Table 5.5
Travel Variations

Took a cruise in the past three years	❖	17%
	➢	22%
	•	27%
Rented a car in previous years	❖	39%
	➢	54%
	•	68%
Possessed a current passport	❖	37%
	➢	52%
	•	74%

Household Income Key
- ❖ $75,000–99,999
- ➢ $100,000–199,999
- • $200,000+

Source: Mendelsohn Affluent Survey, 2004.

group are Canada, the Caribbean, New England, Florida, California, Las Vegas, and New York City. The least affluent group visited Canada, Mexico, Florida, Las Vegas, and New England.

Travel was disproportionately more frequent among the most affluent group. Destinations situated geographically farther from the United States were more frequently visited. Travel is another variable associated with education and high-income families and is one of the reasons that explains the maturity and sophistication of a changing affluent market. The traveler also looks for one-of-a-kind vacations—anything daring, adventurous, and life changing.

Terrorism has triggered many changes in lifestyles for Americans. During periods of uncertainty, vacationers elected to visit traditional destinations such as Cape Cod, Massachusetts; Hilton Head, South Carolina; and Lake Tahoe, California.

EDUCATIONAL IMPACT

Money Magazine has extended the Mendelsohn survey, with coverage directed to education and occupation.[3] Close to 90 percent of the affluent have some college education, and 60 percent are in the managerial/professional ranks, with 27 percent in technical/sales and administrative roles. Table 5.6 shows the increase of people enrolled in college and who in the future may become members of the affluent market. Educational attainment is one of the reasons that explains the maturity and sophistication of the consumer. Amazon.com, Barnes & Noble, and others use Internet selling so that educated buyers find it easier to order books and other products such as toys, CDs, videotapes, and audiotapes.

The new affluent are well educated, and the majority of millionaires are college graduates. Purchasing expenditures were often the result of how much people earned through work, social security, pensions, and investments. Marketers focused their appeals in terms of the individual or the family's buying

Table 5.6
College Enrollments (number of students)

Year	Public	Private
1970	6,428,000	2,153,000
1980	9,457,000	2,640,000
1990	10,845,000	2,974,000
2000	11,795,000	3,340,000
2004	13,092,000	4,003,000

Source: Bureau of Labor and Statistics; www.bls.gov/emp/home.html.

power. Today, many people have sufficient money to purchase most products, and the real question is which products will be bought. Lifestyle marketing based on consumers' educational and occupational background is a better indicator of purchasing behavior. The Mendelsohn survey finds that the affluent income group earning $200,000 or more allocates a large proportion of their spending for home furnishings, personal computers, home improvement materials, artwork and collectibles, women's apparel, watches and jewelry, entertainment appliances, men's apparel, and kitchen appliances, in rank order.

The occupations of family members make a difference in buyer behavior. The purchasing patterns of professional and managerial people are different from those of others. Occupational background often determines the types of clothes, automobiles, residences, and use of leisure time. Money is no longer the only answer to buyer behavior; instead, a lifestyle shaped by education and occupation has become the driving force.

More than half of affluent heads of household work in professional or managerial capacities. The managerial group makes up one-third of the affluent population, and the professional group makes up another third. *Money* magazine found that about 45 percent of Americans believe they would need at least $2.5 million to feel rich. About 40 percent believe that they would join the ranks of the wealthy if they had over $5 million.

One of the greatest determinants of social-class standing is occupation. Various occupations, especially those that require higher levels of education, skill, or training are viewed as higher status. Individuals with the same occupation have a propensity to follow similar lifestyles and values. Education is critical since educational attainment is a reliable indicator of selected occupations, such as medicine, and a determinant of potential income and buyer behavior. The highest-status levels require formal education as an entrance requirement: physician, lawyer, professor, psychologist, or engineer. While entrepreneurs can reach affluence without a college education, it is more difficult.

Educational attainment has been associated with the purchase of books and entertainment activities. Educated consumers desire more information about products. Occupations may affect purchasing behavior for certain types of clothing, selection of transportation modes, and the need for time-saving products. Products and brands also project a symbol of status among various occupations. Internet usage is more likely among high-income groups in communicating and obtaining information. Affluent groups find information about travel and financial products on the Internet. Affluent consumers are likely to subscribe to magazines like *Town & Country*, *Robb Report*, *Elite Traveler*, *Vanity Fair*, and *Gourmet* magazines in addition to *Forbes*, *Business Week*, and *Fortune*. There are also specialized magazines like *Hampton Country* and *Manhattan Style* that target educated men and women ages 26 to 50 with an average annual salary of about $350,000.

When college-educated women marry college-educated men, this has a significant impact on earnings. More than 50 percent of the wealthy, affluent, and upper-middle-class families are comprised of dual-income couples.

Educational attainment helps explain the sophistication of the American consumer. Value rather than low price is an important consideration in making purchasing decisions. The impact of the affluent and upscale female consumer will grow as more women opt to pursue careers instead of jobs. Refrigerator manufacturers in competition for the affluent and upscale female markets are providing new features. For example, for $5,000 Sub-Zero has adjustable glass shelves and a glass front door on its refrigerators in which food can be displayed; and for $6,799, Kitchen Aid-"Architect" has a side-by-side that offers a compressor that is insulated to absorb noise, an ice-maker in the freezer door that allows more space, plus a wine rack.

MANAGING CHANGE

Behind the *Mendelsohn Affluent Survey* and all the figures and facts on expenditures is a living, moving profile of the affluent consumer in the United States. The first impression is one of stability. Since a cashless society is present, many consumers who are not affluent, but upscale buyers and those who wish to trade up in their purchasing can buy many of the goods and services purchased by affluent consumers. The picture of the affluent consumer changes once the figures in the study are subjected to close analysis. A marked contrast is particularly noted in the purchases of artwork and collectibles, home furnishings, and women's apparel. Affluent consumers are now more geographically dispersed. Female professionals and managerial personnel have increased significantly from the 1980s to the present, and education is increasingly paramount to understand the forces behind affluent consumer spending in the future.

Some activities are more related to social class than to income. Concerts and the ballet are available to all people, yet the audience is often from the affluent social class. There are some members of this social class who are likely to spend a relatively large share of family income on housing in a prestigious neighborhood, on furniture that reflects a definite lifestyle environment, and on cultural interests and club memberships. Although social-class segmentation may not always be a relevant consideration for undifferentiated products, it is frequently effective when used in conjunction with other variables such as lifestyle and family life-cycle stage. Life-style market segmentation has been effective as high-end hunting lodges boom. The Paul Nelson Farm in Gettysburg, South Dakota, charges over $3,000 for a three-day pheasant hunt; and the Mesa Mood Ranch, in Grand Junction, Colorado, charges $9,000 for a five-day elk hunt.

Millions of Americans have enjoyed steadily rising earnings. The overall trend has been a shift from middle-class brackets to a growing affluent class. A large number of affluent and upscale consumers are offered a wide array of goods and services that save time. These consumers are willing to spend money for goods and services such as travel, sports equipment, recreation and restaurants, and labor-saving products. They spend a greater percentage of time and money on private club memberships and unique educational experiences for their children. Their homes may be no more expensive than the middle class but have the right address to give a self-image of belonging. Accompanying the growth of the affluent market is the stimulation of economic prosperity that will increase the size of the affluent- and upscale-consumer markets in the future.

There is also a service orientation that places a great value on time expenditures. If gardening is not a hobby, a professional is hired. This is also true of decorators. Since there is mobility in social classes, values, activities, and interests are in a constant state of transition, especially for those members of the upscale market. Most affluent consumers (59%), according to an *Express/Unity Marketing Study*, prefer to spend their money on fine dining and travel rather than purchasing additional products. Only about 20 percent of respondents would prefer personal luxuries such as automobiles, clothes, and jewelry. Many respondents desired activities that would reduce stress. Age and life cycle are important considerations in spending, but vacations, second homes, pets, insurance, security systems, and reading are paramount interests that are associated with future growth markets.

The need to target the affluent market and position products and services effectively to them has become evident as this segment grows. The affluent consumer seeks life-enriching experiences, desires style and quality, and wants to be recognized as knowledgeable and worldly. They operate by word-of-mouth referrals and are better approached by subtler marketing tactics such as invitation-only events, which create an atmosphere of exclusiveness. They can be reached by online services to which they subscribe.

Many affluent and upscale people consider a need for achievement an important personal value. Achievers strive hard for success. The need for achievement influences consumption. Those motivated for high achievement are often good prospects for innovative products, for do-it-yourself products, and for older homes in need of redecorating.

There are actually multiple markets in the United States. Among them are the very wealthy, the new rich, the diminishing middle class, the recent immigrants, and the urban poor and others. Now about 5 percent of homeowners, or 5 million people, own two or more homes. Extraordinarily creative entrepreneurs are among these affluent households. The transition from a manufacturing-based economy to a more knowledge-based one has meant greater reliance on intellectual capital.

The role of creativity is a driving force that has given rise to a new creative social class.[4] The creative social class likes to frequent art auctions, art galleries, and the opera. Education is increasingly important to the creative social class. Richard Florida estimates the creative social class consists of 38 million people in the workforce. This class is responsible for developing new ideas and new technologies. New values have surfaced like creativity, individuality, meritocracy, self-expression, and diversity. The development of such a new social class is of great importance to marketers. A significant part of this new creative social class will be composed of women entrepreneurs. Entrepreneurs are traditionally known for their creativity and individuality. The number of female entrepreneurs increased about 20 percent from 1997 to 2002, and about 28 percent of all private companies were owned by women. The fastest growth rates according to the Census Bureau were found in Nevada and Georgia, and the counties with the most women-owned businesses were Los Angeles County and Cook County in Illinois.

Chapter 6

Affluent Groups and Aspirations

The story of Horatio Alger and others who went from rags to riches is the American dream. Followers of this dream are called *strivers*. They are looking to secure a safe place in their economic and social environment. The strivers look for approval from their peers. Success for many strivers means material wealth and symbolic possessions. Some will achieve what they perceive as success while others will continue as strivers. The *achievers* lead conventional lives structured around family, religion, and business. They purchase products and services that reflect their success.

Those in the *contented affluent* group have attained a measure of comfort in their own minds. The contented are usually well educated and welcome the opportunity to broaden their horizons. They value structure. Some members of this group may be retired or close to retirement, and some will work past retirement age for their own personal fulfillment. Consumption values reflect functionality, value, reliability, and durability. Leisure activities focus on home, education, and travel.

The *sophisticated* affluent group has high self-esteem and the financial resources and personal contacts to make things happen. Those in this group express their taste by acquiring possessions. Some members of this group may have inherited family heirlooms. They have a wide range of interests, seek challenges, and express themselves in a variety of ways. The lives of the sophisticated are characterized by richness and diversity and are governed by a set of principles or actions. They tend to be leaders in their professions and occupations. Personal growth is valued as is a concern of social issues.

There has been historical precedent for affluent groups to band together to accomplish common objectives. For example, automobile purchasers at the turn of the twentieth century were confronted with dirt roads, which made it difficult to travel. Automobile clubs were formed for the purpose of supporting road and highway construction. They lobbied local, state, and federal government to build an infrastructure of roads and highways. Consumer-action groups are a more recent development. They include the National Wildlife Federation and Action for Children's Television. Many people who are strivers, contented affluents, and sophisticates participate in consumer-action groups.

The Sierra Club is one of the leading ecological groups. There is a concern that air and water pollution have reached dangerous levels. Moreover, there are concerns about depletion of the ozone layer due to certain chemicals, the so-called greenhouse gases, and growing shortages of water.

Social-class studies are valuable in understanding how consumers behave in the marketplace as members of different market segments. They differentiate groups by variables such as income, education, occupation, and housing patterns. Buyer behavior among affluent consumers can be divided into numerous market segments and lifestyle niches, which may be as large as baby boomers or as small as the so-called snowbirds, who move to warmer locations when the weather gets cold. Wealthy Asian consumers and physicians, an occupation and professional group, are among the many diverse affluent groups to which marketers may target their goods and services. While social-class stratification has been valuable in the past, it is neither psychologically nor economically sufficiently clear-cut for the purpose of studying consumer behavior. Mobility and aspirations are important moderating variables.

The affluent are more likely to participate in activities such as tennis, sailing, skiing, and power boating than the average consumer. This means they are more likely to join country and yachting clubs. They are also more likely to attend art auctions and galleries, ballet, opera, theater, concert performances, and sporting events and would have more of a desire to join groups that sponsor or study such events. Whereas many golf clubs struggle to compete amid the glut of courses, a select group is thriving by offering top-notch services, incredible amenities, and luxurious facilities. These high-end golf clubs are Dallas National in Dallas, Texas; Mayacoma in Santa Rose, California; Red Sky in Wolcott, Colorado; and Vineyard in Edgartown, Massachusetts. Initiation fees range from $175,000 to annual dues of over $10,000.

Group dynamics impact buyer behavior by the patterns of interaction among its members. Kurt Lewin, an authority on group behavior, stated that "the essence of a group is not the similarity or dissimilarity of its members but their interdependence."[1] Group behavior is based on the premise that two or more individuals share a set of norms, values, or beliefs and that buyer behavior is interdependent. David Riesman wrote that American society was increasingly consumption oriented and that there had been a growing trend toward uniformity in the acceptance of a standard package of consumption goods.[2]

Individuals may view the group as a slight influence on behavior, while others find its impact to be a dominant force on their behavior. Typical groups that can be identified with affluent segments are singles, the gay community, senior citizens, Asians, Jewish people, certain occupations, and affinity associations such as the Harvard or New York University Clubs. A better method for segmenting affluent markets is to delineate the groups by occupation and income. Social class alone is no longer the best method to analyze an affluent segment.

Clothing, jewelry, residence, and the automobile are among the most conspicuous possessions. For example, apparel can be used to express an image. Men high in the corporate world may wear a Paul Smith shirt priced from $190 to $360 and an Armani tie for $135. The suit would be an elegantly slim wool three-button Brioni for $4,295 in black or charcoal and a Patek Philippe watch for about $10,000. Shoes made-to-measure for $3,500 or ready-to-wear made by John Lobbs for $1,000 are worn. Women might wear an Armani blouse priced from $695 to $1,500 and a pantsuit from Jil Sanders for over $1,600. Earrings from Gabrielle Sanchez would be priced at about $800, and shoes from Jimmy Choo at about $500.

Symbolic meanings are conveyed to others when products are purchased. In the past, a high percentage of singles have purchased the Ford Mustang, and today there has been a move to the Volkswagen Jetta and the Honda Civic. Many affluent seniors have purchased a Volvo, Cadillac, or Lincoln. Consumers with rising aspirations may become much more conscious about what they buy so that they are not perceived to be downscale.

GROUP DYNAMICS

Aspirational marketing is the essence of what dreams are about. An aspirational reference group is associated with people who represent the target market that consumers' desire to emulate. The young business manager may choose to "dress for success," dressing like the men or women who are established and respected in the organization's hierarchy. Aspirational marketing strategy can be directed to the nerve center of the individual since it is the embodiment of internal motivation. Aspirational marketing campaigns are most effective when directed to affluent and upscale consumer markets. These aspirations have become apparent for consumers who also trade up in their purchasing as the furnishings, attire, and lifestyle accessories of the affluent have become the prototypes for less expensive versions, such as the K-Mart partnership with Martha Stewart. Designers have created lower-priced lines such as Lands' End for Sears that are still more expensive than brands without consumer recognition.

There are specific groups that have a consumer-relevant impact on individual purchasing behavior, while members who purchase the same items may belong to different groups. For example, the Honda Accord has expanded the definition of its target market to include young single drivers who desire style and empty nesters who are rediscovering style. This target market may be comprised of a high percentage of affluent/upscale consumers or consumers who are trading up. The affluent target falls into precise quantitative measures of income and financial resources. The upscale consumer is only relatively prosperous and stylish, while the consumer who is trading up has made the decision to spend more on a specific product. The dynamics of formal social groups, such as members of ski and country clubs; surrogate groups like interior decorating; and work groups influence the types of products and brand choices of members of their groups. Word-of-mouth recommendations are an important purchasing influence for members of country clubs. Surrogates provide guidance for certain consumer goods to those consumers who use their services. Interior decorators help select furniture and accessories purchased for the home as surrogates, just like financial consultants recommend the purchase of stocks and bonds. Therefore, how the members dress and their viewpoints on various types of goods are of interest to other members of the group.

The dynamics of opinion leaders and reference groups relate to the changing aspirations of members. Reference groups are primarily membership groups, such as family, friends, and co-workers; and secondary groups include clubs, professional groups, and religious groups. Reference groups influence the purchasing behavior of the individual. They include individuals referred to as group leaders or opinion leaders. Opinion leaders are those members whose opinions are sought because of their credibility or expertise. They may act as so-called gatekeepers, filtering information before transmitting the message to others. Consequently, for affluent consumers who are members of yacht clubs, country clubs, or professional associations, word-of-mouth information from opinion leaders is important. Word-of-mouth is persuasive because it involves face-to-face vivid interactions with a highly regarded individual. Depending on the product, it might be difficult for a company to succeed without a word-of-mouth marketing strategy.[3]

Each decade demonstrates how the aspirations of the affluent change. Many consumers who once traded up in their purchasing behavior have experienced increases in their income and have moved up into the affluent market. Status symbols are an expression of affluence. In the time period from 1900 to 1909, radios were desired; from 1910 to 1919, status symbols included Kodak cameras and frontier pens; in the 1920s, vacuum cleaners and electric washing machines symbolized achievement; the 1930s emphasized indoor plumbing, while the 1940s featured air travel and electric refrigerators; from 1950 to 1970, color televisions and Andy Warhol lithographs were status symbols; from the 1970s to 1995, designer jeans, microwave ovens, Internet stocks, and sport utility vehicles were desired; and by the turn of the twentieth century, flat-screen digital televisions and designer accessories for pets symbolized success. Many status symbols have been mainstream items for the middle class and general population.[4] In efforts to attract upscale buyers, Procter & Gamble is upgrading its Olay face creams and marketing them as better than department store brands. When buying luxury goods, affluent consumers continue to seek value and take pleasure in saving money. Discount stores are the favorite shopping source for kitchen appliances and garden supplies, but specialty retail stores and department stores are leaders when purchasing fashion and jewelry. Discount shops are frequented in the purchase of electronics, linens and bedding, and kitchenware and cookware. Over time, these leadership categories for the purchase of luxury goods may shift as reference groups and social influences change.

Group dynamics and aspirations change from one decade to the next. Target, with 1,200 stores in 47 states, has broadened its merchandise line to include Isaac Mizrahi in its offerings. Although Isaac Mizrahi dresses sell for as much as $10,000, the fashion line is now offered for $50 or less and will fill a woman's casual clothing niche for the Target stores. These customers are trading up in their purchasing. Sophisticated shoppers are increasingly mixing expensive and mainstream fashions. Bed, Bath & Beyond has an exclusive arrangement with New York designer Nicole Miller for home furnishings.

Marketers broaden their markets by appealing to upscale segments, such as Starbucks in coffee; Evian in bottled water; and automobile manufacturers Nissan with Infinity, Honda with Acura, and Toyota with Lexus. These firms have used a strategy of designing specific products to enter the high end of the market for growth and improved profit margins. Some marketing strategies divide the market into specialized segments. Honda sells more motorcycles in the United States to a midprice consumer than any other manufacturer. Harley-Davidson dominates the upscale-user market. The demand for a Harley-Davidson upscale motorcycle has shifted to an older consumer with an average age of 46.

Brands marketed to the affluent include Rolex and Cartier in jewelry, Rolls Royce and Jaguar in automobiles, and private store brands such as Tiffany and Harry Winston. Broadening the market to attract the affluent not only places emphasis on brands but on services as well. For example, rentals for private jet planes go for $85,000 for 25 hours as the focus has shifted to rentals rather than sales. Citation Sharer offers 25 hours of travel on three types of planes ranging from $85,000 to $145,000, and Marquis Jet Partners charges from $113,000 to $308,000, depending on the plane.[5]

To target the changing aspirations of various groups, marketers may employ strategies such as the following:

1. Use a proactive rather than a reactive approach.
2. Image development.
3. Capitalize quickly on new opportunities.
4. Encourage innovation.
5. Use brand extension strategies.

The upscale and trade-up market is an integral part of the affluent market. Sales of plasma and flat-panel screens and high-definition televisions are among the best sellers to both markets. Sales of flat-panel televisions have more than tripled. Many of these sets sell for more than $5,000.

PERCEPTIONS OF PRODUCT QUALITY

As consumers' income and educational attainment have increased in recent years, marketers can anticipate pronounced shifts in the demand for different products and services to satisfy these consumers. Changing economic and education conditions are intertwined with psychological and consumer perceptions that modify values and aspirations. The impact of shoe purchases illustrates how different generations have been affected. The older generation was raised believing that leather shoes were of much higher quality than sneakers. Leather shoes were purchased in specialty shoe stores or department stores. Sneakers were considered inferior in quality and purchased in variety stores known as five-and-dime stores. The younger generation was brought up believing that sneakers reflected quality. This generation wears sneakers not only for athletic events but also for walking and for fashionable styling effects. Prices of some brands of sneakers are higher than for leather shoes. The purchasing power of consumers is a function of income, prices, savings, and the availability of credit. The affluent baby boomer generation, which is physically active, wears sneakers not only for walking but for other types of sports activities. A perception and image of brand quality is essential for stimulating purchasing behavior. The brand New Balance was helped considerably when people found that former President Bill Clinton wore this brand.

Goods that affluent consumers once accepted are no longer acceptable. The standards for rating hotels by Mobil and AAA have increased, presenting a challenge to five-star hotel aspirants. The new standards include three phones, with one in the bathroom; prints or lithographs with enhanced matting and frames; an umbrella in every room; an illuminated makeup mirror; two pairs of slippers; and insulated ice buckets. Some hotels may find their five-star ratings downgraded if these standards are not satisfied.[6]

New markets also present themselves as consumers become more affluent. The *Yankelovich Youth Monitor* reported that 57 percent of teenagers from ages 15 to 17 receive an average weekly allowance of $19.30, and 67 percent from ages 12 to 14 receive $11.30. Teenage consumers are considered within the affluent, upscale, or trading-up categories for selected items.

Affluent consumer perceptions of a brand will dictate marketing strategies. In some markets, such as the automobile market, there is a sharp division of consumer segments. The Rolls Royce is targeted to the ultimate segment, the Mercedes-Benz to the gold segment, the Audi to the luxury segment, and the Volvo to the special-needs consumer segment.

When considering the demand for some merchandise items such as designer jeans, prestige pricing is a strategy since consumers will not buy at a price they consider too low. Buyers perceive differences in quality among brands and will focus on a price range. For these goods, consumers establish upper price limits. The situation varies depending on buyer experience in judging product quality. High prices exclude the mass market and give an image of exclusiveness. Products made by hand or not mass-produced often give an image of quality so that the price-quality strategies become important.

When consumers operate under conditions of uncertainty with incomplete information, they rely heavily on price as the indicator of a product's quality. Consumers' quality perceptions are naturally also influenced by store reputation and word-of-mouth. The price-quality relationship generally tends to be product specific and is usually weak for frequently purchased items.

A price-quality relationship strategy can be used to appeal to upscale purchasers. An Audi might lose its appeal for many consumers within its target market if priced for $15,000. The prestige-pricing strategy can be successful if it is in accord with the consumer's brand images. Consumers do not patronize a Gucci specialty store and expect to pay $19.95 for a pair of loafers. Demand would probably diminish if both the Audi and the Gucci loafers were sold at prices lower than consumers expected.

REFERENCE GROUPS AND SOCIAL INFLUENCES

Most individuals interact with other people on a daily basis, and social influences are often motivated by anticipation of satisfying specific needs. Reference groups are frequently selected as a means for realizing these specific needs. A reference group is a set of people with whom individuals compare themselves to guide their activities, interest, and opinions. Reference groups can be described as aspirational and associative.

Aspirational reference groups are groups that are admired and whose behavior is emulated. The individual is not a member but would like to join a country club. There may be a desire to play golf or tennis with its members or just to socialize and interact. Frequently, there is a positive influence on attitudes or behavior.

Associative reference groups are groups where membership is maintained. Work, clubs, and school groups are associative reference groups. Values of the group may or may not be adopted depending on the strength of relationships.

Disassociative groups are reference groups with which behavior is incongruent with the individual's present goals. Joining a rap group would be a disassociative group for some individuals. Other individuals might not desire to join the country club or participate in such sports as sailing by belonging to a yacht club.

Social influences are the forces that other people exert on the individual's buyer behavior. Social forces include social class, reference groups, roles and family, and culture and subculture. A subculture comprises people who share attitudes, interests, and opinions that deviate from the broader culture of society. These subcultures could be based on age, geographic region, and ethnic background, among other factors. Social class, reference groups, roles, and family would in turn influence the members of the subculture or the group.

Many of these social influences can be combined in order to better understand how marketers can target specific groups. To illustrate, Tauck Tours has designed tour experiences that can be enjoyed by grandparents and the entire family depending on financial resources. A nine-day/eight-night trip to the Grand Teton and Yellowstone National Park costs about $7,200 for a family of four, a trip to Alaska costs about $9,600 for a family of four, and a vacation in London and Paris for seven nights is $2,100 a person.

Word-of-mouth carries credibility when products are expensive, risky, or purchased infrequently. Affluent people usually ask others like lawyers, accountants, architects, interior decorators, or financial consultants for referrals. Opinion leaders who have an impact on others through word-of-mouth contact tend to be experts about a product category and socially acceptable. These sources tend to be convincing. Companies such as USAA, an insurance and mutual fund organization, profit from word-of-mouth with very little advertising.

Marketers could be more effective by trying to target opinion leaders in groups such as college students. Frequently, college students will discuss clothing trends, styles, and prices with their friends. Abercrombie and Fitch employs college students as sales representatives to serve a youthful market that is fashion conscious.

THE AFFLUENT SENIOR MARKET

As the members of the senior market grow older there is a renewed pride in family, place, and tradition. Manifestations of buyer behavior direct themselves toward gifts to children and grandchildren, to redecorating residences, and in some instances to purchasing multiple residences. Marketers will find that the gift and special occasion markets are lucrative in cultivating the senior market. The sale of art objects and furnishings for residences is also profitable in targeting this group.

The senior market has a remarkable level of vitality and productivity. With seniors living longer, they typically have 15 to 20 years of time left after retirement. Seniors are joining and enjoying health spas and athletic clubs. Golf, tennis, sailing, boating, aerobic exercises, walking, and swimming are frequent activities. Seniors also participate in volunteer programs.

A high number of seniors live in the metropolitan areas of California, Florida, Illinois, Michigan, New Jersey, New York, Ohio, Pennsylvania, and Texas. This is in contrast to the younger population, who live in selected suburban areas. Seniors who formerly resided in the suburbs have returned to the central cities and desire the convenience of larger metropolitan areas. Between 1990 and 2000, the population of seniors increased 17 percent in Chicago and in Austin, Texas; New Orleans and Los Angeles have also experienced double-digit increases. States with significant senior housing developments are Florida, Virginia, North Carolina, California, and New Jersey. These housing developments include many amenities. Seniors often prefer to remain in communities nearby where they have raised their families, established careers, and have friends. Ninety percent of households with the top 20 percent of income live in metropolitan areas.

Affluent seniors perceive themselves as much younger than their chronological ages. This group manifests a high level of self-confidence, is more interested in fashion, and participates in cultural activities. This market segment does not dine at home as frequently as past generations. Affluent seniors and particularly baby boomers turned seniors make purchase decisions based on an active lifestyle and not age.

The age boundaries for targeting the senior market are not as clear as many marketers would prefer. For example, it is estimated that Nordstrom's customer age range is from 25 to 64, compared to the age range at Neiman Marcus, from 43 to 64. Obviously there is an overlap in markets. At first glance, it would seem that since Nordstrom has a wider age range that would be a differential advantage. While this is true, both department stores present a flexible market offering consisting of products and services that all segment members' value and some service options that segment members' value.

Many affluent senior women demand plus-size fashions. Liz Claiborne sells stylish plus-size fashions, and their brand is distributed by Nordstrom and other upscale retailers. Not only is spending on apparel increased, but spending on home furnishings and pets is also increased. According to the Bureau of Labor Statistics expenditures on vacations, second homes, insurance, and security systems have increased from 11 to 28 percent in the last five years. Growth in housekeeping services also grew. Seniors are also buying camcorders, digital cameras and other high-end gadgets, and $100-plus tickets to concerts.

The most important reasons why seniors purchase goods and services are to replace products that need repair or are obsolete or to reinforce desirable lifestyles. Seniors like to shop since it is a method for meeting friends. They are receptive to new technology and purchase camcorders, VCRs, DVD recorders, large-screen television sets, and the latest in stereo equipment.

The best method for segmenting the affluent senior market is income when targeting buyer habits.[7] The lifestyle term the *contented affluent* is applicable to the majority of seniors even though low-end strivers and high-end sophisticates are present.

THE AFFLUENT SINGLES MARKET

Singles in the 25-to-39 age bracket are a large market segment. The over 39 age group is more affluent. Both groups are unencumbered with responsibilities, have considerable mobility, and can make expenditures on goods and services that those with traditional family commitments could not generally make. Singles as a group can be characterized in the following ways:

- More experimental
- More fashion and appearance conscious

- More active in leisure activities
- More sensitive to social status

Many singles who exhibit affluent and upscale purchasing patterns share common beliefs, preferences, and motives. The single market is subject to lifestyle market segmentation strategies. A divorced person often replaces household goods such as dishes, curtains, or venetian blinds. The new singles purchase new wardrobes, join health clubs, and make new housing arrangements. Many members of the singles market are strivers.

What groups constitute the singles market? There are several million unmarried couples living together. Young people from 18 to 29 living together constitute a part of the singles market, but the majority is older couples who prefer an unmarried lifestyle. Some insurance companies have structured policies for unmarried couples, and some banks have granted unmarried couples loans to purchase homes or to make other large purchases. Marketers have started to target gay and lesbian consumers since this a group has high discretionary income. Logo, a Viacom-owned network, has an audience of about 10 million gay and lesbian consumers. The number of known gay and lesbian actors in major network television programs has increased.

Today's singles are much more educated than previous generations. Part-time students, divorced women, and older men have returned to college. College enrollment is soaring, and the age of the student population has increased.

A large number of professional women under the age of forty have never been married or are separated or divorced. The number of adults living alone has more than doubled in the past 40 years. More adults remain unmarried into their thirties than in previous generations. Singles prefer to reside in close proximity to their work and move into housing such as lofts and condos that families with children usually avoid. Singles are good customers for restaurants and spend more on travel, convenience foods, sporty automobiles, and fashionable apparel.

The increasing size, affluence, and complexity of the singles market creates new opportunities and challenges for marketers. The size of this market is estimated at approximately $600 billion. Single households account for almost one-quarter of all U.S. households. The singles market is indeed complex. Marketers are pushing individual portion packaging that has led to increasing demand. Supermarkets, discount stores, and club stores have stocked large multipacks of snack packs. ConAgra Foods, Chef America Inc., Frito-Lay, and other organizations are all deriving increased profits. But, while the singles market is buying, it is the family market that is causing the increased demand. Family members don't want to share. They desire their own individual package and also want larger individual package sizes. Moreover, families have different time schedules and do not necessarily eat together. Therefore, more than snack food should be considered in marketer's strategies.

Single men and single women have different spending habits. Single men allocate a greater proportion of their expenditures to food consumed away from home, alcohol, transportation, entertainment, tobacco, and to retirement investments than single women. Single women allocate a greater share of their expenditures to food consumed at home, housing, apparel, health care, personal-care services, and reading materials. Both groups of singles use the Internet more than other consumers. There is a desire to reduce shopping time and enjoy time at other activities.

Marketers should be able to further subdivide the singles market based on age. Singles under the age of 25 are the TV generation and the computer-friendly generation. They are heavy readers of special-interest magazines. Manufacturers of luggage, sports equipment, fashion jewelry, cologne, cosmetics, personal-care products, and home furnishings present numerous market opportunities in targeting the singles-under-25 market.

The singles market spends more for housing than many U.S. households. Roommates combine income to live in downtown locations. A flourishing singles culture has helped to developed ski lodges, cocktail lounges, and travel tours. Compared to other population groups, the singles market tends to be affluent, well-educated, highly mobile, fashion conscious, and active in leisure pursuits. Travel and insurance industries will find lucrative opportunities in this market.

THE AFFLUENT ASIAN MARKET

The Spectrum Group of Chicago in their study found that Asian Americans comprise 5 percent of affluent U.S. households, increasing from less than 1 percent in 2002. *Affluent* is defined by the Spectrum Group as possessing more than $500,000 in investible assets. The average net worth of affluent Asian Americans was $2.9 million, and occupations included accountants, physicians, dentists, technical specialists, and business owners. Few inherited their money. Affluent Asians were found to take greater risks with their investments than other affluent groups.[8]

The Asian American market represents $396.5 billion in purchasing power with a population of 11 million. Many members of this market reside in five cities: Los Angeles, San Francisco, New York, Honolulu, and Chicago. There are growing groups of Asians in Seattle, Boston, Atlanta, Washington, Houston, and Dallas. People from the Philippines are the second-largest Asian subgroup in the United States after the Chinese. Their numbers have grown more than 700 percent since 1960. The top six segments are Chinese, Filipinos, Indians, Vietnamese, Koreans, and Japanese.

There are a variety of Asian subcultures depending on region, West Coast versus Northeast and rural versus urban, and social class. A West Coast, urban, college-educated Asian with origins from either China or Japan leads a different life than a Korean small-grocery-store owner in New York City. Many members of these groups are third- or fourth-generation Americans. These offspring of early immigrants have achieved a certain measure of affluence. Newer Asian immigrants come from the Philippines, Vietnam, Cambodia, Hong Kong, and Korea. Already, first-generation Americans from these groups have made progress in becoming either upscale or affluent consumers. According to the latest Census data, approximately 30 percent of the half-million Indian American households had incomes over $100,000 compared with 12 percent of all American households.

Education is highly valued by Asian Americans. They are more likely to obtain a college degree than other Americans. Thirty-eight percent hold a bachelor's degree or higher. They also aspire to managerial and professional status.

Many members of Asian American groups are strivers. Asian American households have outpaced all other population groups in relative spending and have an average household income in excess of $80,000. They have labored hard and struggled in opposition to prejudice. They highly value material possessions and the symbolism of success that is conveyed. They are very receptive to product advertisements and are brand loyal. They have the highest personal computer ownership and the highest rate of Internet use in the United States. They will go online to research a product.

The U.S. Census Bureau predicts that the Asian American market will grow to about 33.4 million people by 2050. Census 2000 indicates that Asian Americans' buying power increased by over 200 percent to $268.8 billion in 2000, from $116.5 billion recorded in 1990. By 2010, the Asian American buying power should be $578.8 billion.

THE AFFLUENT BLACK MARKET

The buying power of African Americans is expected to reach $1,023.4 trillion by 2010. They were at one time the largest nonwhite ethnic group in the United States with a total population of 36.4 million people. Almost 1.5 million of the group have incomes of $75,000 or more. The African American female is an important part of this group. Sales growth to this market segment is significant for household appliances, apparel, and personal products. The growth rate for purchasing new cars is 12 times the growth rate of nonblack purchasers over the past decade.

Affluent blacks have had to overcome obstacles to become successful. Few inherited wealth or businesses but instead assumed a long struggle. Social class is an important concept in comprehending black purchasing patterns as it is for understanding white buyer behavior or that of any other ethnic group. The emergence of the black middle class has been tied to the civil rights movement of the 1960s. The older generation tends to prefer the term *black*, whereas the younger generation likes to be described as African American.

A large proportion of the affluent black market segment can be labeled strivers. More than 25 percent of affluent blacks own businesses. For some years *Ebony* magazine was aimed at an affluent and upscale market, but because of expansion of this market, *Essence* magazine was launched in 2001. *Essence* is now reported as the most influential vehicle for reaching black Americans. Both *Essence* and *Ebony* appeal to black investors who typically are more conservative than their Asian counterparts. Spiegel and *Ebony* magazine jointly produced *EStyles*, a quarterly fashion catalog featuring a new merchandise line of apparel for African American women. Blacks are above-average purchasers of CD players, jewelry, and watches.

Targeting black consumers is different than marketing to a mainstream audience. Advertising requires a different approach. Inserting ethnic faces into traditional advertising campaigns is no longer effective. Communications require an elevated level of cultural awareness. Otherwise, there is a risk of reinforcing ethnic stereotypes and alienating black consumers. The Hallmark Mahogany line of greeting cards, first introduced with 16 styles, has increased to more than 800 and is a good illustration of an effective promotional campaign. The key to targeting the black consumer is respect and credibility.

Affluent blacks are major consumers of luxury brand-name goods. Purchases extend to expensive fashion-conscious apparel and luxury cars. Blacks seem to be more conservative investors than whites and Asians who are more aggressive. Black women have gained professional and managerial positions faster than black men. As more blacks gain higher education they become more demanding as consumers. The growth rate for obtaining post-secondary degrees among black Americans is increasing at a rate five times faster than the general population. Products that demonstrate an understanding of black culture are welcome. This market can be reached by targeted advertising, event marketing, the Internet, and direct mail. There is still an underserved African American suburban market, namely, the baby boomers. Their buying power will rise in every state but Maryland, New York, Delaware, Florida, and New Jersey. Georgia and Virginia will experience the greatest surge according to the U.S. Census Bureau. The U.S. Census Bureau projects that by 2050 the black market will comprise approximately 15 percent of the U.S. population. A significant segment will trade up in their purchasing and will also be upscale and affluent buyers. Among the largest advertisers to the African American market are General Motors, Procter & Gamble, General Mills, Coca-Cola, and Daimler-Chrysler.

THE AFFLUENT HISPANIC MARKET

The Hispanic market is composed of people from Mexico, Cuba, Puerto Rico, South and Central America, and those who are primarily second- or third-generation Americans. They tend to shop as a family. They represent almost 13 percent of the American population, and their buying power should exceed $1 trillion by 2010. The Hispanic market has been segmented by the Spanish language and country of origin. There are differences not only in culture, education, and income but also in purchasing behavior. English is playing a more important role in reaching the market since 76 percent of

Hispanic adults born in the United States watch English-language television. Within 20 years, 80 percent of U.S. Hispanics will be born in the United States. According to the U.S. Census Bureau, Hispanics will represent 15.5 percent of the population by 2010 and 24.4 percent by 2050.

Since many Hispanics are recent immigrants to the United States, a high percentage speak only Spanish. Early immigrants from Cuba, who fled Castro's domination were exceptions and were more highly educated. Many of the early Cuban immigrants are financially successful. The children of the more recent immigrants typically identify strongly with their heritage but have acculturated and are able to communicate in both English and Spanish. The more affluent Hispanic markets are situated in Los Angeles, Houston, New York, Miami, the San Francisco Bay Area, and Chicago.

Cuban Americans constitute only 7 percent of the U.S. Hispanic population but are the oldest Hispanic group in the United States, with a median age of 39; the most affluent; and the most highly educated, with 20 percent of those age 25 or older having attended college. Mexican Americans comprise more than 60 percent of the U.S. Hispanic population. They are the youngest, with a median age of 24, and only about 6 percent have completed college. There is a high concentration of Cubans in Miami; for those of Mexican origin, there are large clusters in Los Angeles, San Antonio, and Houston; and there is a high concentration of Puerto Ricans in New York City. Eight of the top 20 Hispanic-owned companies are located in Florida. Recent trends reveal that there have been shifts to such states as North Carolina, Nevada, Kansas, Indiana, and Minnesota.

The growth of Hispanic households' disposable income has increased from $211.9 billion in 1990 to over $490 billion by 2000, and this amount is projected to be $1086.5 trillion by 2010. Hispanics spent over $735.6 billion in 2005 on goods and services. More than 4.5 million Hispanics earn $75,000 or more. Many Hispanics do not have credit cards, or debit cards. Hispanics have exercised purchasing patterns similar to other affluent groups that had initial language barriers, such as the Asian, Italian, Scandinavian, Jewish, and German immigrant groups.

Hispanics have not integrated as quickly as earlier immigrant groups. Hispanics tend to cling to their language, traditions, values, the role of the family and elderly, and their culture. This is especially true of those of Mexican origin because of their frequent contact with their homeland and their local concentration. Although the average Hispanic person has resided in the United States for about 13 years, only half are fluent in English. Younger Hispanics are most fluent in English and are better able to communicate in English than older Hispanics. Marketing to Hispanics requires more than a translation of a general marketing campaign. In-depth knowledge of Spanish is required in understanding the subtle nuances that vary significantly from region to region. More than 16 percent of U.S. Hispanic households subscribe to at least one direct broadcasting service and receive DirecTV, Para TiVos, or Dish Latino. There has been an increase in the number of Hispanic publications, including regional publications such as *Tu Ciudad Los Angeles*; magazines aimed at men, including *Sports Illustrated Latino* and *Fox Sports en Español*; and *Quina Girl*, a magazine aimed at the 400,000 Hispanic girls who become 15 each year and have Quina-añera parties for their 15th birthdays.

The Hispanic family is strong. But even affluent and upscale Hispanic strivers retain a strong identity. Hispanics own almost half of all minority business establishments, and the Internet is now the most important medium for influencing buyer decisions in the future. Hispanics who access the Internet are on average younger than the general online population. Hispanics have a greater propensity to search the Internet for information—63 percent, compared to 52 percent of the general population—rather than to play computer games.[9]

Marketers need to fully understand the diverse subgroups and subcultures within the Hispanic population. There is also a growing market of wealthy Hispanics coming to America. They own vacation homes in the United States and spend a lot of money as consumers. They buy the best automobiles, foods, wines, clothes and furniture. Among the largest advertisers to the Hispanic market are Procter & Gamble, General Motors Corp., Sears Holdings Corp., Wal-Mart Stores, Verizon Communications, Toyota Motor Corp., Ford Motor Company, PepsiCo, and Johnson & Johnson. Hispanics represent 6 percent market share of the United States automobile market, and it is anticipated that this will increase to 12 percent by 2020.

MANAGING CHANGE

Aspiration levels are influenced by achievement or failure, and one goal usually leads to another. Should success be achieved, a hierarchy of goals is constructed. For example, junior executives proceed to midlevel career status and then to senior career levels. The ownership of a starter home in a respectable neighborhood precedes the purchase of another home in an exclusive section of town. A reality orientation and group reference points are established as to possible achievement levels for various activities and interests. Affluent people tend to be achievement oriented in their work and in their social lives.

Group membership exerts a powerful influence on the purchasing decisions and the behavior of individuals even without consultation. Purchasing similarities exist in the consumption behavior of "statistical" income groups, age groups, and life-cycle groups. Purchasing behavior is motivated by a changing environment that is dynamic and changeable over time.

Affluent individuals continue to belong to groups. During the 1980s, wine tasting was a common basis for group get-togethers. This presented marketers with the opportunity to contact these groups to make their products known. The 1990s had its book clubs and investment clubs. Book stores such as Barnes and Noble had game night every Tuesday, where patrons played chess, Scrabble, or backgammon in the café of their store. Every Wednesday from noon until 2:30 P.M., classical musicians play in the café; and every Monday evening, great books such as *Dr. Zhivago*, *To Kill a Mockingbird*, and *All the*

Presidents' Men are discussed. Readers attend book and poetry readings and participate in discussion groups. Highbrow socializing has fostered discussion groups featuring casual conversation and current events.

Marketers need to adjust their marketing strategies and policies as seniors, singles, and ethnic groups experience changing characteristics. The focus of marketing campaigns should be on changing values and lifestyles. The selection of media and the message should reflect sophistication and maturity. For example, the gay market is a subgroup of the singles market and a lucrative one. Members of the gay market are more likely to be in professional jobs, more likely to own a vacation home, and more likely to own stocks as compared to the typical American. Firms like Merrill Lynch and Smith Barney are competing for business from gay and lesbian investors. Same-sex couples have special needs since under federal and most state laws they are not recognized as legally married. Financial advisors must know which laws are either applicable or not applicable to their clients in order to satisfy the needs of same-sex couples.

The senior group will grow appreciably with the aging of the baby boomers, creating a culture once fixated on youth that will respond more favorably today to marketing campaigns that make sense. Marketers are increasingly challenging the stereotype that seniors are only good buyers of real estate, jewelry, automobiles, and various types of recreational pursuits. Marketers are learning that seniors also desire the latest in technology as seniors purchase $1,200 camcorders and $5,000 home-theater systems. Marketers are beginning to change their obsession with youth to include seniors in their strategies.

In the future, Asians striving to become affluent will become contented joining other ethnic groups. Blacks and Hispanics comprise 25 percent of the population, and Hispanics are currently the fastest-growing minority group in the United States. The ethnic groups integrate and adopt the culture and purchasing patterns of the established affluent population. According to the U.S. Census 2004, the three major ethnic groups combined will grow at six times the rate of the nonethnic United States population. Already, the combined ethnic percentage of population exceeds more than 50 percent in Los Angeles, Houston, Miami, and New York and 40 percent in Chicago and San Francisco. The University of Michigan and Florida International University in their survey found that blacks and Hispanics are twice as likely to establish business organizations as whites.

An understanding of affluent groups and their changing aspirations cannot be fully understood unless it is realized that in 1900 only about half a million people in the United States were Hispanic, and by 2100 it is estimated that one-third of Americans will be of Hispanic origin. In 2003 the Census Bureau designated Hispanics as the largest minority group, with a 14 percent share of the population versus 12 percent for blacks. Marketers already realize that there are large markets of Hispanics in California and Texas, but there are new and emerging populations in Washington, Nevada, Florida, Georgia, and Colorado. There is potential for profits in these markets that has been undeclared because of cultural barriers.

The approach for studying affluent groups is interdisciplinary. Disciplines such as psychology, sociology, social psychology, cultural anthropology, and economics play an important role in helping us understand how and why customers behave the way they do in the marketplace. Marketers are increasingly combining multiple variables to identify and reach smaller, more precise target groups.

Chapter 7

Segmenting the Affluent Market

Every society has its beliefs, values, and norms to guide individual behavior. Changes in the cultural and social environment affect purchasing patterns. Years ago the family home had a room that was its showcase, and it was the living room with a plastic covered sofa off-limits to children. It was not uncommon for the family to take off their shoes before walking on wall-to-wall carpeting.

The baby boomers and their children have grown up buying homes with family and living rooms, master bedroom suites, numerous bathrooms, and three-car garages. The family feels squeezed for time and more harried than ever. Husband and wife are in the workforce and being pulled in different directions by jobs, soccer, PTA, music, and tennis lessons. They desire convenient shopping and time-saving services and products.

The dramatic increase in the number of dual-income families has not only affected the magnitude of spending but the types of products purchased as well. Dual-income families have a propensity to purchase convenience-oriented products such as riding lawnmowers, microwave ovens, and leisure-related recreation services such as travel and dining out. New types of services have been made available to affluent families, such as nannies and live-in housekeepers, and security systems with alarms and visual systems that monitor the entire house.

The increased number of women striving to further their careers has led to smaller families. Parents and grandparents, with fewer children, are willing and able to spend more money on each child.

The contribution of new and changing technology is reflected in new products for affluent families. Time organizers, cable television, and home theaters are just a few of the many products now used in the home. Advancements in medical science have led to cosmetic operations that make people feel good about themselves.

Marketers typically have an abundance of data about product attitudes but scant information about lifestyle values and preferences. This is unfortunate since the marketplace is shifting from product-based considerations, such as quantity, tangibles, and money, to lifestyle characteristics like quality, intangibles, and time. The affluent market desires products that provide lifestyle experiences rather than just product satisfaction. The proliferation of income for the affluent has created consumers who can purchase almost anything they desire, but not everything. Affluent consumers are confronted with a continual process of making choices from a wide array of goods and services. The complexity of decision making has increased and should therefore stimulate more research in affluent consumer purchasing behavior.

Customized marketing is one of the most advanced strategies used for the development of tailor-made products for satisfying the needs of affluent consumers. Marketers adjust product, price, promotion, and distribution strategies to each target market, with more costs but greater opportunities for a larger market share and increased profitability. Clothing such as shirts and suits can be made to the specifications of individual consumers. Golf clubs and furniture can be designed to the specifications of individuals. Homes can be constructed in a mass-produced stage, but with a number of available options to be chosen by consumers. Information can be customized and personalized. Customization also has its negatives—it is difficult to implement for complex products, customers may not be willing to pay increased costs, and the product may prove hard to repair. However, for some products, such as laptop computers and skincare products, customization has worked well.

CHANGING ORIENTATIONS TOWARD THE AFFLUENT MARKET

There is a greater variety of goods and services available, and almost anything can be ordered regardless of location. The affluent segment has a tremendous impact on certain markets including automotive, electronic, financial management, travel and leisure, estate planning, tax advisors and charities.

There is a greater amount of information not only about products and services but customers as well. Business organizations find it easier to reach customers who are likely to be interested in their product offerings. Consumers find it easier to compare the offerings of business organizations. All of this facilitates improved interaction between buyer and seller. There are some new products referred to as discontinued innovations that require the establishment of new consumption patterns. New behavior adjustments are developed to use fax machines, home computers, videocassette recorders, medical self-test kits, video text, cell phones, and CD-ROM players.

New opportunities have been made possible by changing technology. There has been a substantial increase in buying power and in the numbers of affluent and upscale consumers. Business organizations are now able to serve markets on a 24/7 basis. Companies will need to change their strategies as the marketplace changes.

HOW MARKETERS CAN RESPOND

- Affluent consumers expect higher quality and exhibit greater price sensitivity as they seek value and show less brand loyalty. Marketers should respond by increasing product quality and offering desired services. The goal is to establish long-term profitable customer relationships. For example, Patek Phillippe advises customers that its watches are not owned but passed on to the next generation.
- Fiercer competition is prevalent targeting affluent consumers. Companies should respond by offering the customer lifetime value. This is possible if the product needs repair or adjustment over the years. E. T. Wright Shoes and Allen Edmunds will both restore and refinish old shoes and try to make them appear new. L. L. Bean has been successful in developing an image for customer satisfaction in the postpurchase phase by not only refunding the purchase price on merchandise if the customer is not totally satisfied, but also by making adjustments for merchandise that has been worn out or damaged too early.
- Affluent consumers desire positive atmospherics. Increasingly affluent consumers are purchasing over the Internet and by mail order. Luxury retailers need to respond by offering an environment of drama and showmanship. Neiman Marcus in the past has sold camels and midget submarines by mail order. Victoria's Secret has penetrated an upscale market for elegant intimate apparel with showmanship. Victoria's Secret dominates the lingerie category with new product introductions each year supported by television advertising and lingerie fashion shows. This position is then reinforced by a catalog, Internet selling, and an active direct-marketing program.
- Affluent consumers desire special attention. Customization is a strategy to individualize messages and offerings. Every employee should be customer focused. The entire organization should coordinate the marketing program.

The affluent consumer desires to feel special, and this motive is dominant in purchasing unique or exclusive merchandise. The individual affluent customer wants to be treated as an individual. The focus of companies serving the affluent market should be on satisfying individual needs and wants.

Companies that have the resources to collect information on customer demographics, lifestyle, purchasing preferences, and customers' past transactions are in a better position to practice one-on-one marketing. Technological advances such as database software, computers, the Internet, and factory customization make possible the strategy of one-on-one marketing. One-on-one marketing is not for all companies. Those companies that are able to collect a great deal of data about customers, offer a wide assortment of products that can be cross-sold, and offer products that need upgrading and have a high premium value can best be effective with one-on-one marketing.

THE SOCIETAL CONCEPT

As more consumers become affluent, there is increasing concern over the social responsibility of business as consumers deal with tobacco products, no-return bottles, food with high taste appeal but low nutritional value, liquor, and the proper disposal of trash. The problems of ecology are holistic in nature and encompass air pollution, water pollution, noise pollution, overburdened travel arteries, decaying cities, overpopulation, poverty, and the conservation of natural resources. Many of these challenges have become political issues.

Ben & Jerry's ice-cream company has directed many of its appeals to a market segment that is concerned with ecological environmental challenges. The proceeds from its Rain Forest Crunch ice-cream flavor went to save the Amazon. Ben & Jerry's was a pioneer in recycling packing materials. Ben & Jerry's constructed a water-treatment plant and the company is noted for its energy conservation within the manufacturing process. The corporate structure is still the antithesis of the large corporate bureaucracy since a fun and laid-back atmosphere is promoted and encouraged even though Ben & Jerry's is now part of Unilever.

The Body Shop specializes in natural cosmetics, such as skin creams and lotions made from fruit and vegetable oils rather than animal fats. Unlike other cosmetic stores, plastic bottles are recycled, sales literature is printed on recycled paper ,and animal testing of new products is prohibited. Competitors include Estee Lauder with its Origins natural line and the Bath and Body Works brand. The Body Shop has developed small-size bottles that make a splurge appear less extravagant.

Both Ben & Jerry's and the Body Shop see cause-related marketing as an opportunity. They believe that customers will buy from companies that have a responsibility to society. Social responsibility goes beyond supplying rational and emotional benefits and directs itself to higher needs. Interest in these high needs is more common when physiological needs are satisfied and higher needs become paramount.

GENERATIONAL AND COHORT MARKETING

Generational and cohort marketing define lifestyles and social values. They focus on a generation in terms of external events that occurred during their member's formative years. The distinction between lifestyle generational marketing and cohort analysis is that generation marketing holds that it is important to target each generation based on the times in which it grew up—the movies, music, and other events of that period. Cohort marketing focuses on groups of people who share experiences of major external events that have made a penetrating impact on their attitudes, values, and preferences. The

Great Depression, World War II, and the Vietnam War would be examples of these external events. Some marketers may target baby boomers, and others may prefer to target a World War II cohort. Each generation feels a bonding because they shared similar experiences and consequently use and depict images and icons that were prominent during those periods. The use of cohort marketing is more focused than generational marketing, but each can be effective when used appropriately and can be combined together. Values help to define the cultural environment to which a group belongs, and a social system develops with its own norms.

A marketer, by understanding generations' characteristics and core values, may better develop products and strategies to attract customers. Naturally, as members of a given generation mature, age, income, gender, and environmental experiences help modify a sense of the future. Each generation has its dream. For baby boomers, that dream has been early retirement; but for many, this dream will not be realized. The dream of Gen Xers is to be entrepreneurs—not necessarily to establish their own businesses, but to individualize their experiences.

Every generation goes forth with its own challenges caused by external events. How they confront these events becomes a memorable part of history. These generations are united by common experiences and bonds. After World War I, a war to end all wars, a generation wandered around Europe disillusioned and made its headquarters in Paris. This generation was known as the lost generation. As history evolved, other generations emerged that shared common bonds and experiences that were to influence their purchasing patterns. Marketers, to be effective, must in some way appeal to these generations with realistic strategies.

THE GREAT DEPRESSION—OVER 80 YEARS OLD

This generation experienced adverse economic conditions and many also served in World War II. Many members of this generation preferred to avoid debt and used credit sparingly. Savings were a high priority and low-risk investments were preferred. Big-band music helped to define this group. Affluent members of this generation exhibited hard work and thrift. Family heirlooms such as jewelry, dishware, and furniture were left to offspring. Estates were treasured by a younger generation.

THE GREATEST GENERATION—AGED 75 TO 80

There is some overlap between the Depression and the Greatest Generation, but focus should be on the vast majority that contribute to an affluent lifestyle. Some members of this group built small businesses from World War II loans. These businesses grew and prospered. Many attained a college education on the G.I. Bill and subsequently became successful. This generation, because of the war, rationing, and the economic depression, was raised with a spirit of self-denial. Like the Great Depression, they were influenced by radio and motion pictures. Their favorite music is swing. Sports figures such as Joe DiMaggio and Ted Williams were influential spokespersons for promoting products to this cohort.

THE SILENT GENERATION—AGED 55–75

This postwar generation entered family businesses and became affluent. Their teenage years presented memories of economic growth that followed World War II. The uncertainties of war and attack remained fresh in their minds as they endeavored to ease their lives by acquiring material possessions. Although many were involved in the Korean conflict, they silently marched off to war. This generation faced life as it evolved and acquired a more balanced perspective toward spending and savings than either the Great Depression or the Greatest Generation cohorts. This group has fond memories of Frank Sinatra, and they enjoyed the movie *The Wizard of Oz*. Home ownership gained momentum with this generation.

THE BABY BOOMERS—AGED 45–55

These 78 million people are one of the most powerful forces shaping the affluent marketplace. Approximately 17 percent of the boomers are minorities, and 29 percent have a college degree or higher. More than half of all boomers live in nine states: California, Florida, Illinois, Michigan, New Jersey, New York, Ohio, Pennsylvania, and Texas. Baby boomers feel younger than their actual age. Since many affluent women are in the workforce, this generation desires convenience, which has resulted in a demand for home-delivery services for items like appliances, furniture, and even groceries. The desire for convenience has manifested itself in the demand for microwave ovens and prepared takeout foods.

Affluent boomers patronize health-food stores, use personal trainers, and purchase exercise equipment. There is an increased demand for skin treatments, hair coloring, hair transplants, and the luxury of spas. Men join women in this adventure to remain youthful. Baby boomers are replacing furniture purchased early in their marriage. Home theaters are in demand, and furniture from retailers like IKEA, the Bombay Company, Pier 1 Imports, and Williams-Sonoma are in vogue. Affluent baby boomers are a moving target. Baby boomers from ages 45 to 64 will have increased by 8.7 million people by 2009. Affluent baby boomers desire new experiences as well as close relationships with their children and grandchildren. Sports products, marketers, entertainment, and technology industries will find boomers receptive to their offerings. Affluent boomers are among the first to purchase new products and constitute about 25 percent of the baby boomer market.

The early baby boomers born between 1946 and 1954 are more affluent than those born between 1955 and 1964. The early baby boomers are today's entrepreneurs and professionals. Many of these early baby boomers have from $100,000 to $1 million to invest, with an average account of $200,000. Although the early baby boomers are well educated, they have found it more difficult to realize their dreams. However, since the baby boomers comprise at least 50 percent of all those in professional and managerial occupations, they are an important market segment.

Some baby boomers have been referred to as so-called yuppies, which is an acronym for young, urban professionals who are well-educated college graduates interested in their personal fulfillment. These yuppies have matured but still tend to be materialistic and prefer branded products like BMWs and Rolex watches. This group desires the best of everything. This group has been achievement oriented and has shifted as they aged to more suburban and family-oriented lifestyle purchases.

The older baby boomers born between 1946 and 1954 remember the Vietnam War, and the assassinations of John F. Kennedy and Martin Luther King Jr. This segment embraces the values of youthfulness, freedom, and instant gratification and has been referred to as the Woodstock generation. The earlier baby boomers grew up with television programs such as *Father Knows Best* and *Leave It to Beaver*. Watergate took its toll, and there was a loss of faith in the political system. Gratification was a prized value, but so was an interest in a clean environment. This group was highly influenced by television.

GENERATION X—AGED 28–44

This segment is comprised of individuals born between 1965 and 1976 and is referred to as the so-called baby busters. This is the first generation of latchkey children, whose parents worked or were divorced or separated. They are in no hurry to marry or start a family. Generation X, unlike their baby boomer parents, will not neglect their families to obtain career advancement or higher salaries. For this generation, it is more important to enjoy life and have a lifestyle that provides freedom. They are more interested in golf and camping equipment than in luxury condos.

Generation Xers do not believe that they will do materially as well as their parents. Generation X is sometimes referred to as the boomerang kids. These are Xers who live with their parents at home well into their thirties or until marriage. This financial savings allows more discretionary income for new cars, stereos, vacations, and sports activities. This segment constitutes an important part of the singles market. Since marriage has been postponed, this generation has more savings to spend for household goods and furniture when marriage happens. This generation spends a high percentage of their discretionary income dining out. When they eat out, they go to full-service restaurants to reconnect with family and friends. There is also a high percentage of Internet usage. This generation of consumers is more sophisticated in product evaluation.

GENERATION Y—AGED 23 TO 27

Generation Y is referred to as the Internet generation, the echo boomers, or the dotcom generation. This generation numbers over 73 million and has more money to spend than the other generations did at their age. Generation Y favors L. L. Bean, J. Crew, Motorola Flex Pagers, and Mountain Dew.

The Internet Generation is comfortable with computers and wireless technology and finds that using digital technology is no more challenging than the use of a toaster. Hilfiger jeans are replacing Levi's. Baggy jeans, power beads, and the Backstreet Boys are in the forefront. Marketers with established brands are challenged to cultivate via the Internet the largest generation since the baby boomers. The term *viral marketing* has developed from the new behavioral patterns of Generation Y, influenced by the Internet and encompassing word-of-mouth advertising, direct mail, telemarketing, electronic mail, and the Internet. Viral marketing is a strategy that helps marketers to develop closer relationships with customers.

Although many members of Generation X are sophisticated users of the Internet, it is Generation Y that has had formal instruction in its use. The software industry has directed most of its products toward targeting Generation Y. Titles such as Baby-Rom are designed to help infants learn from the computer.

Generation Y is more diverse than the baby boomers since changes in family structure, technology, and demographics reflect attitude modifications of this generation. More than half of Generation Y has working mothers, and one in three is not Caucasian. As many as 10 to 15 percent of Generation Y children have been born into a household where a foreign language is spoken. A broad spectrum of cable and satellite TV channels and niche magazines using a generational or cohort approach have been used to target this generation.

BASIS FOR SEGMENTING AFFLUENT MARKETS

Each generation can be segmented by variables such as family life cycle; education; occupation; income; gender; and behavioral variables such as occasions for purchases, product benefits, user rates, and psychographic factors including lifestyle. Some of these variables can be used alone, but it is more likely that when combined, a more effective strategy will result. Marketers need to use demographic segmentation variables in conjunction with behavioral variables to define markets precisely.

A company cannot serve all customers in a broad market such as automobiles. The customers are too diverse in their purchasing preferences. A company needs to identify the market segments it can satisfy effectively and efficiently. The market for automobiles, for instance, may be segmented into three price categories—high, medium, or low—by type of car, family, luxury, and sports. Any one of these segments can be further subdivided.

A firm's image, even though favorable, cannot necessarily be successful with each new generation. For example, Cadillac's success with the senior market limits its effectiveness with younger consumers. Younger customers do not want to drive a luxury automobile perceived as their father's car. Present Cadillac owners are over 60 years of age, and although likely to remain loyal, cannot be viewed as an attractive long-term market.

Products that are no longer acceptable among the affluent may become popular again. The martini has reemerged as a sophisticated drink, and the liquor industry has been restored to its earlier esteem. There are other products from the past that if altered or modified may become successful in the future.

LIFE-CYCLE STAGE AND AGE

Consumers' desires and abilities change with age and their stage in the family life cycle. The majority of affluent people were not born into wealthy families but have gained affluence through their education, occupation choices, and hard work. Consequently, age and life cycle are tricky variables. Age has an impact on marital status and the presence or absence of children in the household, and the ages of children impacts spending behavior. Generally, affluence comes with increased maturity and occupational success.

Life cycle position is an important determinant of buyers' behavior. In an effort to attract new affluent mothers, hospitals are constructing deluxe maternity wards. Hospitals are expanding luxury services and offering perks such as a Jacuzzi tub that costs patients extra. St. Vincent Women's Hospital in Indianapolis, Indiana, offers complimentary massage; and a baby portrait studio provides a disk with digital pictures. Gaston Memorial Hospital in Gastonia, North Carolina, has 52 rooms with a sofa bed, refrigerator, whirlpool bath, and DVD players. Siblings can play in the children's library. The young married couple with children under age 10 has different needs from those of a couple in their mid-50s whose children have graduated from college and are not living at home. Middle-aged couples without children typically buy more expensive home furnishings and automobiles, and they are more likely to use financial services.

Abercrombie & Fitch, in an effort to serve young adults better, has opened Hollister for high school students and Ruehl for young adults in their 20s. Abercrombie & Fitch believes that it is beneficial to develop marketing approaches for each group.

The family is the most important reference group in society. The family unit influences individuals' values and lifestyles. These values and lifestyles are manifest in purchasing expenditures. The increasing numbers of families with two incomes and the greater number of women seeking careers are causing changes that affect spending patterns. Past generations delegated spending for certain types of goods to the wife and others to the husband. More couples are exercising joint decision making in purchasing expenditures. Awareness of household structure is paramount in designing marketing strategy. Different strategies may be developed when the following information is collected:

- What percent of affluent households are without children?
- With children?
- Living alone?
- Female-headed families?
- Male-headed families?
- Members of the opposite sex living together?
- Members of the same sex living together?
- Who makes the purchasing decision?
- Who influences the purchasing decision?
- Who makes the actual purchase?
- Who actually uses the product?

The over 50 population is not only wealthier but healthier. This generation accounts for more than half of leisure and travel expenditures. Marketing research shows that age is a meaningful variable for product segmentation strategy. For example, unlike the baby boomers, who share many characteristics, seniors aged 60 to 90 are increasingly heterogeneous. There are significant differences in health and income between seniors from 60 to 70 and those over 80.

GENDER

Gender segmentation has long been applicable in apparel, cosmetics, and periodicals. Some recent changes are that men do more of their own personal and family shopping. Women are purchasing more tools than ever before in stores like Home Depot and Lowe's. Teenagers and tweens have more discretionary purchasing power to make purchases alone than in previous generations. Women constitute at least one-third of the luxury automobile market. Single women are purchasing homes and condominiums. Changing family purchasing patterns reveal that women either make or greatly influence buying decisions of homes, medical care, and vacations, whereas their influence was not as strong previously.

Citigroup, Merrill Lynch, and American Express have developed programs for female clients. The greater involvement of women seeking financial advice spans a demographic spectrum from the middle class to the very rich. Women are deciding not to wait for divorce or widowhood to develop a financial plan. Citigroup offers investing advice, loan services, an online newsletter, financial classes, and other services. Merrill Lynch provides advising and educational services for wealthy women, including business owners, executives, and philanthropists. American Express sponsors seminars offering the basics through more advanced investing techniques. These firms are anticipating a wave of baby boomers, widows, and those who will inherit great wealth from their parents' generation.

OCCUPATION AND ECONOMIC CIRCUMSTANCES

Occupation has an important impact on an individual's consumption patterns. An executive will purchase expensive suits, belong to a country club, and own a sailboat. They will likely be a heavy user of air travel. Occupational groups such as physicians, attorneys, and other professional and managerial personnel have an above-average interest in buying certain products and services. A company can design products for certain affluent occupational groups, such as a computer software company targeting engineers, lawyers, and physicians. Corporations may be targeted by hotels that have extended-stay features and amenities such as refrigerators, fax machines, and computers in their rooms for relocated employees.

Product choice is affected by economic purchases such as luxury automobiles, jewelry, and vacations. Economic circumstance such as savings and assets, debts, and how much is needed for financial security also determines consumption patterns.

GEOGRAPHICAL SEGMENTATION

Marketers are able to target affluent populated areas based on zip codes. Products targeting the affluent can be directed to geographical areas such as Gladwyne, Pennsylvania, and Atherton, California. Streets such as Rodeo Drive in Los Angeles, North Michigan Avenue in Chicago, and Fifth Avenue in New York City include retailers catering to affluent consumers.

Blockbuster is able to track video preferences in different states, regions, and cities. Blockbuster maintains a higher inventory of videos portraying gay relationships in San Francisco and a higher inventory of family movies and dramas in Chicago. Technology allows business organizations to invest in complex databases that divide the market into different geographical areas.

Many in the affluent market have multiple residences located in different parts of the United States. A primary residence may be located in Kenilworth, Illinois; the summer residence in Cape Cod, Massachusetts; and the winter residence in Vail, Colorado. All of these residences would need to be furnished.

Geographic segmentation is not the most effective marketing strategy. Variables used in conjunction with geographic location are more important in determining which types of apparel or furniture would be well received in the marketplace. Often, when product usage or some other variable, such as ethnic group, is used in conjunction with geographic segmentation, the strategy is more successful.

Whereas geographical segmentation is not always a sound strategy when used alone, it is an important link between geographic preference and economic opportunity for home-improvement centers. The sun belt states have attracted population growth from other regions with harsher climates. Therefore, the housing market in the sun belt states has offered much better opportunities for firms like Home Depot and Lowe's. Population mobility ranges from 17 to 21 percent each year; tends to possess affluent characteristics; and is an attractive market for upscale furniture, appliances, and garden and yard equipment.

BEHAVIORAL SEGMENTATION

Behavioristic segmentation divides buyers on such variables as occasion, the basis of need-satisfying benefits derived from product use, the rate of product usage, the degree of brand loyalty, and an understanding of consumer readiness to purchase the product. Affluent consumers are thus targeted based on their knowledge, attitudes, responses, or uses of the product. Buying situations vary depending on the circumstances that the consumer finds at the time. Purchasing situations have an impact on product benefits sought, product usage, readiness to buy, and the purchasing conditions of the moment. The lowly sandal or flip-flop is worn as warm-weather footwear and is meant to be casual. The popularity of beach shoes worn with more formal clothing has increased. Manolo Blahnick targets the affluent with an alligator toe-ring sandal priced at over $1,000, and Lillian's Sandals targets the upscale market with shoes in faux snake priced at about $100. Newport News targets those consumers who trade up with a $25 sandal. Some products are used as conscious or unconscious symbols that designate various social categories. Many affluent consumers like to demonstrate refinement and understate restraint and discipline in their consumption activities. Attire for affluent females may include cashmere sweaters, flats, and a small leather handbag for leisure. Jewelry might include a small bracelet or necklace. Colors are subdued, and apparel is conservative.

OCCASION SEGMENTATION

A special situation will drive product preference and selection, such as a family event or a holiday. Upscale candy producers have done a good job targeting Valentine's Day and Mother's Day to sell more products. Other brands such as Rolex have targeted birthdays. Charter airlines serve groups who fly to a vacation destination.

A. T. Cross has a relatively low share of the total pen market but by clever niche marketing has become profitable. A.T. Cross has successfully targeted itself in the high-priced writing instruments market with its gold and silver products. Birthdays and graduations have become specialized markets for gifts. A. T. Cross has offered high value to the upscale consumer, charged a premium price, and established a strong brand culture.

BENEFIT SEGMENTATION

Benefit segmentation is related to purchase occasions, purchase intentions, and psychographics. Benefit segmentation strategy explains a cause-and-effect relationship that helps a marketer influence buyer behavior. As consumers become more affluent, their attitudes, values, lifestyles, and postpurchase habits are modified; and benefits sought in specific purchasing situations change.

Benefit segments are based on the reasons why consumers buy. For example, affluent consumers who vacation may desire to be with their families, travel for educational purposes, or travel for the fun aspects of travel such as gambling.

The marketing strategy of benefit segmentation is useful for the breakfast cereal industry in enabling it to appeal to adults who value proper eating habits. Natural-food enthusiasts favor natural, ready-to-eat cereal and bran and high-fiber bread, granola bars, and rice. These consumers are more likely to be college graduates, younger, and in the upper-income bracket.

Benefit segmentation is valuable in the analysis of markets and is able to pinpoint the reasons why affluent consumers are purchasing. Demographic, behavioral, or psychographic variables can then be used to direct the marketing strategy to the target market.

PRODUCT-USAGE SEGMENTATION

Product-usage segmentation categorizes consumers in terms of product, service, or brand-usage characteristics. The most common categories are heavy, medium, light, and nonuser. People who buy the product, brand, or service over and over again show brand loyalty. Frequent usage programs to reward loyalty may take the form of memberships that provide special accommodations and services. Airlines such as Delta and Continental provide private clubs at airports where members can relax and work. Frequent travel awards can be granted for travel to Europe, Asia, or within the United States after accumulating a sufficient number of miles. Affluent consumers are likely to be frequent fliers, either for business or personal reasons.

When identifying a market based on usage situations, marketers are able to target different segments even when the customers are similar. For example, some affluent consumers may purchase relatively inexpensive table wines for everyday consumption and expensive wines for special occasions. Heavy users may not necessarily be brand loyal but may purchase heavily within the product class, and heavy users do not necessarily make purchases for the same reason. Product-usage segmentation used as a single variable may be difficult to explain, but when used with behavioral and lifestyle analysis, it is more effective.

Insurance firms, as the ranks of affluent consumers have increased, are offering new policies for the wealthy. The new rich are an expanding client base as the number of people in the United States with more than $1 million in financial assets grew approximately 10 percent in 2004. Wealthy individuals desire excess liability policies and comprehensive policies, which protect assets from personal injury or property damage. AIG Private Client Group offers up to $100 million in excess liability coverage that includes a defense lawyer from a panel provided by the insurer; Chubb offers coverage up to $100 million and includes coverage for serving on nonprofit boards and for worldwide automobile rentals.

VALUES SEGMENTATION

Strategies target consumers by core values that are more penetrating than attitudes and behaviors at depicting people's choices and desires over the long term. For example, strivers place more emphasis on material and professional goals than other groups. Altruists are interested in societal welfare and the environment, and creatives have a strong interest in education, knowledge and technology.

PSYCHOGRAPHIC SEGMENTATION

Psychographic segmentation is the strategy of measuring and categorizing consumer lifestyles using personality and motivation variables. Personality, as an independent variable, has proven useful as a moderating factor. Lifestyle is a broad concept that sometimes overlaps personality characteristics and is useful in segmenting markets. The manufacturer of Porsche automobiles recognizes that those consumers who are successful have high personal and professional goals and therefore target this segment.

The SRI International Values and Lifestyles (VALS) framework has gained widespread acceptance. These are the major characteristics of the four groups with greater resources:

Actualizers: successful and sophisticated with purchases that reflect cultivated tastes for relatively upscale, niche-oriented products

Fulfilled: mature and comfortable with tastes that reflect durability, functionality, and value in products

Achievers: successful and career oriented and purchase products that show prestige and success to their peers

Experiencers: young and impulsive and spend a high portion of income on clothing, music, movies and videos, and fast food

Lifestyle is an important psychographic category composed of a combination of factors such as activities, interests, and opinions. Eddie Bauer, recognizing the importance of lifestyle segmentation, developed itself as a leading brand of casual lifestyle products. Eddie Bauer has carved out a distinct niche in the mid-to-upper segment of the market, offering apparel and home furnishings for the casual lifestyle.

Lifestyle market segmentation strategies have become increasingly important. A relatively new occupation, lifestyle designers, has developed to serve those people who have made unexpected business fortunes. These members of the newly rich hire lifestyle designers whose advice ranges from wardrobe selection to home décor to party planning to gift-giving to the selection of perfect automobiles. The newly rich are insecure socially and desire such guidance.

Affluent consumers can be appealed to on the basis of rational, emotional, and patronage motives. For example, Mercedes-Benz and Jaguar appeal to status-related motives. Life-insurance companies appeal to emotional motives. Stores such as Tiffany appeal to patronage motives.

PRODUCTS DESIGNED FOR A MASS AFFLUENT MARKET

As the older affluent generation disappears, marketers will need to reach out to a new affluent generation, many of whom are in dual-income families. This generation will include those consumers who have aspirations for joining the affluent ranks and those who just like to treat themselves to certain types of goods and services. For example, learning what wines go with fish or meat and the different types of wines for various occasions leads to a feeling of sophistication.

The difficulty in reaching a mass affluent market is sometimes hard to understand because the market is divided into so many segments. More importantly, marketers have been able to customize their products to each of these segments.

A NEW WAVE OF UPSCALE PRODUCTS

T-Shirts

There are many fashion authorities who believe the modern renaissance of the T-shirt is tied to the rebirth of designer jeans. A T-shirt manufactured by Three Dots retails for about $103; by C & C California, $53; and James Perse, $60. Michael Stars, Park Vogel, Sass and Bide, and Velvet also manufacture pricey T-shirts. There are many variations in fabrics, colors, cuts, and decorations.

The mass affluent market would find it difficult to wear jeans priced at $200 and a T-shirt for $20. Bloomingdale's has increased the number of T-shirt brands it carries to satisfy consumer demand. Many of their female customers are wearing expensive T-shirts under a Channel suit.

Cell Phones

Since cell phone subscribers have increased from about 11 million in 1992 to over 140 million in 2002, this growth has presented market opportunities to penetrate an affluent market. Cell phones can be for both personal and business use and therefore are even more attractive for market-segmentation strategies. Samsung, a Korean company, has introduced cell phones with luxury designs and technological innovation. Samsung is targeting the high-end consumer and establishing its position in a niche market. Industry analysts define high-end cell phones as those with a retail price of more than $300. Samsung is manufacturing cell phones with more expensive materials, and there are plans to sell a titanium phone in the United States.

Samsung is marketing a camcorder phone that can store two hours of moving images. Consumers are developing an emotional bond with this product. More than 100 designs give consumers new choices. Female consumers tend to view their cell phones as fashion accessories, and the aim is to satisfy this desire.

Home Products

Buying the best is the way upscale consumers set themselves apart and bolster their self-image. Home products that are displayed or that can be shown to guests convey elegance. There are many new affluent and upscale consumers who “want it all” and wish to demonstrate that they are participating in the good life.

The International Home and Homeowners Show in Chicago revealed a number of housewares to please baby boomers. By 2005, this market will have more than 75 percent of the financial assets and almost 60 percent of the discretionary income in the United States. Baby boomers constitute more than one-third of the population. Baby boomers love high-tech items.

L. G. Electronics offers a side-by-side refrigerator with a 13-inch color TV embedded in the door. The suggested retail price is $3,000. An Internet model comes equipped with a 15-inch LCD computer monitor, stereo speakers, and a digital camera. The cost is $8,000. Glass tile in the kitchen, in the bathroom, and on the floors is also available. The tiles come in opaque and glossy styles. Prices start at $10 per square foot and increase to $100.

MANAGING CHANGE

An assumption is often incorrectly made that affluent consumers have similar desires regarding product attributes and that firms view differences among market segments as minor. Dual-income families have become more the norm, and marketers have broadened their definition of the low end of the affluent market.

Purchase decision making in affluent families is changing as family related roles shift. Given the number of women in the workforce, more men are involved in household tasks. Marketers must be especially sensitive to how shifting family roles affects their marketing strategies. Men are purchasing not only more of their own apparel but are doing the grocery shopping as well. Women in professional and managerial jobs need clothing that reflects this new role.

In the purchase decision-making process, certain family members assume the following buying roles:

- *Influencers:* provide information to other family members about a product or service
- *Gatekeepers:* control the flow of information by informing or withholding information about a product or service
- *Deciders:* family members who make the final decision whether to purchase a product or service
- *Buyers:* family members who actually make the purchase
- *Users:* family members who use a specific product or service
- *Disposers:* those who decide to discontinue the use of a particular product or service

These roles shift depending on the situation and the product or service. The role of influencers, gatekeepers, deciders, buyers, users, and disposers as well as the number of the family members who assume these roles varies from family to family. Sometimes, a single role will be performed by two or more family members, and in other cases, products may be consumed by a single family member or used directly or indirectly by various family members. There are instances when two or more people, either family or friends, shop for clothing or furniture items, to pass time, or just to have fun. These shopper groups desire pleasant company or the presence of someone who has more knowledge or more experience with a desired product or service. The challenge in either turbulent or changing markets is to anticipate changes over time.

A family's decision-making style is made based on the degree of affluence and the extent of financial contributions of individual family members. When conflict arises, it may be resolved if one member of the family has more expertise or information about the specific product or service. There are instances when one family member influences the others based on the position in the household. Through bargaining and negotiation behavior can be influenced.

The affluent family may look for guidance to opinion leaders or authorities who serve as information sources. Although few individuals have the knowledge of Peter Lynch, the former financial manager of the Fidelity Magellan Mutual Fund, and John Bogle, the former head of Vanguard, many can identify with their expertise in financial management. An opinion leader from a reference group would be significant in the decision to buy a specific mutual fund. Today's affluent families travel more frequently, take extended vacations, and are likely to purchase a second home in a warmer climate or buy a time-share unit that all family members enjoy. They have higher disposable incomes because of savings and investments. These families are an important market for luxury goods, automobiles, furniture, apparel, jewelry, and vacations. The increasing number of dual-career families has had an impact on family behavior. Dual-income affluent families will spend more than other families on child care, dining out, and services and are more likely to use catalogs and the Internet for purchasing.

Strategic planning begins with studying the environment. The environment presents new opportunities and threats as a result of changes in the marketplace. The changing affluent market continues to cause many shifts and surprises. The following strategies may be beneficial:

- Upscale appeals
- Psychological appeals to a loyal customer base
- Image upgrade and maintenance
- Brand positioning
- Effective use of new technology
- Shift to nonprice variables
- Total customer satisfaction
- Superior customer service
- Improve and differentiate service offerings
- Enhance value of services

Dynamic socio-demographic changes in society have resulted in many nontraditional family stages, such as childless couples, couples marrying later in life, single parents, unmarried couples, same sex unions, and single-person households. Many of these households undergo changes in brand and patronage preferences. These nontraditional households are becoming increasingly important to marketers considering the targeting of specific market niches.

CHAPTER 8

Upscale Strategies Are Not a Panacea

Change is the driving force that impacts marketing strategy as it affects the affluent consumer. New strategies are needed to direct products and services to the affluent consumers as the needs and wants of these customers change. An element of risk is present. Marketers will need to seek ways to minimize these risks. Long-range sales forecasting is frequently ignored to cut costs but can actually reduce costs and win new markets. Forecasts are part of strategic plans, and firms must be willing to absorb the costs of developing strategies based on research and planning while building market share in the affluent market. With increasing uncertainties and environmental changes, including those brought about by political and economic events beyond the control of a company, marketers' planning becomes very important. Forecasting and planning activities call for a leadership style in an organization that is proactive. The following situations are especially critical as a firm tries to penetrate the affluent market:

- When the uncontrollable environment is subject to accelerating rates of change due to the economy and events beyond the control of the company
- When the firm is considering entering new geographical regions
- When the firm's basic business is closely tied to a single factor, such as a sole source of supply or distribution

Both innovation and technology have a paramount impact on strategic planning and forecasting. Innovation includes not only invention but also adjustment and adaptation. Innovation involves an idea and its implementation. For example, the way consumers purchased toys from discounters and over the Internet led to the bankruptcy of FAO Schwartz, a retailer whose customers were affluent and upscale consumers. Changing technology and innovation by Japanese marketers in the watch industry caused the decline of Swiss manufacturers, and Seiko and other brands became more dominant. These changes called for an adjustment of behavior in strategies for firms in the affected industries.

Defining the corporate mission is a crucial part of total corporate strategy. A clear-cut corporate mission specifies the scope of the firm and its emphasis and values. A firm should reassess its mission to ascertain its fit in a changing environment. Answers to questions such as what is the company business, who is the customer, what does the customer value, and what should be the company business help define the corporate mission.

From a marketing perspective, upscale consumers and those who occasionally trade up in their purchasing behavior, as depicted in Figure 8.1, identify with groups of people who share common ideas about how life should be lived. Whereas income influences purchasing behavior through availability of resources, cultural and psychological perspectives affect how consumers spend their income. Lifestyle and socioeconomic status are to a great degree inseparable. Consumption patterns are largely expressions of socialization with particular groups where people learn appropriate values and preferences. Upscale consumers use role models to reflect purchasing behavior. These role models would likely live in such places as the Upper East Side in Manhattan, along Lake Shore Drive in Chicago, or in the Pacific Heights section of San Francisco. At the heart of upscale purchasing behavior is the desire to enhance self-image and social status. Aspirations are the key to understanding the basis for strategies to target the upscale consumer. There are aspirational differences present in the market. For one family it may be a weekend getaway at a Four Season's Hotel instead of a Holiday Inn, and for another family it may be the purchase of a Lexus instead of a Toyota Corolla. Whether the aspiration or the dream is great or small, it is real and an important variable in purchasing behavior. The challenge for marketers is to take advantage of this opportunity by devising strategies that will trigger upscale consumer motivation.

Millions of individuals have achieved varying degrees of affluence. Many newcomers to the ranks of upscale consumers are women and members of ethnic groups. Some marketers have adopted a two-tier strategy targeting two different but distinct groups composed of affluent and upscale consumers. Mercedes and

Figure 8.1
Strategies to Target Upscale Consumers

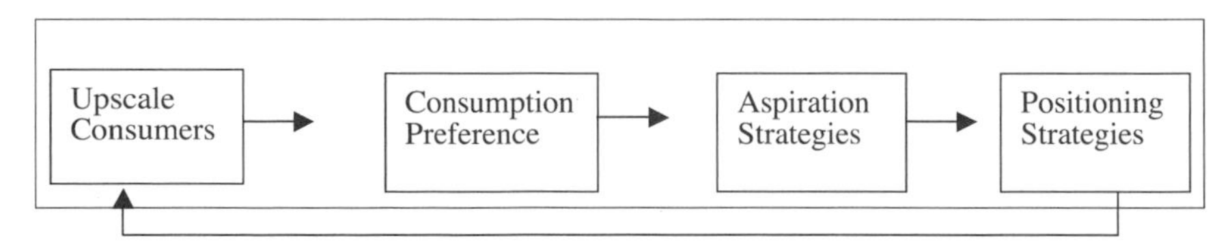

some automobile manufacturers are using this two-tier strategy to attract upscale and affluent consumers. Lands' End, Ralph Lauren, and Isaac Mizrahi are also following this strategy. Upscale consumers, like their more affluent counterparts, desire goods that save time, enhance the physical self, and maintain a youthful appearance. Goods and services that support mobility, such as cell phones, laptop computers, and instant photography are in demand. Services from financial planners and home decorators are desired.

Upscale consumers seem to "want it all" and purchase products with the symbols and attraction of elevated status. Treating oneself to the best and occasionally splurging bolsters self-image. Marketers frequently use messages that convey sensual and provocative images. Many product categories that were formerly regarded as purely functional, such as beach sandals and kitchen aprons, have become fashionable and expensive. Services such as professional lawn care have also become an upscale, intangible symbol of success. New consumption preferences such as the buying of organic food are gaining the interest of upscale consumers. Porsche has positioned itself as one of the world's best sports cars, and Lenox positions itself to convey elegance with such products as fine crystal, china, table linens, and napkin rings.

The challenge in many instances is to develop a strategy that separates the upscale buyer from the affluent consumer. Coach sells last season's accessories and irregular products at discounts in their factory stores. Coach has situated its factory outlets at least an hour's drive from its full-price stores in order to avoid the tarnished image problems of Calvin Klein and Tommy Hilfiger when their brands were sold through discount distribution channels. Coach refuses to allow their regular stores or department stores to mark down their products. The full-price customer is about age 35, college-educated, and a single or newly married working woman. In contrast, factory outlet customers are about age 45, college-educated, and likely to allocate about 80 percent of their Coach dollars at factory outlets; they are as brand loyal as the full-priced customer. The factory store targeting the upscale customer has a sales growth of more than double that of the full-price stores.

Upscale strategies can be made more effective by customizing the product or service offering to individual needs and by focusing on customer retention. For example, Fidelity, Vanguard, and other financial institutions have developed tailor-made portfolios for their retired customers. Portfolios were prepared ranging from aggressive to conservative based on the personality and financial resources of the individual. Financial institutions are sponsoring customer satisfaction studies in efforts to close the gap between customer expectation of products and services and actual performance.

Company objectives have an impact on the length of the product line over time. There are some companies that will serve only an upscale market. For example, Porsche makes only expensive automobiles. A firm can either down-market or up-market its product line. Honda introduced the Acura to up-market its line, and Tiffany down-marketed its diamond engagement ring line. If the firm is in the middle of the affluent market, it is possible to up-market and down-market its line. As market conditions change, it will be necessary for firms to broaden their markets.

MARKET OPPORTUNITY

A market opportunity exists when the correct combination of circumstances occurs for the firm to enter a market and make a profit. Based on all data, the affluent market is growing. This market represents a lucrative opportunity for many products and services. Each organization needs to assess the affluent segment and particularly look at the costs, the firm's resources in terms of strengths and weaknesses, and the competition.

Nestle targeted an upscale market for coffee with Taster's Choice, a decaffeinated brand. However, the size of the market segment does not always mean profitability. Relatively small market niches may be profitable if a unique and sustainable competitive advantage can be maintained. E. T. Wright, known for producing high-quality shoes, could not keep up with demand due to the distribution channel it had selected. In the 1980s, department stores accounted for 30 percent of its sales; then the stores found it unprofitable to stock this expensive brand because of high inventory costs. The Wright brand appealed to older affluent men who purchased them only when a pair wore out. Wright, at this time, manufactured only dress shoes and declined to broaden its merchandise line. Confronted with a declining market, E. T. Wright made an important strategic decision and decided to compete with its own retailers. They became a mail-order manufacturer. Wright also decided to broaden its offerings to young professionals with brands such as Hush Puppies, Rockport, and New Balance. Wright changed its policy to manufacture casual shoes as well as dress shoes to satisfy the needs of a changing target market.

Niche marketers like Hanna Anderson and Mama's Earth, baby apparel manufacturers, are now targeting "yoga moms" with clothes that cost 50 percent more than from Sears. Yoga moms are usually between ages 25 and 45, college-educated, and working or former career moms whose income ranges over $60,000. These yoga moms purchase the trendiest diaper bags made by manufacturers like Petunia Pickles Bottom and Fleurville, which costs more than $150 and is eight times the cost of a Pooh bag at Target. Yoga moms care about education, child development, and the environment. Marketers can reach yoga moms through Web sites such as Babycenter.com, and parents' magazines like *Brain Center*, as well as through the Learning Channel and Lifetime network. However, the favorite source of information of these upscale consumers is word-of-mouth from other yoga moms. Yoga moms are willing to forego luxury items for themselves to enrich their children's lives.

POTENTIAL FOR GROWTH

An affluent consumer base that is likely to attract a wider market in the future is preferable to one that has a stagnant position in a mature market.

The affluent can be reached by manufacturers and retailers who are willing to adapt their promotional messages, and other parts of the marketing mix to this market.

Pier 1 changed its image from the 1980s as a store targeting college-educated working women between the ages of 25 and 45 to a furniture store with more than 70 percent of the items exclusive to them. The typical customer is an upscale consumer with a much higher income than the average U.S. household, and more than one-third have a college education. The store carries furniture, decorative accessories, bed and bath, and housewares. Pier 1 Imports dominates a niche that it created by importing furniture and housewares. Pier 1's furniture and furnishings satisfy the consumer looking for distinctive products.

Even the lowly sandal referred to by many as the flip-flop has the potential for growth. The evolution of the flip-flop from dime-store item selling a few years ago for $12 changed when designer Sigerson Morrison came out with an $85 version in 2003. Presently, Jimmy Choo offers a jeweled sandal at $650, and the upscale market has been penetrated as Stewart Weitzman competes with a jeweled sandal for $235. The price online is also aiming toward the affluent since Zappos.com is offering styles priced at $500 or more.

COMPETITIVE INTENSITY

A basic criterion in targeting the affluent market is to consider the degree to which consumer needs are satisfied by a particular product or service. A "me too" brand has little competitive advantage. If a differential exists, then a strategic window is open to satisfy the specific needs of this market. For example, Stub.com challenges eBay by selling event tickets. Stub.com built a reputation by selling tickets to Broadway shows, football games, concerts, and other events and by guaranteeing that you would have the tickets in time. This niche strategy has impacted the market served by eBay.

There have been numerous environmental and health concerns that were not addressed by marketers in the past. In applying these concerns to the soft-drink industry, bottled water is taking the place of soda. Neither Coca-Cola nor Pepsi-Cola were marketing bottled water and addressing environmental concerns when bottled water companies entered the market. In the product introductory stage, bottled water was sold only in health-food and gourmet shops. Consumers' concern over their tap water caused bottled water to be in greater demand. A strategy was devised to distribute bottled water in supermarkets and to place the product in the same aisle as soft drinks. These companies had successfully used a product-positioning strategy to capture a larger market share of the soft drink industry. They positioned their product in consumers' minds as an alternative to soft drinks. Their objective was to not only intensify the distribution of their brand but to also serve that part of the market segment that desired an elegant drink. The target market composed of upscale, well-educated, health-conscious adults had now been broadened to include many consumers who were dissatisfied with their local water supply. Pepsi-Cola has a commanding presence with Aquafina. San Pellegrino targeted upscale bottled water drinkers and obtained distribution in upscale restaurants. Evian and other brands profited from innovation that allowed bottled water to be carried in gym bags.

SUCCESS DOES NOT GUARANTEE CONTINUED SUCCESS

There are many firms that either dominated their industries or exhibited enviable growth records and were relatively secure in serving the upscale or affluent market segments. Yet these companies succumbed to reverses at the height of their growth and success. Complacency lends to resistance to change in a business organization because these changes can be traumatic and disruptive to what has previously been successful. Success encourages the viewpoint that the past will be indicative of the future. Should such an attitude permeate the organization, a changing competitive environment can be undetected for a long time. Firms such as Brooks Brothers, Brentanos, Haagen-Dazs, and Harley-Davidson all experienced enviable growth records. Some of these organizations learned from their errors and were able to survive. Even the most successful organizations make mistakes.

Success promotes vulnerability. Success may leave a firm open to competitors who desire to either emulate or surpass the established firm. Competitors may also devise more profitable ways of serving the same affluent target.

The affluent market has exhibited a changing demand pattern driven by a combination of demographic and cultural shifts. The affluent market for many items now includes those consumers who are trading up in their purchasing behavior. A broader affluent market is more discerning than in the past since consumers have attained higher levels of education and worldliness. New brands have displaced older brands in the luxury market. For example, BMW and Mercedes-Benz have replaced Cadillac and Lincoln; Viking Range has replaced AGA in kitchen appliances; Coach has replaced Louis Vuitton in leather goods; Sam Adams has replaced Heineken in beer; and in lingerie, Victoria Secret has replaced La Perla. In contrast, Lacoste shirts have a strong pricing policy. Prices are deliberately established at high points to reach all segments of the affluent market. Lacoste perceives that the luxury market is now a mass market for some products and that quality products with correspondingly high prices no longer limit a firm to a niche.

Oscar de la Renta and Valentino have reinvented themselves as important fashion designers by attracting a younger generation without losing their traditional customers, who are wealthy women. Valentino emphasizes evening gowns priced from $3,000 to $15,000, and de la Renta designs luncheon suits ranging from $2,500 to $7,000. Attempted comebacks by Yves Saint Laurent and Hubert de Givenchy have failed largely because their loyal customer base was not retained. A major problem is that unless promotion is continuous, loyal customers will lose interest, and younger customers will not have brand recognition. Both designers have made efforts to offer other products such as a $150 white, tattooed T-shirt to reach younger consumers.

Neiman Marcus and Nordstrom have had long success records in serving the affluent market, and until recently, Saks Fifth Avenue shared this enviable record. Its current strategy, however, is flawed. Saks Fifth Avenue attempted to target customers who might seek less-expensive goods elsewhere by unsuccessfully offering moderately priced merchandise particularly in its private-label apparel line. Neiman Marcus took the opposite approach—that their customers would not trade down—and was successful.

Saks endeavored to broaden their base by attracting younger customers. But Saks' traditional customers, ages 45–54, felt alienated with styling changes. Finally, a campaign promoting cashmere sweaters was ineffective. Saks' sales decreased in comparison to Neiman Marcus and Nordstrom and lagged the entire luxury sector.

BROOKS BROTHERS

Brooks Brothers did not consider the changes around them or thought that because of their reputation for quality products serving the affluent market, these changes would not have an impact on their operations. Brooks Brothers had a distinguished history that included being one of America's oldest clothing stores, founded in 1818 and selling suits to Theodore Roosevelt, Ulysses S. Grant, and Woodrow Wilson that they wore when taking their oaths of office. Authors such as Ernest Hemingway, F. Scott Fitzgerald, and Somerset Maugham depicted characters in their novels who wore Brooks Brothers' suits. Movie stars who patronized Brooks Brothers included Fred Astaire, Burt Lancaster, Elizabeth Taylor, and Katharine Hepburn. Before Brooks Brothers realized it, their market was declining, and the organization was walking a tightrope endeavoring to serve their loyal customer base and adapting to the needs of a changing consumer.

The conservatism that has characterized the apparel made by Brooks Brothers is one of the factors that has made the firm a legend. Their personal service is outstanding. It is not uncommon for generations of a family to patronize Brooks Brothers and deal with the same salesperson. When the firm was purchased by Julius Garfinckel & Company of Washington, D.C., in 1946, customers feared that this conservatism and personal service would terminate, and changes were often resisted by loyal customers. The firm's operations continued, but profits were diminishing; and in 1988, Marks and Spencer, a British firm, purchased Brooks Brothers.

The perception that Brooks Brothers sells only three-button "sack suits" with a center vested jacket needed to change for the store to survive. Brooks Brothers now offers more two-button versions, suits with a tapered fit, and suits for athletic men with broader upper bodies. Brooks Brothers, moreover, had to broaden their target market to include women in executive and professional occupations. A larger assortment was needed to serve these female professionals, and this incurred increased costs and risks.

After years of selling its famous button-down oxford shirts, Brooks Brothers added purple gingham shirts and turquoise striped ties to the product line. At one time, the average age of the customer was 55, and now it is close to 40. The merchandise line now appeals to a younger customer. Salespeople are more receptive to the twenty-something customers. Employee-training programs were implemented to prepare new-customer-friendly salespeople.

Brooks Brothers concentrated on improving its product lines, customer service, and the availability of merchandise. It had missed out on the trend for apparel to be worn on casual days or dress-down days. A transformation took place as khaki pants, casual shirts, and a selection of brightly colored shirts and ties made the merchandise more appealing to fashionable, affluent, and upscale shoppers.

Brooks Brothers has expanded and now has stores throughout the United States. Brooks Brothers is doing a balancing act with a brand franchise that has strong significance to the professional person and upscale customer. The challenge confronting Brooks Brothers is to attract new customers, including women and younger adults, without losing older customers.

It is axiomatic that if Brooks Brothers wishes to succeed, they must become closer to their customers needs and emphasize enhanced customer relations. Brooks Brothers is confronted with a changing affluent customer and the desire to develop new approaches to reach these customers.

BRENTANOS

Upscale strategies do not necessarily guarantee continued success. Brentanos, a prestigious book store, learned that upscale strategies do not necessarily guarantee continued success as new competitors entered the marketplace. Brentanos did not foresee the success of discounters and book sales on the Internet. While personalized service was important, it was not as important as Brentanos envisioned. Brentanos failed to grasp the importance of entertainment and fun in shopping. Barnes & Noble and other competitors realized that the old fashioned book store was going to disappear.

Brentanos was founded in 1907 and became a cultural center, selling art objects and jewelry as well as books. Brentanos store image was upscale. A purchase made at Brentanos in Chicago, New York, Boston, or any of the branches was virtually analogous to making a purchase at Neiman Marcus in Dallas or Tiffany in New York. On July 31, 1995, Brentanos closed its doors.

Brentanos numbered among its customers Andrew Carnegie, Henry Clay Frick, J. P. Morgan, Theodore Roosevelt, and other celebrities of the period. In 1981, Crown Books moved into the Chicago area with its discounting policy. B. Dalton instituted discounting in 1985, but Brentanos waited until 1991. Their management maintained the belief that Brentanos' excellent service and knowledgeable staff would suffice and that discounting was unimportant. They did not believe affluent consumers would engage in cross-shopping behavior when purchasing books.

Much of Brentanos' strength had stemmed from its employees. Human resources were an integral part of its past success, but the competitive environment had been misjudged, and price was more important than management had considered. A competitive strength was its foreign book collection and periodicals that were unobtainable elsewhere. Brentanos' rare book collection and first editions and its series of cultural events that attracted hundreds of people were held in high esteem by customers.

With competition from Crown Books, B. Dalton and others, factors like location and the slowness in realizing the importance of new technology also brought about the demise of Brentanos. Shopping traffic shifted from downtown areas where Brentanos was situated. The firm was also hurt by superstores and competition in suburban shopping malls. Moreover, computer technology, which Brentanos was slow to adopt, had placed a much greater emphasis on cost control and inventory management. Brentanos had lost opportunities because it did not sufficiently realize the long-term benefits of effective financial analysis, planning, and control; and it ignored the sale of books through the Internet, and specifically, through Amazon.com and BarnesandNoble.com.

The lesson that can be learned from Brentanos is that you cannot sit still. Market threats are ever present, and adaptable behavior should be the basis for strategy development.

HÄAGEN-DAZS

Häagen-Dazs, founded in 1961, is a superpremium ice cream. The premium brands accounted for an increasing percent of the ice-cream market. Surprisingly, superpremium brands, despite their high butterfat content and the health concerns, reported higher sales than other ice-cream market segments. The Häagen-Dazs name with its foreign connotation conveyed quality and distinction. Upscale consumers believed that Häagen-Dazs ice cream was a treat.

Häagen-Dazs was an innovator in the superpremium ice-cream market. Häagen-Dazs successfully targeted the self-indulgence of the "me generation." Even though some consumers believed that they could not afford a new car or expensive stereo equipment, luxury ice cream was affordable.

Ben & Jerry's in a few short years had successfully linked a product with a social mission: to sell a high-quality ice cream with innovative flavors that would improve the community. For example, one of their flavors was named Rain Forest Crunch, which was a manifestation of their social mission. Although Häagen-Dazs had been the innovating firm, a new motivating appeal of environmental activism attracted upscale consumers.

There is a combination of reasons for the loss of market leadership of Häagen-Dazs. One reason is that Ben & Jerry's has been successful with their cause-related marketing efforts. There is also a danger that consumers who are concerned about fat will switch to Breyers, Sealtest, Dolly Madison, or Louis Sherry, which are perceived as more medium in price and richness. Upscale consumers are more likely to read the new government-ordered nutritional labels than typical consumers. Another reason is that conflict developed between Häagen-Dazs and its retailers. Owners of franchised Häagen-Dazs stores rebelled when they found that their product would be sold to supermarkets. Retailers claimed their marketing efforts were undermined. Furthermore, Häagen-Dazs did not market frozen yogurt and other health-oriented desserts. Social and cultural patterns in the United States are changing rapidly, and many of these changes are reflected in eating habits and therefore must be anticipated by the food industry.

HARLEY-DAVIDSON

Harley-Davidson is a favorite among the affluent. The company has a reputation of a company that cares. Many of the new bikers are women. More than 4.3 million women rode motorcycles in 2003, up 34 percent from 1998, according to the Motorcycle Industry Council. The impact of the female motorcycle rider has become such a significant buying force that BMW and Suzuki are designing bikes that complement female physiques.

Harley-Davidson in the early 1960s dominated the motorcycle industry with a market share of 70 percent of the industry. It was inconceivable that within a decade Honda and other Japanese manufacturers would seize a commanding share of the motorcycle market and Harley-Davidson's market share was to decrease to 5 percent. Harley-Davidson did not believe in the lightweight motorcycle market but believed that motorcycles were sports vehicles and not transportation vehicles.

Honda desired to instill the idea that riding a motorcycle is fun. The association of black leather jackets and rowdy behavior patterns with motorcycles was a stigma that manufacturers had to remove in order to market the motorcycle. Since Honda first introduced the theme "You Meet the Nicest People on a Honda," dealer organizations more than doubled, and sales increased approximately 200 percent. Social acceptance was finally achieved. At this time, the target market was composed of mainly young riders under the age of 40.

Since the 1960s, Honda and other companies have captured the mass market for motorcycles, while Harley-Davidson successfully reached the high end of the motorcycle market, composed of people over the age of 35 with an average annual income of $75,000. Harley-Davidson lost the larger market because of marketing myopia. The company could not believe that there was a need for change in strategies and maintained that the environment was stable with little potential growth. Since there was no competitor that would compete in the large motorcycle market, and Honda was entering the lightweight market, Harley-Davidson could not envision a change in the market and consumer preferences. It had lost significant market share because it underestimated the competition and did not react to the changes in consumer tastes.

The entrance of women into the market and an older affluent consumer means that Harley-Davidson needed to change its strategy. A sizeable segment of the Harley market is composed of professionals or managers who desire to become so-called weekend warriors. A new generation of yuppies, generations X and Y, has emerged and the market has changed.

Harley-Davidson has licensed its name to such products as cologne, wine coolers, and polo shirts. This branding strategy could well reflect a basis to develop further inroads into an upscale motorcycle market.

COMPETITIVE MARKETING STRATEGIES

The use of market segmentation accompanied by market flexibility is needed to penetrate the affluent market. The use of competitive strategies with varying degrees of emphasis on price, promotion, product assortment, service, and distribution is needed. Implicit in penetrating affluent markets is strong brand recognition and a high level of customer service. To illustrate, Dunkin' Donuts is challenging Starbucks by going upscale, expanding its menu with snacks that can substitute for meals.

NICHE STRATEGY

The heart of developing competitive advantage in the affluent market is adopting market niche strategy. The selected market segment of the mass affluent market should be of sufficient size and have growth potential. The firm should have the required expertise and resources to effectively serve the segment. Customer goodwill is often the best way to combat a competitor.

The market-niche strategy is appropriate for smaller business organizations competing with stronger firms. Without a niche strategy Lance Crackers could not have gained a competitive advantage. Lance, in 1988, became the first in the snack-food industry to respond to the changing environment that emphasized consumer health concerns. Lance changed over to cholesterol-free, low-saturated fat, low-salt, and low-sugar snacks. Many affluent and upscale consumers look for more healthful products.

Lance has become a master of niche marketing. Niche strategy has enabled Lance with limited resources to compete with industry giants such as Nabisco, Frito-Lay, Borden, and Keebler. Niching can be profitable since the market niche is known so well that it can satisfy needs better than competitors who are casually selling to this niche. Lance had found an ideal market niche since it had growth potential and the market of health-conscious consumers was of sufficient size and purchasing power to be profitable.

Niche strategy is a broader concept than market segmentation, encompassing management direction, overall marketing strategy, and product differentiation. Companies that adopt niche strategies are customer driven, observe trends, and are creative marketing strategists. Research is emphasized and valued.

Innovation was an important variable as Williams-Sonoma was one of the first retailers of fine-quality cookware in the United States. The chain includes Williams-Sonoma stores, the Pottery Barn, and Hold Everything outlets. Its 4.5 million customer database accounts for much of its success as well as the development of effective mail-order businesses for its retail store operations. Williams-Sonoma has defined the market to serve the key customer segments called niches. Williams-Sonoma offers culinary and serving equipment for the consumers interested in furnishing their kitchens. The Pottery Barn features items in casual home furnishings, flatware, and table accessories for either dining rooms or kitchens; and Hold Everything offers innovative storage products. These retail stores serve niches for different areas of the home. The development of a positioning strategy for a targeted market segment is an important dimension of niche strategy. There are other aspects of niche strategy that differentiate it from market-segmentation strategy:

- The company designs products and services to satisfy the needs of the niche segment.
- Market opportunity is closely tied to finding new and better ways to do things.
- Since the focus is on satisfying specific target markets, efficiency is maximized.

Ann Taylor, once considered *the* store for urban career women in their 30s and 40s, has gone through difficult times. The Ann Taylor chain became a fixture in malls in the 1980s. But by the 1990s, Ann Taylor's product line did not fit in with the career woman's new style. Ann Taylor compounded its problems by a number of marketing mistakes. First, it purchased inferior products and sold them at a high markup. Second, a costly expansion program drained company resources. Customers noticed the higher prices and inferior goods and deserted in droves. Subsequently, prices were reduced, stores were redecorated, and new management arrived. A heavy promotion program was implemented to regain consumer confidence.

Ann Taylor had difficulty in establishing a fashion identity. Sales competition from other apparel stores had made inroads to the existing customer base. Ann Taylor eventually carved out a niche making its image more fashionable than Talbot's. Ann Taylor is less trendy than Limited's women's stores and tends to charge less in big-ticket categories like business suits and evening wear than Saks and Nordstrom. The Ann Taylor label has returned to a sign of belonging for the career woman in the business world. Clearly, upscale strategies alone were not a panacea for Ann Taylor.

POSITIONING STRATEGY

Positioning strategy is important in lifestyle market segmentation. Position is the process of distinguishing a company or product from competition along such dimensions as product characteristics or values that are meaningful to consumers. Dior is positioned as a French designer. Positioning strategy can be useful if aimed at the affluent segment to achieve a desired position in the potential buyer's mind. A company segmenting a line of perfumes might develop different positioning strategies for self-indulgent, socially active, or inner-directed segments. Positioning strategy must have a firm foundation. There is the need to first define a target segment before developing the position strategy. The linkage between positioning strategy and market segmentation is apparent as the market segments are defined and products are positioned to satisfy the needs of these segments.

Positioning a service is more difficult that positioning a product because benefits are often intangible. Hilton Hotels developed Embassy Suites, a luxury hotel chain of multiple-room suites targeted at upscale business travelers with computer and Internet equipment. Merrill Lynch established CMA as a brand identity for its cash management account. American Express sent consumers a wallet-sized card with information on tips concerning the purchase of insurance. Banks try to extend the distribution of services by means of ATMs.

Positioning aids customers in evaluating competing products or brands so that they can select the one with the most value. For example, Hyundai and Subaru are positioned on economy; Mercedes and Cadillac, as luxury; and Porsche and BMW, as performance automobiles. Other strategies are to offer a specific balance of price and quality—such as Saks Fifth Avenue, which offers high quality at high prices—or to stress specific-use occasions, like Gatorade satisfying an athlete's thirst.

Creative positioning uses emotional appeals based on product characteristics, benefits, usage occasions, and user category against a competitive product. These strategies direct themselves to participation by the customer. Positioning also includes the emotional reaction of individual customers.

MONITORING EFFECTIVE STRATEGIES

Social and cultural patterns in the United States are changing. Changes in technology have led to buying on the Internet. These changes are reflected in the purchasing behavior of the affluent. Among the considerations in reaching affluent consumers are the following:

- Social movements dictate strategies in penetrating the affluent market. Concern for environment, for better health and nutrition, and for better working conditions are important issues in making purchasing decisions.
- Continuous experimentation and long-term planning are necessary to maintain success. New product offerings that maintain and improve the environment are vital. Products with the right balance of ingredients that improve health and nutrition are sought after by this market.
- Product quality and diversification is essential. Service is tied to customer satisfaction. The saving of time is an important consideration.

- There is a need for growth. DeBeers has established retail stores in affluent shopping centers. This challenges Tiffany and others in the diamond trade.
- Image development is paramount. The image of firms or brands such as Neiman Marcus, Rolex, Cartier, Saks Fifth Avenue, and Lady Godiva Candy has spelled success in a competitive marketplace.

Consumer taste for specialty foods is also changing. Customers who purchased gourmet foods were usually in their 50s, and now more young people in their 20s and 30s are willing to pay higher prices. The growth in specialty foods from 2003 to 2005 has been a spectacular 18 percent.

MANAGING CHANGE

A firm's image is established after a long and satisfying relationship with its customers. If a firm has developed a quality image serving the affluent segment, it is not easily imitated by competitors. Such an image enables the firm to charge higher prices and to distribute the product through luxury specialty retailers.

Some marketers lose their favorable image through inattention and complacency. A firm may be inclined to coast on the mystique that its name or brand has developed over the years. Aggressive competitors enter the market and all is lost.

American Express has long cultivated an affluent clientele. Visa in 2004 launched a marketing campaign to challenge American Express' control of the affluent market. The affluent consumer has a propensity to charge higher amounts on credit cards and defaults less than ordinary consumers. Visa has aimed its Signature card at the affluent consumer with a minimum of $125,000 in household income. Each company defines their high-end segment differently based on their particular situation so that $125,000 household income is not a standard from industry to industry. For Visa this is a sizeable market, and it is offering perks such as concierge services to attract the affluent market.

Real-time marketing, mass customization, and creative positioning are only the beginning of strategies developed to satisfy individual customer needs. Real-time marketing has developed from mass customization. Customization is reflected in products such as a washing machine that selects its wash cycle based on the weight of dirtiness and type of wash load and a vacuum cleaner that adjusts its suction pressure based on dirt level on the carpet.

Mass customization has been able to target the upscale consumer in the housing industry. A house can be constructed with many different models. After construction, the consumer is given the choice of type and color of tiles, carpeting, and lighting. The consumer can also select from patio and front door overhang variations. Additions such as placing extra cabinets or a desk in the kitchen can also be selected. Rooms can also be designed as home offices, with high-speed Internet access.

Differentiation positioning seeks a smaller market niche that is less competitive in which to locate a brand. For example, a television manufacturer may segment the quality market with the aim that their brand is the most expensive television set available. Firms that penetrate the affluent market make a commitment to understanding the customer, innovation, product improvement, marketing flexibility, product reliability, and after-sale service.

Upscale strategies are not a panacea without a precise company mission. Broadening the target market line is an appropriate strategy. For example, Mercedes covers the affluent market with cars priced from $30,000 to $100,000 and up.

Toyota's Lexus and Nissan's Infinity have decided to enter the high end of the market for more growth, higher margins, or to position themselves better. Starbucks in coffee and Haagen-Dazs in ice cream have developed upscale segments. Rolls-Royce and John Deere have both down-marketed their product lines to compete with competitors who have attempted to up-market their product lines.

One way to target upscale consumers is to provide offerings to all at affordable prices. Disney, for example, allows customers to bypass the line for an extra fee and grants a membership pass. A second strategy is to introduce new models of luxury items that are affordable. Fractional ownership and renting such items as luxury automobiles, art objects, the latest products in technology, and vacation homes make these items available to the nouveau riche. There has been a new shift in consumption in a mature affluent society that will continually test the creativity of marketers.

CHAPTER 9

Redefining Affluent Consumer Lifestyles

America's middle class has acquired greater wealth and purchasing power than ever before. In the next decade, baby boomers, born between 1946 and 1964, will number about 70 million; Generation Xers, born between 1965 and 1979, will number about 60 million; and Generation Yers, born between 1980 and 1999, will number over 80 million. Many of them will comprise a large segment of the affluent market.

As the economy shifts, Wal-Mart is attempting to redefine itself by redesigning their store and offering trendier merchandise to attract upscale consumers. Wal-Mart sales in 2004 were more than 7.5 percent of all nonauto retail sales in the United States but seemed to have reached a plateau. Wal-Mart, by advertising in *Vogue*, is endeavoring to demonstrate that more stylish merchandise is carried. A caveat exists that this strategy will alienate their traditional customer base in targeting upscale consumers, but Wal-Mart understands that the affluent consumer is a significant market.

Luxury has been redefined. The focus in the past was on material possessions; today the emphasis is on the experience of luxury. For the new rich, who constitute the mass luxury market, spending reflects feelings and experiences. These experiences include fine dining, travel, entertainment, and cultural and sporting events. Personal luxuries such as automobiles, fashion, and jewelry are not as satisfying as in the past.

How do the new rich redefine themselves? Consumption patterns tend to reflect the types of goods and services purchased, used, and discarded. These consumption patterns are made in a manner consistent with prevailing values and will reflect activities, interests, and opinions of the individual. For example, affluent consumers who value fun may tend to learn how to ski or do more skiing. Those who value family and children are more likely to purchase gifts. Marketers, in turn, need to identify affluent consumers who have a common set of values that reflect specific activities, interests, or opinions that are different than others. To illustrate, one automobile manufacturer may appeal to one group that desires high-tech features, and another automobile manufacturer might appeal to those who value achievement. Many of the new rich have not inherited their wealth, and these consumers embrace many of their old values but desire to adopt new values. Each individual generally assigns priorities before purchasing goods and services and may redirect their activities and interests. These priorities are subject to change and may not be rational.

In the past, values were considered to be relatively permanent before being transmitted from one generation to another. However, it has become increasingly apparent that some shifts in values and lifestyles are occurring at a more rapid pace. For instance, new values have emerged related to dual-career families that have significant effects on consumer behavior.

Defining values of the new rich is a difficult undertaking since the new rich are composed of a variety of subcultures. There also has been a rapid change in the population composition of the new rich, which makes it difficult to monitor cultural values. The new rich adopt almost unconsciously the beliefs, values, and norms of the society in which they live or want to live. These values define their relationship to themselves and to others. The values of self-respect, security, warm relationships with others, accomplishment, a sense of belonging, self-fulfillment, and enjoyment of life as value segments will vary in importance and priority from decade to decade. As these values shift in importance, age, education, occupation, gender, and stage in the life cycle will have greater significance. Since many members of the new rich are redefining themselves and many subcultures exist, such as seniors and various ethnic groups, marketers need to identify and market products that will address core and secondary needs. For example, some members of the new rich may purchase what they perceive to be dream automobiles or dream vacations. Products such as cruise travel may manifest activities that promote social support systems. The new rich who love nature may be motivated to purchase package tours to wilderness areas. Since only half of the highly affluent feel financially secure, old values are blended with new values.

Marketers cannot change basic value systems, however, they can monitor and adapt to changes. It is possible to influence some consumer attitudes and fringe values. For example, affluent consumers can be influenced to accept new clothing fashions and recreational activities. Levi Strauss was the innovator in the 1850s, selling inexpensive jeans that were strong and durable to gold prospectors in California. As the market for pricey denims escalated, Levi Strauss needed to reinvent itself. Among the strategies planned is to sell jeans for $100 in a partnership with the Andy Warhol Foundation to create a collection based on the famous art styles of Andy Warhol, who wore Levi's. Consumer perception is important since brands selling for more than $100 are only 1 percent of the $6.8 billion jeans market.

Reference groups provide a means of social comparison and are instrumental for understanding changing lifestyle behavior patterns. This concept suggests that the individual's purchasing behavior can be compared to other members of the reference group. It is possible that an individual may be influenced by a variety of reference groups. Norms exist for both small and large groups and subcultural groups such as singles and teenagers. Although the degree of influence may vary in particular situations, lifestyle and purchasing behavior can be swayed by group norms.

Core values may act as a justification for the acquisition of certain goods and services. The core value of individualism may motivate the purchase of customized products. Those who value efficiency may purchase products that save time. The value of youthfulness may stimulate the undergoing of operations that restore youthfulness, such as face lifts. Traditional food manufacturers have modified their ingredients to target health-conscious consumers. There are many more core values, and each of these values varies in importance to members of the new rich. Marketers will need to determine how they will provide an effective basis for segmenting markets.

EMERGING VALUES

Cultural creatives subscribe to a new set of values that have been adopted by nearly one in four American adults.[1] Cultural creatives have a propensity to be affluent, well-educated and believe in environmentalism, feminism, global issues and spiritual searching. Their food habits are characterized by ethnic cooking and the use of natural and health foods. They tend to purchase more books and magazines than the average consumer.

Four fundamental core values have emerged in today's society.[2] The first core value is time driven as many consumers cope with time-crunched lifestyles. Greater affluence results in less free time because the alternatives competing for their time have expanded. Retailers respond to time problems by stocking labor-saving devices; increasing store hours; prewrapping gift items; adding special services, such as fashion coordinator; and expanding in-home sales efforts by telephone, direct mail, and the Internet. Affluent consumers want the best and fastest service.

The second core value is referred to as the connectedness craze. The connectedness craze serves to reinforce personal connections to important people, events, or experiences. Heirlooms, family photos, and souvenirs connect as symbols in our memories. Consumption rituals observed during Thanksgiving or Christmas maintain traditions familiar to each family. A higher value will be placed on spiritual possessions, objects, and places. Artifacts from John F. Kennedy or such leaders as the pope are regarded by many as sacred. Many consumers will visit the Lincoln, Jefferson, World War II, and Vietnam

Memorials; and powerful emotions will be evoked. Religious holidays, weddings, and births can also be identified as sacred. Special possessions such as pets, achievement symbols, and collections are also included. Consumers use the Internet as a source of connectedness to information, as a method of contacting sellers of merchandise, to obtain services, and to stay in touch with friends and family. The interactive features of the Internet will be used to satisfy very specific, individualized needs such as access to medical, financial, and entertainment information.

The third core value is known as the body versus soul uncertainty. For instance, consumers will adopt a fitness agenda and may even hire a personal trainer but also buy junk food. More time will be allocated for home enjoyment, but consumers will desire more entertainment outside the home. A higher value will be placed on spiritual possessions, objects, and places.

The fourth core value is the triumph of individualism. Marketers will no longer just target a woman, but instead, a single mom, a buyer of full-size fashions, a bicycling enthusiast and a purchaser of mutual funds. Individualism will also encompass ethnic markets, and fashion trends will be driven by the expansion of ethnic markets. Cocreating personalized experiences is a strategy as firms move toward microsegmentation, the market of one. Customers have already become cocreators for such products as greeting cards and flower arrangements by selecting from menu features.

REDEFINING THE AFFLUENT FAMILY

What factors have caused the affluent family to be different from past generations? The new affluent include dual-career families; the growth of the over 55 age segment; the increase of entrepreneurs; and more women, ethnic groups, and gays and lesbians in high-earning jobs.

The role of the entrepreneur in the United States has made a significant impact on becoming rich. The average net worth of households of the self-employed increased from $714,500 to $1.2 million between 1992 and 2001. The number of people who operate their own businesses is at a level five times greater than the past 10 years.[3] The failure rate can be high, but none-theless those individuals who are successful have an opportunity to strike it rich. Women have been particularly successful as entrepreneurs, and many have become millionaires.

Affluent family values have been redefined through the past four decades. Many people now believe that success is self-defined rather than defined by conformity to the expectations of others. The value of quality of life is associated with success. High on the list of values that are paramount are having a good family life with loved ones, getting one's time under control, managing money well, enhancing health and personal appearance, and becoming more conscious about the environment. Although many believe that family life is more strained today, families are now better off than their parents were at a comparable stage in life.

Family roles have an impact on buying behavior. Decision-making roles, especially the roles of spouses and children, have a propensity to vary significantly depending on the goods and services purchased. Traditionally, husband-dominant decisions were made for automobiles, insurance, and financial planning. Joint decision making was more evident when vacations and housing were considered.

Traditional household purchasing patterns in affluent families are changing since women are now engaged in careers. Shifts in social values have also changed as men do more of the grocery shopping and undertake household tasks. Home Depot and Lowe's have found that a large percentage of their products are purchased by women.

Another shift in purchasing behavior has been the greater influence of children over the purchasing decisions of their parents. Since in many affluent households both spouses are in the workforce and short of time, children participate more in family decision making. Children may be greatly influential in the purchase of food and the choice of restaurants. Even though children may not be the actual purchasers, they may still be influential in the purchasing decisions regarding toys, clothes, vacations, recreation, and even automobiles. The Internet has become a valuable medium for reaching children.

As the roles of women, men, and children shift from the purchase of traditional items such as the automobile (women purchase about half), marketers will need to change their promotional programs. Evening and Sunday business hours in stores in suburban shopping centers have encouraged more joint decision making in two-career families. The thrust of marketing strategy should change as the role structure of the buying decision varies. When, for instance, only one individual is involved, marketing can be more concentrated than when several people are involved.

Not only are the roles of affluent family members changing, but values are also changing. There is greater tolerance and acceptance of pluralism. Interfaith and interracial marriages have increased. More ethnic food products have been mainstreamed. Many consumers appear to believe that kosher certification is a sign of quality and purity. For the health conscious, a kosher designation is important. Since 1990, more than 1,000 new or newly certified kosher items have been placed in the marketplace. Growth is estimated at more than 5 percent annually. There are 60,000 kosher-certified packaged food products. Kosher foods are in about one-half of the nation's supermarkets, and nearly 75 percent of Hebrew National customers are non-Jewish. This is also true of Empire Kosher that sells mostly poultry products.

Another changing value is that there is greater personal responsibility for health. Today, the focus is on physical fitness and appearance. This means that more money will be expended on spas, fitness centers, vitamins, and health-food products. Both women and men will have surgery that will make them appear younger. A symbol of wealth will be the hiring of a personal trainer and a personal cook who will serve nutritious food. Many affluent people concerned about the environment will purchase more expensive organic food.

Increased affluence is also changing values in relation to work and leisure. There is the belief that work should serve self-expressive needs. A manifestation of this belief is dress-down days in the office. As a result of dress-down days, casual clothes became more popular than in previous years. More corporations have realized the change in values relating to health, leisure, and work and have established recreational facilities for employees.

Individual consumers and their families share values, interests, and activities. Affluent consumers try to have their purchasing expenditures reflect good taste and graceful living that may manifest itself in purchasing quality merchandise and expensive hobby and recreational equipment. Individual expression can be demonstrated in the purchase of art objects, books, and travel. Many affluent people believe that they should possess the good things in life.

Educational values are important to the affluent family. Many parents enroll their children at birth in private schools hoping to eventually secure their admission into Ivy League colleges. Among these schools are Deerfield Academy, Phillips Exeter Academy, Choate Rosemary Hall, Lawrenceville School, Westminster School, and the Sidwell Friends School. Tuition ranges from $20,000 to $40,000 a year. In previous generations upon graduation, girls entered society through the debutante ball, and boys were members of various clubs.

The children of the new affluent consumers are rapidly becoming known as the Millennials. They were born between the early 1980s and 2002. They prefer structure because they grew up with play dates and other organized activities. They will expect more attention from marketers and retailers. They are confident, achievement oriented, and want to be heard. They will be more sophisticated consumers. They are the children of the so-called helicopter parent, parents who place themselves in a strong position to oversee the welfare of their children. It is expected that this generation of children will focus more on work-life balance than their parents.

REDEFINING THE AFFLUENT MARKET FOR CHILDREN

There are a number of demographic characteristics favorable for targeting the affluent children's market. There are more grandparents with fewer grandchildren and with more discretionary income. There are more dual-income families with more money to be expended on children for products such as furniture, toys, and apparel. More is spent on children today than in the past. Internet shopping has helped to extend the buying season for products such as toys that once were centered on special holidays.

Parents are purchasing for young children brands like Eddie Bauer and Tommy Hilfiger and purchasing upscale luxuries such as beauty products and organic baby food. About one-third of apparel purchases for young children are gifts. Children generally function as independent consumers in the first grade. Delta Airlines has initiated a Fantastic Flyer program for children as a technique of generating future customers. Delta targets children ages 7 through 14 with birthday greetings, special foods, and gifts during flights.

The tweens are the age group most affected by the social phenomena known as age compression. Age compression means that the tweens are acting older and growing up faster than in previous generations. Tweens are ages 9–12. Tweens are more accepting of new technology, styles, and trends. Retailers aiming for the tween market now carry sophisticated designs such as beaded Capri pant suits, reflecting a more mature taste. Tweens learn about fashion trends by surfing the Web and reading magazines such as *Seventeen*, designed for their older sisters. Designers such as Tommy Hilfiger, Ralph Lauren, and Steve Madden aim their advertisements to that market segment.

Many teenagers drive their own automobiles and some are employed part time. The degree of independence is the most paramount distinction between tweens and teens. Teenagers travel more than their parents and wield increasing influence in household purchases. They are not inclined to postpone purchasing gratification, yet there is a trend among many affluent teenagers toward saving and even owning financial instruments like stocks and bonds. Affluent parents have a tendency to pay for leisure class goods that were previously paid for by teenagers. This can be attributed to smaller family size and higher disposable income.

There are a number of changes that have taken place by manufacturers and retailers in redefining the affluent market for children. Furniture and décor makers have followed the trend of the fashion world by introducing grown-up looks for children's rooms. A Venice bed costs $8,000 and is an iron replica of a Venetian antique. A little Molly Mermaid chandelier is priced at $1,100 and has five ceramic mermaids with garlands made of Austrian crystal. Ethan Allen offers kids a $1,300 dresser with six drawers and a jewelry tray identical to the company's adult version. Affluent parents have indulged their grade school children with trainers. An estimated $4 billion was spent on personal training and coaching in 2000. Trainers may charge as much as $100 an hour. Strive Enterprises has developed miniaturized machines with metal plates to protect little fingers. Their KidzSmart line is designed for 9–14 year olds. Velocity Sports Performance targets middle-school students.

Many affluent parents aware of the dangers of latchkey children are hiring nannies. There were over 900 nanny employment agencies in 2004, compared to 45 in 1987. Nannies for young teens and tweens is a challenging job. Nationally, nannies average $590 a week, and college-educated nannies are usually paid 20 to 60 percent more.

Financial institutions have developed special materials for young people in their teens or 20s, although some include children as young as age 7. For instance, Weatherbridge Partners, LLC has developed programs for children age 7 and older and also their parents. Typical clients are families with $100 million or more in wealth. Both Citigroup and J. P. Morgan have developed courses ranging from five days to two weeks that are free for clients with $10 million to $25 million to invest.

REDEFINING MARKET OPPORTUNITIES

The affluent market is not homogenous. There is a high, a middle, and a low end. There are opportunities to penetrate a mass market for such items as automobiles, travel, leisure, and financial management products and services. Automobiles such as Mercedes and Cadillacs are products for the affluent mass market. Niche, positioning, and word-of-mouth strategies can help to penetrate a mass and fragmented market. Affluent people who desire to buy sports cars, coins and stamps, or rare books represent opportunities for many firms.

The world of golf is perceived differently in the market of consumer affluence. Two golfers may see the same advertisements and possibly buy the same driver, but one may be wealthy and the other middle class. The distinction between the two is that one may be splurging and may play on a public course, while the other may pay a high price to play at a private country club. There may be other distinctions in the purchasing of apparel and other items. Moreover, the use of credit to purchase other items might be an instrumental equalizer. A firm like New Balance might use a product concept for its sneakers by developing a variety of athletic shoes specific to certain occasions such as running, walking, tennis, or basketball.

The implementation of a plan to redefine the corporate strategy requires reaching a market segment efficiently. For instance, if the firm desired to sell video instruction material to sailboat owners on navigation, selected media such as *Yachting* and marine supply stores would be critical for success. It would be difficult to reach this market by advertising in *Sports Illustrated* or through general book stores.

Although a market opportunity may be present to redefine strategies, the firm must have the knowledge and resources to take advantage of this opportunity. Charles Schwab had an identity crisis after targeting the affluent consumer. Potential customers were not certain if the organization was a discount brokerage or full-service firm. Schwab had to return to its roots as a discount brokerage firm as Merrill Lynch, Morgan Stanley, Citigroup, and others were able to charge and offer more for their services.

The luxury goods market includes upscale consumers and those who on occasion trade up. The mass luxury market consumer buys goods and services because the process makes them feel good, because they feel it has been earned, because they desire an indulgence, because they enjoy spending, and because expectations need to be satisfied. Spending is closely tied to personal identity. Living in a certain type of home, ordering the right bottle of wine, decorating with tasteful furnishings, and attending cultural events supports a particular type of self-image to themselves and hopefully to the world. Aspirations are an important part of comparing lifestyle and possessions to those people who are respected and whose values are similar. The value of bargain hunting is still a fascinating endeavor as the rich will shop in Target, Costco, and Sam's Club.

REDEFINING THE FASHION MARKET

Fashion has its roots in psychological and sociological factors. Affluent people yearn to look and be somewhat different from others. They often make purchases that reflect good taste and afford them the opportunity for self-expression. Consumers usually buy luxury apparel and accessories in department stores such as Neiman Marcus and specialty luxury retail stores such as Ann Taylor and Gucci. Jewelry and watches are usually purchased first in specialty luxury stores such as Cartier and secondly in department stores.

Affluent people desire clothing with a subtle look, such as sportswear found in an L. L. Bean catalog. In contrast, middle- and lower-class consumers have a propensity to purchase T-shirts, caps and other clothing items with a mark of identification, such as Nike or the name of an admired person like Martha Stewart. There is a desire for the individual to reflect his or her self-image, which includes the individual's perception of his or her own social-class status.

Although fads, fashion, and styles are related concepts, some distinctions can be made among them. Fads are of shorter duration than fashions and seem to be more personal. Styles are permanent and do not change, whereas fashion does change. Colonial furniture is a distinctive style. Not every style becomes a fashion because it may not be popularly accepted. For some years, Brooks Brothers sold only three-button "sack suits" with a center-vested jacket and boxy fit to affluent consumers. Brooks Brothers now offers more two-button versions, suits with a tapered fit, and suits cut for athletic men with broader upper bodies.

Target has redefined the luxury market by making luxury more about design than price. Driving some segments of the luxury market is accessibility rather than exclusivity. Anyone can purchase a Channel handbag. Luxury brands such as Coach and Tiffany appear to have maintained their status, but some brands have now become more mainstream. When a watch costs $100,000, this is obviously an object for the connoisseur. But it is still obvious that some high-end brands have embraced a democratic trend.

Dr. Stephen Fox, a psychologist, maintains that luxury addresses psychological needs like restoring connectedness, easing boredom, and satisfying the need to be the best and feel in control. Dr. Fox believes that for some people, luxury is a need rather than a want.[4] Opportunity exists for luxury brands that desire a broader market and for pure luxury brands that want to retain their status.

Luxury marketers Coach, Godiva, and J. Crew have all increased their prices to maintain their luxury status. Coach has introduced a Mink Frame Evening Bag for $698, while Godiva Chocolate offers a limited edition G Collection line including a $350 African Wenge Wood box, and J. Crew has raised its luxury image by creating only about 50 of its $1,500 Shearling Toggle Coat. Distribution is important as Godiva offers its exclusive G Collection in limited quantities solely in luxury retailers Neiman Marcus and select Saks stores and through their Web site. Even the battered briefcase gets a makeover as Hartmann Inc.'s top-of-the-line attaché sells for $1,495. Accompanying their attaché cases is the guarantee to offer lifetime servicing, much like Allen Edmunds does with shoes.

Formerly high-end retailers such as Tod's, Prada, and Burberry believed that global expansion required a strong, consistent brand that would be easy to identify throughout the world. Today, these international brands have redefined themselves by moving away from standardization by varying stores and merchandise. For instance, Prada opened a store in New York that departed from traditional green and beige décor and sold vintage clothing not offered in other Prada stores. Burberry sells antique cufflinks in London and customized trench coats in New York. Tod's will sell only 19 of its new pink crocodile bags and stores in New York, Los Angeles, Chicago, Hawaii, and Las Vegas; will stock only one of its $9,900 handbags, and only three or four pairs of $3,800 loafers. This strategy is aimed at the international travelers who desire exclusive merchandise.

Neiman Marcus has chosen to maintain the luxury image of its 35-unit store chain. The average shopper at Neiman Marcus spends about $11,000 a year, and the stores' top 100,000 customers generate $1.2 billion in sales. A frequent shopper program was introduced in 2004 that required annual spending of more than $5,000 and offered awards ranging from a limited edition Emilio Pucci silk scarf to a complete Sony home movie theater to an eight-night trip through India. The frequent shopper program had over 100,000 customers with an average income of approximately $600,000.

The average shopper at Neiman Marcus is about 43 years old, well educated, well traveled,, sophisticated, and desires quality and fashion. Household income averages over $200,000. The belief is held by Neiman Marcus that affluent consumers have an insatiable appetite for luxury. Although many retailers believe that their customers will trade up in their purchasing, Neiman Marcus maintains that the competition will be unable to offer the designs and quality that has separated them from the competition.

BROADENING THE LUXURY MARKET

Not only are affluent consumers redefining themselves but manufacturers and retailers are also endeavoring to reposition themselves. Nicole Miller made its reputation by designing $400 dresses and $65 printed ties for mainstream consumers. Now, the company is broadening its image by creating a home megabrand. Nicole Miller is launching a top-tier Signature bedding line starting about $250 and bringing chic to sheets. The Nicole Miller home collection will be sold exclusively through Bed, Bath and Beyond Inc.'s 600 stores. Plans are underway to also market shower curtains, picture frames, and tableware. Nicole Miller is trying to duplicate the success that Ralph Lauren's upscale bedding and home collection was for Bloomingdale's in the 1990s.

Volvo and Porsche are attempting to compete with successful Mercedes to broaden their markets. Both companies are introducing smaller, less costly automobiles. Volvo and Porsche will offer prices slightly less than BMW and Mercedes. This strategy was once successful for BMW, and Mercedes and both Volvo and Porsche hope to increase sales volume with lower price offerings.

In the past, Calvin Klein and Jaguar have marketed their brands by using a strategy of massification of luxury. Critics maintain that it dilutes the value of the word *luxury*. Luxury brand names have been extended into everything from coffee to bed sheets. Consumers today believe that luxury is in the eye of the beholder; perceptions no longer depend on category or price. The challenge that confronts marketers is to link their product with an experience that is valued by the consumer.

Bentley, one of the fanciest manufacturers of super luxury cars priced well into the $300,000 range, has introduced the Bentley Continental GT at $156,000 and the $165,000 Lamborghini Gallardo. This shift in focus to less-expensive models has arrived at the low-end of the high luxury car market. Although these superluxury automobiles sell in small numbers, substantial profits are generated. Bentley appears to be successful in exceeding its sales target. Buyers of these luxury vehicles are typically from ages 38 to 49 and have approximately $5 million in assets, not including the value of their homes.

The cigar, once viewed as a symbol of success and subsequently perceived as a product that smacked of politicians and gangsters, has reemerged as a symbol of success for both men and women. This product has reinvented itself as a connection to a new emerging culture. Furthermore, until the early 1990s Godiva chocolates were sold only in Neiman Marcus. Now Godiva is sold in more than 2,500 stores.

Finally, Tiffany in an attempt to target the mass affluent market has created a separate identity for a new brand. Tiffany already offers cultured and natural pearl lines at its 55 stores in the United States. But the goal is to have the new Iridesse brand stand alone without referencing Tiffany in any advertisements. Tiffany plans to open four Iridesse stores in 2005, bringing the total to six. Tiffany is trying to create an all-pearl concept. Fundamental to this strategy is the concept that the affluent already have diamonds, but the new rich need a different focus.

REDEFINING WANTS VS. NEEDS

People are driven by specific needs at particular times. There is a hierarchy of needs ranging from the physiological to safety to social to esteem to self-actualization. The affluent consumer is driven by each of these categories of needs, but lower needs have already been achieved and therefore higher needs are sought. The higher needs generate tension in individuals and they try to reduce it through the purchase and consumption of goods and services.

Rather than endeavoring to proceed from one need to another, the affluent individual seeks enrichment by acquiring goods and services and by fulfilling activities and interests. Goods and services perceived by one generation as wants, such as central air-conditioning systems, are perceived as needs by another generation. Thus, today's luxury goods and services that are wants will be perceived as needs by another generation.

Today, everyone wants to live their dream. The purchase of luxury goods and services has become commonplace. It's not just the superrich who are acquiring luxury goods and services but many consumers in particular situations are demonstrating upscale preferences in their purchasing behavior. Affluent consumers have become less materialistic and have sought to possess more leisure goods and services.

Affluent consumers have responded to some important shifts in culture. There has been a refocusing in the importance of values placed on family, relationships, and community. This value has taken the form of seeking connections with others. For instance, the travel industry is experiencing a growing trend at conference and trade shows of executives bringing their families along. Moreover, there has been a housing boom of first and second homes and all related areas of home decoration. Sales growth of stores like Crate & Barrel and Bed, Bath & Beyond has soared. Spending on home related goods continues to exceed as expenditures on apparel and the sales of second homes are strong.

There are other trends that indicate that a new concept of luxury is present. Expenditures on pet health are increasing. Health therapies such as CAT scans and MRIs, kidney transplants, root canals, and chemotherapy treatments once reserved for people are now extended to pets.

Affluent consumers are seeking quality of life values. They find joy in satisfying wants as distinct from needs. Increasingly these wants have become needs, and these needs are not necessities. Many consumers purchase upscale items and trade up in their purchasing behavior. The mainstreaming of affluence has increased sales of products like cell phones, plastic surgery, Starbucks coffee, and sushi.

The affluent market desires an emotional experience that will help them escape from the tensions of modern life. This means that purchasing patterns reflect the buying of high quality, high performance, emotionally satisfying goods and services. The spread of the desire to purchase luxury items is reflected in the sales of boats, BMWs, Williams-Sonoma, and premium chocolate. This desire for luxury items has created a market for premium coffees, bedroom sheets, and vodkas such as Belvedere. Marketers interested in penetrating the affluent market need to promote brands that develop a sense of internal well-being and to create a model for enriching services.

Fractional ownership is still another strategy for a segment of the affluent market. Buyers purchase a share of an expensive asset such as a jet plane, a yacht, a Bentley automobile, an RV or a time-share vacation property in an exclusive place like Jackson Hole, Wyoming, or Jupiter Island, Florida.

The buyer pays the seller fees to administer scheduling and maintenance. For instance, through Exotic Car Share, a Bentley can be purchased for $30,000, which is a one-fifth share and a $10,000 maintenance fee. A 2003 Silverton Motor Yacht 453 can be purchased for $102,000, with a $7,200 maintenance fee through Great Lakes BoatShare. The purchaser, in turn, is able to use the yacht four weekends a month and 15 weekdays between May and October.

Exclusive Resorts is a time-share vacation club with vacation units in Hawaii, the Bahamas, and on luxury cruise ships. The exclusive vacation clubs appeal to people who travel with large families, friends, nannies, and pets and who need lots of room. Annual fees range from $12,000 to $18,000 with a refundable deposit of $200,000. The Ritz-Carlton and the Four Season Hotels have also entered this field, and in 2003 over 3 million consumers in the United States owned some form of time-share.

A number of affluent people have personal chefs. The American Personal Chef Institute and Association reports that 72,000 clients used personal chefs in 2003 and estimate this number will increase to 300,000 by 2010. Senior citizens constitute about 20 percent of the membership. Unlike a private chef who is employed full time for one person, a personal chef works on a contract basis from once a week to once a month.

Senior citizens are redefining themselves both on intellectual and physical levels. Seniors are enrolling in college courses throughout the United States. More than 1,000 seniors a year audit classes at Boston University and at the University of Pennsylvania. Seniors may audit classes with undergraduate students, provided space is available. Some other colleges that mix seniors with undergraduates in class are Florida Atlantic University, Dartmouth, Oberlin, and the University of South Florida. Seniors are purchasing Harley-Davidson motorcycles, getting face lifts, joining fitness clubs, and buying low-cut jeans.

CREDIT CARDS HELP UPSCALE SHOPPERS PURCHASE LUXURY

Consumers are bombarded with advertisements for expensive automobiles and large-screen television sets. The Federal Reserve reported that consumers spent half the money from refinancing their homes in 2001 to pay for home improvements, cars, vacations, and other purchases. Households possessing at least one credit card owed more than $9,200 in 2003, a 23 percent increase from 1998 after adjusting for inflation. More consumers are using credit cards to finance lifestyles than their current incomes cannot support. Credit cards assure a financial flexibility. Consumers are seduced by such television programs as *Desperate Housewives*, which take upper-class life for granted. Upscale purchases and those people who trade up find it easier to purchase luxury items that may range from premium coffee to superpremium ice cream to jewelry and automobiles. Home improvements such as new kitchens and bathrooms are on the top of the list of luxury goods.

Credit card companies market a wide spectrum of offers that segment the market. American Express offers the Centurion card, introduced in 1999 and offered by invitation only to customers who spent at least $150,000 a year on American Express cards. Cardholders pay an annual fee of $2,500 and receive such services as a personal travel counselor and concierge available 24/7. Among the other perks included are provisions for taking a companion abroad first class for free and the concierge arranging for parties and obtaining hard-to-get reservations.

Asian Americans are a significant segment of the new rich. Asian Americans are more likely than whites, blacks, or Hispanics to have a credit card and to use credit cards more often each month. More than two-thirds of Asian Americans pay their balances each month. The Asian American market has high brand loyalty and high word-of-mouth buying. Education is an important goal. Asian Americans are more likely to obtain a college degree than the average American.

THE ULTIMATE IN CROSS SHOPPING

Although dollar stores are the five and dimes of the twenty-first century, households with incomes of more than $50,000 represent their fastest-growing market. The core shoppers at dollar stores are families with incomes under $30,000, but 40 percent of households with incomes of more than $70,000 still shop regularly at dollar stores. The three largest retailers are Dollar General, Family Dollar Stores, and Dollar Tree Stores.

The affluent market is willing to splurge on automobiles and home theaters, but on everyday items, they want discount prices. They love the adventure of finding bargains. They consider themselves shrewd, careful shoppers. Therefore, many dollar stores are expanding into the suburbs to attract an affluent consumer educated in online price comparison shopping and bargain hunting. These shoppers can well afford a $5 greeting card but would rather purchase greeting cards at two for a $1. A dollar store known as "99 cents stuff" has sold shopping bags imprinted with the Channel name to develop a favorable image in carrying purchases. Items such as candles, craft materials, flowers, and even food products are purchased by their customers. Dollar stores are expanding faster than any other type of retail institution, and it is only a matter of time before items priced at $50 or under will be added to their merchandise assortment.

NEW PRODUCT INROADS INTO THE AFFLUENT MARKET

Many external considerations must be accounted for in the process of targeting the affluent market. Some of these considerations include knowledge of the particular segment of the affluent market that will purchase the product or service as well as the external constraints that are placed on their decisions.

Buyer behavior has become an important aspect for targeting the affluent market as well as knowledge gained from other disciplines.

Product success may be due to proper matching of product differentiation and market segmentation strategies to satisfying the wants and needs of the affluent market. Some product failures may be attributed to the failure to consider the benefits of the product, its difference from the competition, and its suitability for the affluent market. The question remains, What products and services will the affluent market desire and accept? The following products and services have gained a foothold in the affluent market:

- Gift shops at some art shops in museums next to the postcards and stationery sell $3,250 Eames lounge chairs, $1,200 Naguchi coffee tables, $175 Jasper Morrison coffeemakers, and Alessi teapots. Among the museum shops offering home design items are Cincinnati Contemporary Arts Center and the San Francisco MOMA.
- Giant luxury motor coaches that sell for more than $500,000, such as Featherlite Luxury Coaches.
- Kids programs at hotels, such as West Virginia's Greenbrier and Georgia's Sea Island, which give craft lessons with artists and lizard viewings with naturalists, and the Breakers of Palm Beach, Florida, which has golf clinics for children.
- Appliance manufacturers offer new colors that include terra-cotta, aubergine, pewter, wedge wood blue, and yellow. These new colors sell for much more than the traditional colors.
- Tote bags that sell at Coach and Saks Fifth Avenue. A Prada bag sells for more than $800, a Tumi tote bag measures 20 × 16 × 4. A Louis Vuitton bag can carry about 15 pounds and measures 16 × 18. Large, oversize bags are purchased by many professional women with numerous responsibilities.
- Vacation Home Frontiers featuring member's only communities with airstrips; ski hills; and seclusion, security, and privacy. These vacation communities include: Carnegie Abbey in Portsmouth, Rhode Island, starting at $3.5 million; Ford Plantation in Richmond Hill, Georgia, starting at $1 million; The Hideaway in LaQuinta, California, starting at $1.5 million; Mountain Air in Burnsville, North Carolina, starting at $800,000; and Yellowstone Club in Big Sky, Montana, starting at $3.8 million.

WINNERS IN THE AFFLUENT MARKET

There are many industries that have lucrative possibilities, but marketers need to identify changing needs and wants in order to satisfy the affluent market. Although success stories abound, there will be some industries and marketers that will fail unless there is a comprehension of the new rich in some depth and breadth. For instance, the consumers' search to appear different from one another is a threat to luxury brands in the fashion industry that rely on selling status as a mass product. Affluent consumers can easily find firms marketing handbags by shape, color, and fabric on the Web.

The toy industry is an example of an industry that has not understood the affluent consumer. FAO Schwarz had been in business since 1862 and targeted an upscale market with stores in more than 40 cities in the United States. Customers desired unique toys. Yet, FAO Schwarz was unable to compete with Toys "R" Us, Wal-Mart, the Internet, and discounters. Lionel has been a troubled toy train manufacturer for some years; and A.C. Gilbert, once a pillar of the toy industry for 58 years and known for its Erector set, microscopes, and chemistry sets, failed to realize that the market was changing.

Differentiation is the process of adding uniqueness to product or services. The goal is to help achieve a differential advantage over the competition. Affordable differentiation is the process of adding a set of valued differences to the product or service that the buyer finds significant enough to warrant paying extra. Thus, men may desire membership in a health spa if golf clinics are provided or if hotels provide special accommodations for family reunions. An umbrella with a mink-trimmed handle may be perceived by a buyer as a valued product addition. Firms in such sectors as health and fitness, travel, financial services, technology, and other areas need to create affordable differentiation for their products and services in targeting the mass affluent market.

HEALTH AND FITNESS

Purdue University is the first college nationwide to offer a four-year degree program in personal fitness training. Included in the program are internships in commercial health clubs and cardiac rehabilitation centers. According to the Bureau of Labor Statistics, employment of recreation and fitness workers is anticipated to increase by 35 percent by 2012. These new trainers will have to pass the American College of Sports Medicine's new personal trainer exam to become certified workers.

The number of spas has more than doubled to over 12,000 from 1997 to 2003, with revenue accounting for $11.2 billion in 2003. Luxury product marketers, personal-care companies, and private-equity firms are all endeavoring to serve other growing markets. Firms such as Starwood Hotels and Resorts Worldwide Inc., North Castle, which purchased Elizabeth Arden, and Mario Tricoci have entered this lucrative market. Among the services offered by these spas are hairstylists and pedicures.

Upscale salons and spas are developing strategies toward the lucrative men's market. Men currently account for over 20 percent of spa visits according to the International Spa Association and marketers desire to attract more males in the future. Strategies include decorating in warm, earthy colors; hiring both male and female therapists; and offering special classes such as golf clinics or sessions with exercise consultants. Privacy is essential for men. The best way to reach men is through a wife or girlfriend who has purchased a gift certificate for them. Print ads are also helpful.

TRAVEL

Many affluent people spend a great percentage of their income on travel. The hotels have developed new programs that satisfy the needs of busy professionals. The Four Seasons in Atlanta has developed a program whereby the parents of busy professionals can accompany them at special rates, and as a result, the hotel has witnessed a 10 percent increase in elderly people accompanying their children on business trips. The Benjamin Hotel in New York has seen these types of reservations increase from 15 to 25 percent in a year. As the baby boomers age there is more desire to spend additional time with parents. In response, the Renaissance Chicago O'Hare Hotel gives elderly guests 50 percent off on a second room, and the Carlyle Hotel in New York offers a free Sunday stay.

The hotels have responded to another family need by encouraging family reunions at special rates. In this way, family members who reside in distant states can meet each other. The Arizona Biltmore in Phoenix has organized a treasure hunt for family enjoyment. Hotels such as the Sonoma Mission Inn in California have offered such elaborate services as gourmet chefs to cook family recipes, photographers, and experts to help trace genealogy.

FINANCIAL SERVICES

Financial service professionals view affluent consumers as a major market. Most surveys of consumers demonstrate that there are an insufficient number of the affluent to permit an analysis in any level of depth or breadth. Fortunately, there is one database that allows detailed analysis of the finances of the affluent. The Federal Reserve Board publishes the Survey of Consumer Finances every three years. Many financial organizations divide the market into four segments based on financial assets: mass affluent—$250,000 to $499,999; affluent—$500,000 to $999,999; high net worth—$1 million to $4.9 million; and pentamillionaire—$5 million or more. If the mass affluent and the affluent are combined, they represent close to 9 percent of the population, while the high net worth and pentamillionaires constitute no more than 2 percent of the population. In 2004 those with $5 million or more in assets increased by 38 percent to 740,000, up from 480,000 in 2001 and more than three times the number from 1997. Affluent households allocated 24 percent of their money in stocks and bonds, 23 percent in managed accounts, 14 percent in IRAs, 13 percent in mutual funds, 9 percent in alternative investments, 9 percent in deposits, and 8 percent in other investments in 2004.[5]

Merrill Lynch, Smith Barney, and Morgan Chase are advising the ultrawealthy. There is no dominance of this market by any single firm. Since industry experts anticipate a great transfer of generational wealth from the baby boomers to their children in the future, many firms are starting to enter this market.

About one-third of the wealthy manage their own investments, and about half of the wealthy seek advice from professionals. The number of certified financial planners has grown from over 23,000 in 1991 to 45,000 in 2003, according to the Certified Financial Planners Board.

TECHNOLOGY AND GADGETS

The backyard solar system is for the environmentally conscious. Improved solar technology is allowing homeowners to illuminate unplugged everything from lighted patio umbrellas to small water fountains to walking stones that brighten walkways. Costs range from a bird bath with a small fountain at $200 to a table umbrella with bulbs built in at $200 to a mailbox post at $200.

For many people, the umbrella is a $5 item; but for others, it can cost more than $100. For example, F. Lippincott sells umbrellas with sterling silver or mink trimmed handles for $120 to $1,500. Giorgio Armani stores sells a logo iridescent polyester or matte cotton umbrella from $95 to $225. Designers and retailers have turned the umbrella into something precious. Sales at retailers like Bloomingdale's and Neiman Marcus have been brisk.

The Neiman Marcus catalog sells items that are out of the ordinary such as a Mr. & Mrs. Potato Head set encrusted with more than 50,000 Swarovski crystals at $16,000. Neiman Marcus also offers a $10 million 12-passenger Zeppelin air ship, a $1.7 million personal submarine, or a $1.45 million bowling center. In the past, camels have been offered for sale since there are some wealthy people who enjoy purchasing unusual items.

MANAGING CHANGE

There are many seniors who still have a need for achievement. The Department of Education has reported that nearly 85,000 men and women over 50 are full-time students in undergraduate and graduate programs. Approximately 435,000 are part-time students, and about 120,000 are earning graduate degrees. Intellectual activity often leads to creativity that is reflected in purchasing behavior.

Colleges and universities are competing for students with luxurious amenities. Ohio University has constructed a three-story entry rotunda in 2005 with a 250-seat theater, a food court, a ballroom, and a five-story atrium that links the upper campus with a lower campus down the hill. The University of Massachusetts at Boston has completed a $75 million student union that features a curved-glass façade overlooking Boston Harbor. The University of North Carolina at Chapel Hill has completed a sports bar with 40 video games, including a helicopter simulator. The University of Cincinnati constructed a $50.8 million 90-foot tall atrium with a skylight, an 800-seat auditorium, and a 600-seat food court.

The television networks are reinventing themselves by targeting the richest viewers. Shows with the highest concentration of an audience aged 18 to 49 from households with income over $75,000 are *The Apprentice*, *Boston Legal*, *The Office*, and *Desperate Housewives*. Nielsen Media has made this type of competition feasible with the ability to measure high-income households through technology.

Demographic changes coupled with technological innovations, among other factors, has helped to redefine consumer lifestyles. Census Bureau data has confirmed the multiculturalism of America. Particularly noted has been the inclusion of Asian, Hispanic, and black Americans into the affluent market.

Family structure has also included a higher percentage of single-person households that has gained in affluence. There has been recognition of the entrance of gays and lesbians into the affluent market. New family structures including those couples choosing not to have children are reshaping the affluent mass market.

The emergence of the affluent market has spread to an affordable luxury market with premium brands. Starbuck coffee, designer pet foods, Godiva chocolates, premium ice cream, and personal-care products by Bath and Body Works have encouraged reinvention through brands. The popularity of remaking the body is represented by Botox and a number of cosmetic surgery procedures through which people remake their appearance.

There is a profound cultural connection to reinvention and the redefining of affluent consumers' changes in purchasing patterns. A new openness to change has made an impact on gender roles, ethnic makeup, and family structure. Technological innovations have empowered the individual to help manage a busy daily life with products such as navigation systems available in luxury automobiles and the L G Internet refrigerator, which takes inven tory of contents and transmits a shopping list to a service like Peapod. These innovations give affluent consumers feelings of more control and choice and the ability to simplify their lives.

The affluent market, which includes consumers who make upscale purchases and who trade up on occasion, has been targeted by designers such as Isaac Mizrahi, who has produced a line of apparel for Target stores. Design is a movement toward aesthetics, and manufacturers are now making it more accessible to everyone. There are manufacturers who are emulating this trend by offering goods and services not only in apparel but in automobiles, appliances, entertainment, vacations, and financial services that are now perceived as new luxury items.

Marketers will need to use their creative imagination to devise strategies to satisfy the upscale needs and wants of a new affluent generation. Even American baseball has joined this trend. Minor-league parks have gone upscale with luxury skyboxes, wine gardens, and hot tubs. For example, the Dayton Dragons in Dayton, Ohio, offer skyboxes with leather couches; and the Kane County Cougars in Geneva, Illinois, offers hot-tub seating for eight at $175.

Revenue for minor-league teams has increased 90 percent a year for the past 10 years, and the average minor-league ticket increased 12 percent in 2005.

The trend is for consumers to reinvent themselves. Marketers need to do the same. Abercrombie & Fitch, for example, is developing a chain of 300 stores called Ruehl that focuses on consumer experiences and feelings. Ruehl will sell merchandise at about 30 percent higher than its parent company. Ruehl's will reflect a business-casual style in accord with a Greenwich Village neotech approach. Décor of the store will look like a studio apartment with photographs, couches, and bookshelves lined with Museum of Modern Art books.

CHAPTER 10

Myths, Realities and Predictions

Many American families have witnessed gains in the value of their assets over the last five years. According to the Federal Reserve Bank, families had an all-time high level of wealth in 2005 due to the rising values of housing and ownership of stocks. Median household net worth was estimated at more than $100,000 in 2005 with assets rising in value faster than debt. This means there are now tens of millions of Americans who are part of the affluent market, purchasing flat-panel HDTVs, the PIP or Nokia E-70 phones, Pierre Marcolini chocolate, the Sony DSC-N1, the ISong book, Goyand leather goods, and many other products. This same phenomenon is taking place in Europe and Asia. Upward mobility is a goal.

There have also been social changes affecting the purchasing behavior of affluent customers that will shape the activities, interests, and opinions of these customers for decades into the twenty-first century. New information technology has given marketing better insight into buyer behavior. Companies like Abacus help marketers identify the best customers by combining and analyzing offline and online data mined from over 1,900 retailers. Abacus recognizes that past purchases are the best documentation of what customers will buy in the future. They track more than 90 million shoppers' buying habits. Abacus provides information on shoppers with details about household income and education. They provide customer intelligence to help companies identify, select, and target a market niche.

For many years, marketers believed that affluent consumers were a relatively small, slowly growing, and stable market segment. This belief is now challenged by new evidence. Significant changes are occurring in the lifestyles of affluent consumers. Changing technology and economic and social forces have made affluent consumers more imaginative and creative. These consumers are sensitive to environmental issues and to the need for social change. Other changes include inter-generational upward mobility. Smaller-size families have more money to spend on their children and themselves. Attitude changes, in the short term, have occurred in establishing spending priorities for affluent families with few children.

A second change is in group norms, values, and memberships. Many affluent consumers belong to country and social clubs and participate in community affairs.

A third change is characterized by technological innovation, which includes increased use of the Internet. Many affluent consumers make purchases online and through the use of cell phones. Information about brands, products, and prices is learned by accessing appropriate sources.

The final dimension of these changes that has impacted the life cycle, group norms and values, and technological innovation is its consequences. There has been a sociocultural, radical change in affluent consumer buyer behavior. There is a conflict between the newly rich and the established values and attitudes of the old rich.

There are five myths associated with affluent consumer purchasing behavior, and it is necessary to look at these myths in light of new marketing intelligence.

Myth #1. Luxury merchandise is dependent on brand identification with products and services sold through prestige stores.

Reality #1. This statement is questionable with the changing face of affluence. Luxury customers are brand conscious and seek high-end experiences along with high-end products. Even the once dowdy apron has ascended to new heights. A new line of aprons known as Kitsch'n Glam is priced from $42 to $62 and ranges from sophisticated prints to kitschy black and white French-maid styles. This merchandise line is available at more than 100 boutiques scattered throughout the United States. Designers of fashion aprons have not established department store channels yet but sell products through clothing and gift boutiques, specialty cooking stores, and their own Web sites. Sur La Table, a Seattle-based national cookware chain estimates that sales will grow 15 to 20 percent a year.

Creative marketing strategies are necessary as marketers try to reach the new affluent consumer. Mars, the candy manufacturer, is emulating Starbucks as upscale chocolate lounges are established in the Chicago area. Godiva has also introduced its first in-store beverage in 270 stores, and Hershey is adding seating areas and a bakery to an existing store in New York's Times Square.

In apparel, fashion has been added to plus-size women's wear. Nordstrom and Bloomingdale's are emphasizing the latest fashion trends in selling their collections. Only a decade ago, the latest designs in fashion were not offered, and mainly dowdy styles in dark colors were available for plus-size women.

Luxury brand manufacturers such as Coach, Ralph Lauren, Guess, and Liz Claiborne have opened retail outlets in competition with department stores. Polo stores are Ralph Lauren's fastest growing marketing channel. Plans are underway to open 70 to 85 stores in the next few years. Guess plans to open 24 new stores in the next year. Designer brands such as Christian Dior are using e-commerce sites to market their merchandise and are experiencing higher profit margins than those garnered by selling their merchandise through department stores.

New luxury merchandise previously sold through prestigious status retailers is now distributed through Costco, Sam's Club, and B. J.'s Wholesale Club. Costco, the largest warehouse club is selling a Suzuki grand piano for $8,000 and a 100 C. D. Wurlitzer jukebox for $6,000. Sam's Club, the second largest wholesale club is offering a Hummer H3 golf cart, priced at $8,998, and a 180-bottle wine cooler for $1,500. B. J.'s Wholesale Club, ranked third, is offering a $1,900 Baja Motorsport go-cart. These items are sold in addition to merchandise such as fancy cookware and fine wine to take advantage of cross-shopping patterns.

New luxury products in contrast to the old luxury goods are now able to generate high sales volumes despite their high prices. Customers are willing to spend more for experiences ranging from better service to one-of-a-kind adventures. The middle market is eroding as high-end producers gain prominence. Low-priced goods in the past, such as sandals and aprons, have been made upscale to take advantage of the new customer. Luxury is a changing target. Today's luxury is tomorrow's necessity. Cashmere, once considered a luxury item, is now targeted for the masses.

Myth #2. Men have dominated affluent markets and will continue to do so in the future.

Reality #2. Women are challenging men's domination of affluent markets. It is thought that the domination of males over females starts early in grade school. However, the facts are that females develop faster. The average boy is developmentally two years behind girls in reading and writing. Boys also make up most of the special education students. According to the National Center of Education Statistics, girls outnumber boys involved in student government 27 percent to 19 percent; in music/performing arts, 4.6 percent to 3.5 percent; in yearbook/newspaper activities, 29 percent to 21 percent; and in academic clubs, 36 percent to 28 percent in high school in 2000. Consequently, women will exert a greater influence in affluent markets.

Projections indicate that by 2010, 142 females to 100 men will hold bachelor's degrees and 151 females to 100 men will hold master's degrees. Women are closing the gap in medicine and constitute almost half the students in law school. Women outnumber men in occupations such as education, pharmacy, veterinary medicine, and in the visual and performing arts. More than one-third of women students are enrolled in nontraditional curriculum majors such as business, computer science, and the physical sciences; and these percentages are estimated to increase in the future.

Marketers have traditionally ignored women in selling technology products. The viewpoint was held that women cared little about technology and only men would buy technology products. In 2005 women accounted for one-half of technology purchases. Women were expected to outspend men in the $122 billion technology market, according to the Consumer Electronics Association. Samsung has increased the number of women on its consumer panels, and this has resulted in an increased number of design awards. Dell has worked to get women's magazine editors to write more about their computers, televisions, and pocket PCs. Marketers are realizing that women are the key to their growth strategies. Best Buy has relaunched 60 stores, changing their appearance with pastel colors, rather than using the chain's traditional dark blue and yellow scheme, to attract female customers. As we have watched the mommy track, where young professional women left the workplace in their 30s to raise families, we now see successful women in their 50s making a similar choice. They are the baby boomers, the first group of women to rise to the top of their professions and to leave their jobs to care for elderly parents. Sociologists have labeled this the daughter track. This phenomenon has a significant impact on marketers interested in selling to affluent women with new family responsibilities requiring different products and services. Since more than 20 percent of women in America earn more than their spouses, they exert a greater influence on family purchasing decisions.

Myth #3. Private-label or store brands are considered inferior merchandise by affluent consumers.

Reality #3. Macy's, Saks, Federated Department Stores, J.C. Penney, and the May Company have targeted affluent consumers with store brands. Private-label apparel sales are increasing approximately 5 percent each year. Macy's is selling such items as a $375 silk quilted coverlet, Italian made duvets for $1,350, and $275 pillowcases under their own private brands labeled Hotel Collection by Charter Club. GAP and Victoria's Secret stores are using brand extensions by putting their names on lotions, shampoos, shower gels, and perfumes.

J. C. Penney is selling a $275 velvet and jacquard comforter set in its Home Collection and men's apparel under its Stafford label. Saks is selling under its Platinum line $1,000 jackets and $500 cotton dress shirts and women's sportswear under its 5/48 label featuring its own in-house designer. The May Company offers the Context and Valerie Stevens's labels for upscale buyers, with a new merchandise line of tailored and casual separates. Federated distributes their own store brand, Tasso Elba, offering Italian-inspired men's suits and sportswear. Traditionally, department store private-label brands were placed in the least expensive category, but increasingly, department stores are increasing their store brands in prominence, quality, and price. Although the name on the product is important, the luxury customer is concerned with the services the store provides such as guarantees, free repairs, convenient parking, and an easy return policy.

Myth #4. Customer services are the same as in the past.

Reality #4. New services are demanded by affluent consumers. Affluent consumers want more individualized services. According to the Luxury Institute survey of wealthy customers, about 80 percent desire to bypass automated phone systems and speak with an individual directly, and nearly 75 percent want front-line employees empowered to make immediate decisions. Another 75 percent maintain that companies should have quick and easy return policies, and 65 percent believe that firms need to know individual purchaser's preferences about conducting business with the company.

The most successful companies targeting this market are personalizing their messages and differentiating their services. The diversity of the service industry defies generalization, with affluent consumers wanting individualized medical treatment, legal advice, financial information, and services associated with travel and the purchase of luxury goods and collectibles. These customers value the relationship more than the specific product or service. To illustrate, there are some medical doctors who limit their practice to individuals who pay a flat fee for their personalized services.

A wide range of standard services are now provided to employees by corporations, with employees paying for these services. BEA Systems has allowed car detailers, massage therapists, a roving farmers market, and Weight Watchers representatives to carry out services with employees at the workplace. Electronic Arts Inc. has brought in an acupuncturist. Google operates free shuttle services to employees living in San Francisco, and the vehicles have wireless Internet capability so that work can be performed during the trip. Firms in many instances permit haircuts, car washes, and oil changes for busy workers during their work hours. This saves employees personal time so that more time can be devoted to professional duties.

Companies serving the affluent realize the importance of satisfying service needs. Swissair wants to have more than 96 percent of its passenger's rate its services as good or superior, thereby maintaining the highest standards. Hyatt Hotels tries to excel in responding to customer complaints in record time. Nordstrom trains its personnel to adhere to the highest service standards. John Deere endeavors to make their product-support services a competitive advantage, and more than 50 percent of their profits are derived from these services

Myth #5. Luxury goods are in ample supply for affluent consumers.

Reality #5. The demand for luxury goods exceeds supply. *Forbes* magazine has tracked the Cost of Living Extremely Well (CLEW) Index since 1976, which rose 4 percent compared to the consumer price index (CPI), which rose 3.6 percent. The price of luxury goods reported by the CLEW index increased 680 percent since 1976, compared to the CPI increase of 344 percent. The price for color televisions in the 1950s, computers in the 1980s, and other such items from decade to decade in the introductory stages were initially high and demand was high. It was only during the mass production stage and the acceptance of color televisions and computers by the general public that supply caught up with demand. Eventually, luxury goods are no longer considered luxury items.

The definition of luxury goods has been broadened to include cell phones, eyeglasses, beach sandals, and the apron. The definition of luxury goods will continue to be broadened in the future. Consumers are using nontraditional media to sell these luxury products. The 30-second television spot is being used less as companies spend more for online video advertising. It is estimated that by 2009, video advertisements will account for more than 20 percent of all advertising spending. Video ads include blogs and mobile ads. Satellite radio with channels targeted to specific listeners' interests is another medium that will be used to reach affluent customers.

MORE MYTHS AND REALITIES

The affluent society of John Kenneth Galbraith is no longer intact. It has matured. No longer are luxury goods sold only through prestigious retailers. Luxury goods are sold through the Internet, eBay, cell phones, and mail-order catalogs to customers who in the past have been cautious in their purchasing behavior and protective of their financial resources.

Wealthy people in the past knew that they were rich. Today, many affluent people do not believe that they are rich because they come from middle-class backgrounds. Ivy League colleges were the training ground of the wealthy in the past. Today, a significant number of Ivy League colleges enroll more minorities, foreign students, and more students who are in debt upon graduation. The prep school students of former years are a distinct minority at many Ivy League colleges. Half the students who graduate from Yale and 75 percent who graduate from Mount Holyoke are in debt

The size of the affluent market before World War II was stable. Today, the affluent market is huge and growing. Senior citizens; entrepreneurs; celebrities; and groups such as Hispanics, Asians, African Americans, and gays and lesbians are joining the ranks of the wealthy. Since the Census 2000, multicultural marketing in all its forms has continued to evolve in research funding and in its importance.

Marketers in the past viewed affluent consumers as a conservative segment in purchasing behavior. Research today reveals that affluent consumers comprise a high percentage of innovators and early adopters for purchasing new goods and services. Even affluent seniors are not afraid of new technology. Large numbers of seniors were among the first market segment to purchase computers, camcorders, and the latest in stereo equipment. This segment, which is part of a 3.8 million affluent empty-nesters market is growing rapidly. The market includes households with an annual income of $100,000 or more. These consumers are looking for experiences rather than just buying another product. There is a waiting list of more than 300 people willing to pay $65,000 to reach the top of Mount Everest each year.

Stereotyping can mean missed opportunities. There is a myth that senior citizens are interested only in traveling, shopping, watching sporting events, and playing cards and bingo. The reality is that seniors make up the fastest-growing market segment of the fitness industry. According to the International Health, Racquet and Sports Club Association, seniors accounted for 25 percent of health and fitness membership in 2005, and this is a six-fold increase since 1993. The fitness industry, in response, is starting to redesign workout programs and equipment.

The gay and lesbian segment of this market is also growing. Firms such as Wells Fargo, Bank One, and Olivia Records have targeted this market. Market size is estimated at over 18.5 million with spending power of more than $500 billion.

Marketers need to comprehend the distinction between a fad and a trend in the affluent market. The green movement among affluent consumers is a trend, not a fad. Eco-friendly consumer products are increasingly aimed at the affluent market. For example, Serfontaine is selling jeans for men and women tested with natural enzymes rather than chemicals for $178 to $318 at Bluebeeonline.com, and UJeans is selling custom-made jeans in denim treated with chemical-free dyes and rinses at $107 at Ujeans.com.

There is a segment of the affluent market that is not interested in the ownership of luxury assets such as houses, boats, exotic cars, and private airplanes. There is now a "membership-ification" of luxury assets. This allows the customer to have these items available on an as-needed basis for a membership fee. This trend is now trickling down to other luxury products such as apparel and furniture.

There is an old axiom, "If it's not broke, don't fix it." However, fragmentation strategy in the affluent market is based on not only demographics but also imagination and creativity. Fragmentation marketing is more profitable since the affluent market is not homogeneous. Many marketers previously thought that luxury goods were expensive and had to be priced over $100. Along came Starbucks, and luxury goods were viewed from a different perspective. Marketers like Mercedes, Coach, and Tiffany have developed products for the affluent and buyers who wish to trade up. There has been a recent democratization of luxury products so that they are now available to the mass market.

Major changes have been occurring in retailing as many affluent consumers are shopping in stores previously not serving the affluent. Marketers thought that affluent consumers would only patronize retailers such as Neiman Marcus. Now, stores like Costco, Sam's Club, Target, and Wal-Mart are attracting wealthy and upscale buyers. These retailers are introducing new marketing strategies to be more competitive. Brands such as Ralph Lauren and Liz Claiborne are sold through nontraditional marketing channels.

FIVE REALITIES FOR SETTING MARKETING STRATEGIES

Companies may decide to target a single-segment concentration, such as Porsche selecting the sports car market, or provide a number of products to reach many segments, such as Coach offering a number of fashion accessories. Neiman Marcus specializes in serving the many needs of the affluent market and has gained a strong reputation in serving this customer group. Manufacturers seek out Neiman Marcus as a channel to reach the affluent market. The following are new realities that influence marketing strategies for this market.

1. Affluent customers will focus on new experiences. The affluent customer is better educated and is willing to take more risks in trying new products and services. Time has become more valuable to these customers. They are willing to pay a premium for the goods and services valued. To illustrate, in the bookstore sector, retailers have targeted children and mystery readers. Niche strategies will be more useful in targeting affluent markets in the future. Consumers who comprise niche markets have pronounced purchasing characteristics and motives.

Niche strategies that emphasize individualization or personalization of products will gain a favorable reception in the affluent market. For example, customers are encouraged to design a custom label for their wine bottles. A personalized label placed on a bottle of wine can cost $250 or more. The task of marketers is to use their creative efforts to allow customers to personalize desired products. A pleasurable sense of satisfaction can be derived from showing these personalized products to friends, and this also allows for inward emotional experiences.

A new high-end home catalog launched in 2005 under the name 10 Crescent Lane from Home Depot has a mailing list of 1 million people who are primarily upscale buyers. Home Depot is attempting to extend and expand its presence in the upscale market. Upscale catalog sales are increasing beyond expectations.

Home Depot is competing with such competitors as Frontgate, Horchow, Williams-Sonoma and Restoration Hardware. Offerings include mother-of-pearl candlesticks, a mirrored parsons table, Yves Delorme bedding ($540 for a coverlet), Silk Trading Company window treatments, and $1,100 headboards. Strategies in the future include carrying exclusive goods that will be unique from competitors.

EBay has seized a competitive advantage over department stores and boutiques by providing fashion distribution and marketing. Competitors must wait months to receive orders, but eBay offers a timing value to online customers who don't want to wait for fashion items. The clothing, shoes, and accessories category was launched in 2002, and in 2005 it reached $1.3 billion in sales compared to Tiffany's $1.9 billion at its 120 stores worldwide. Among the brands sold by eBay are Louis Vuitton, Prada, Manolo Blahnick, and Hermès Birkin handbags that sell for about $10,000.

2. Promotion on the Internet will facilitate global competition for the affluent market. Waterford Wedgwood PLC launched an e-commerce site, WedgwoodU.S.A.com. The site sells the Wedgwood brand of fine china and Hasperware collectibles and other brands such as Vera-Wang china and Emeril kitchenware. The upscale British retailer Harrods Ltd. and the British luxury shoe company Georgina Goodman Ltd. have established online shopping sites. Foreign companies have targeted the affluent market with the following Web sites: Aurorafernandez.com with fine swimwear from Spain, gentrydeparis.com with fine lingerie from France, and eccousa.com. with fine shoes from Denmark. Many of these firms are testing the market before opening stores in the United States.

A promotional pull strategy is especially appropriate for foreign manufacturers. A pull strategy operates well when there is high brand loyalty and consumer involvement. Eventually, consumers responding to Internet promotions may be induced to request intermediaries to order the product. If the promotional pull strategy is successful, a strong consumer demand for the product has been stimulated. Generally, a pulling strategy involves large expenditures for promotion. Limited financial resources often prevent a small firm from using this strategy, and the firm may embark on a partial pulling strategy. Firms that have well-established luxury brands after setting up Web sites might be well advised to use direct selling to resellers. A successful record of Internet sales would help to convince intermediaries to stock the brand.

Companies targeting the affluent market need to think globally. The number of multinational corporations in the wealthiest countries has more than tripled in the past three decades. Many countries are relaxing trade barriers and encouraging free trade alliances.

Globalization has been made possible through faster communication, transportation, technology, and financial access. Products marketed in one country, such as Gucci purses, Mont Blanc pens, Armani suits, and Rolex watches, are accepted in the United States and other countries. American firms such as Hallmark cards; Mattel dolls and toys; Johnnie Walker whiskey; Hyatt Hotels; Border Books and Music; and University Games, a software company, have made inroads into affluent markets in foreign countries.

Counterfeiters from Asia and Europe, as the luxury industry becomes global, not only deceive consumers but continue to plague the luxury industry. Imitations of Louis Vuitton handbags Cartier jewelry and Rolex watches are sold to unsuspecting consumers. The total value of counterfeit goods seized by U.S. Customs Officials has increased from $50 million to $140 million from 2000 to 2004. Marketers will need to identify their luxury goods more carefully as a precaution as competition for luxury goods becomes more international.

The spread of luxury stores in airports, both in the United States and foreign countries, has helped to internationalize luxury brands. Cartier and Hugo Boss have established stores in John F. Kennedy Airport in New York; Brooks Brothers and Victoria's Secret have established stores in Pittsburg International Airport; Coach and Esprit have opened shops at San Francisco

International Airport; and Fossil and Swarovski have established stores at McCarran International Airport in Las Vegas. Overseas, Channel and Gucci have stores at London's Heathrow Airport; Mont Blanc and Hermes have stores at Frankfurt International Airport; and Prada and Dior have opened stores at Hong Kong International Airport. Airport retailing has become more difficult since September 11. Increased security measures result in people arriving at airports earlier with more time to shop. High-end retailers have been established in foreign airports in past years, but now more and more luxury retailers are considering United States airports as a new channel of distribution.

3. Niche strategies dominate the future in affluent markets. This is the age of niche marketing as companies segment the affluent market. Niche retailers in the bookstore sector have established stores that target history and science-fiction buffs. In the footwear sector, chains such as Footlocker aim at the sneaker and athletic market segment. In the furniture sector, Pier 1 Imports dominates a niche that desires exotic imported furniture and housewares. Niche retailing and Internet selling has been a catalyst for change as manufacturers reexamine and revise their distribution systems to better serve retailers and consumers.

Many markets have grown as a result of niche marketing. Apple Computer built itself on the hobbyist market. Many of the early users of personal computers in education, small business, and the business professional market came from hobbyists. Affluent consumers who comprise niche markets have clear and pronounced purchasing characteristics and motives.

Retailers like Abercrombie & Fitch successfully used niche marketing to reposition themselves. This organization was founded in 1892 and has reinvented an established brand. Abercrombie & Fitch, at the beginning of the twenty-first century, has adjusted its target market to include teens and young adults and established itself as a popular specialty store serving a youthful market.

Williams-Sonoma is a diversified niche retailer and includes the Pottery Barn and Hold Everything Outlets. Williams-Sonoma offers culinary and serving equipment for those consumers interested in furnishing their kitchens. The Pottery Barn features items in casual home furnishings, flatware, and table accessories for either dining rooms or kitchens. Hold Everything offers innovative storage products. Since the focus is on satisfying specific target markets, efficiency is maximized.

The prevalence of niche marketing is present in the proliferation of new magazines. Magazines target special groups such as gay and lesbians; those interested in health and fitness or pets; and there is also *Aqua*, a bimonthly magazine for divers and those who snorkel.

Niche marketing is international in scope. For example, Hohner, a German-based firm, has over 80 percent of the world harmonica market; and Becker has half the world's oversized umbrella market. Niches would seem to be the norm in serving international global markets. Companies that are successful in serving affluent world markets emphasize continuous innovation, offer superior performance, and maintain regular contact with their customers.

4. Product life cycles have accelerated in affluent markets. Products directed to affluent consumers may have a limited life, especially if these products are new. Products pass through distinct stages—introduction, growth, maturity, and decline. Affluent customers who adopt new products are usually among the innovators in the introductory stage of the product life cycle and among the early adoptees in the growth stage. Fast fashion is a trend that Target and J. Crew have adopted that shortens the fashion cycle. Fast fashion shortens the cycle from design to finished product to 6 to 10 weeks compared to an industry average of 7 to 9 months. Mango, Zara, and H & M are the originators of this fast-fashion model. Charlotte Russe, Bebe, J. Crew, and Chico are copying some of these fast-fashion strategies that were introduced in Europe and dominate about 18 percent of the market. If other American retailers adopt fast-fashion strategies, the apparel market could be changed significantly and will give consumers a choice of a new and fresh merchandise lines frequently. Luxury jewelers such as Cartier and Bulgari have followed the apparel industry by having shorter product life cycles and seasonal collections.

Affluent consumers may contribute to the acceleration of the fashion cycle in uncertain periods of the economy and in their personal lives. These affluent consumers desire to remain at the top of the fashion cycle as a reward or, when feeling depressed, as a form of self-indulgence. To illustrate, in 2005 suede bags and shoes were acceptable, but in 2006 it became important for these affluent consumers to purchase crocodile or alligator bags and shoes. Prada's green crocodile bag was sold for $5,765. When other items such as black gloves and their belts became dated in 2005, other items such as colorful gloves and wider belts gained acceptance in 2006. Affluent consumers in purchasing fashion merchandise respond to a definite need in their lives that is consistent with their values and other societal trends.

The manufacturers of premium brands of jeans are introducing other luxury products because of their success in this market. The premium brands of jeans accounted for almost 20 percent of department store sales of jeans in 2005. In many urban areas, jeans are considered status symbols. To complement its $300 jeans, Paper, Denim and Cloth has introduced men's leather computer carrying cases at $400, blazers for men and women from $375 to $400, and men's shirts at $165. The computer cases are made out of distressed leather. The wool blazers are lined in cotton, and the men's shirts are made of Italian cotton. Chip and Pepper, known for the distressed look of its jeans, is now offering leather jackets for men and women that retail from $600 to $1000, velvet and cotton pants for women that sell from $150 to $180, and T-shirts starting at $55. The T-shirts feature the logos and mascots of 15 well-known colleges in the United States.

Product improvement coupled with declining prices is another aspect of the accelerating product life cycle. Since the price of labor to repair products is high, it makes little sense to repair products that are out of warranty. In many instances, shoes, watches, and other products are not repaired but discarded. The idea of inexpensive chic has penetrated the furniture industry with young professionals ready to trade up from IKEA to the West Elm retail brand.

Products that were once deemed the possessions of the wealthy have been successfully mainstreamed to all customer groups. Status symbols that were an expression of affluence were once radios, Kodak cameras, vacuum cleaners, electric washing machines, color televisions, microwave ovens, and designer jeans. Now, they are available to everybody in the mass market. With the increased size and changing aspirations of the affluent market, marketers are confronted with new challenges and opportunities to serve a significant and viable market.

The perception of affluence has changed over the years. Once upon a time, consumers were happy with one telephone, one television set, and an automobile. Homes had one or two bathrooms and one or two car garages. Affluent customers now demand ownership of multiple items, such as four or five bathrooms and three or four garage spaces. Every family member has their own computer. Opulence has arrived, and art has been integrated into the existing culture, presenting broader opportunities to serve affluent upscale markets.

5. The competitive environment requires continuous innovation. Distribution channels will constantly change in serving the affluent market as technology evolves. More companies are able to sell their services directly to customers without intermediaries. The Internet, e-mail, fax machines, cell phone, and online services that complement catalogs, direct mail, and telephone marketing firms are able to reach affluent consumers. For example, Affluent Lifestyle is a small direct marketing firm located in Boca Raton, Florida, that confines its business to targeting upscale consumers. The company has produced mailings for the Sinatra Theatre and the Palladio Italian Gourmet Market. EBay and Amazon.com also target affluent and upscale consumers. The Direct Marketing Association estimates that there about 10,000 mail-order catalogs of all types and about 200–300 are launched each year. The catalog business has been aided by the Internet, and it is approximately a $90 billion industry. Lands' End has added essays by such famous writers as David Mamet to target their well-educated customers.

Technology has dramatically increased the power of information transmission to shape brand presence. Not only are consumers given more information, but it is easier to get the information quickly.

Increasingly in the future, marketers are building alliances to gain acceptance and inspire their images. For example, Starbucks has extended its brand presence through alliances with Barnes & Noble, a reseller of books; and Ben & Jerry's, an upscale ice-cream firm. Wal-Mart, in its efforts to reach upscale buyers, has teamed with Hewlett-Packard in selling relatively inexpensive electronics. Hewlett-Packard is selling a desktop computer with a 15-inch flat-panel monitor for $398, a notebook computer for $398, a digital camera for $98.88, and a photo printer with LCD for $198.72 at Wal-Mart. The challenge is to select partners that extend and reinforce brand positioning. Firms such as IBM are learning that alliances are needed to either complement or leverage their capabilities and resources.

The world of affluence has even had an impact on McDonald's. After its customers defected to rival chains like Panera Bread, McDonald's assumed a risk. McDonald's responded with an upscale pricing strategy with some upscale menu items that successfully overcame resistance from their price-sensitive customers.

CONCLUDING COMMENT

It is impossible to develop one profile for all affluent consumers. There are affluent consumers who tend to be more social, more satisfied with their lives, more open-minded, and more confident about their future. There are also affluent consumers who do not believe they are affluent, who never left their neighborhoods, who drive older automobiles, and who still look for bargains at discount stores. There are affluent consumers who are financially confident. They are concerned about their image. They believe the house in which they live, their clothing, and their automobiles are reflections of themselves. They prefer brand-name merchandise, adopt new technological products quickly, and shop where they are recognized by salespeople. No matter how you describe the affluent consumer, you can assume they work hard and lead busy lives. Marketers recognize that affluent consumers represent a large and growing market that can only be reached successfully after careful research.

To collect information about this market, there are a variety of approaches available, from using materials in the library, company files, and the Internet to collect historical and current information to conducting surveys using mail, telephone, mall intercepts and personal interviews. There is the hard quantitative data that leaves little room for interpretation and the soft qualitative or behavioral data, which is used to explain why affluent consumers act the way they do in selecting and purchasing products and services. You can collect information by ethnography, which is the direct observation of individuals in their homes, at their jobs, and at social gatherings. The methodology is based on the belief that behavior occurs in a setting and that to understand why a consumer acts in a particular way in that setting you have to ask them in that setting. By using this research methodology, you are collecting information about social interactions when they take place. You are combining observation and discussion that includes hard and soft data to learn why the consumer behaves in a particular way before, during, and after the sale is made.

The affluent customer is concerned more about relationships than products and services. Marketers are interested in having a better understanding and knowledge of this market so that they can position their products and services to effectively meet the needs and expectations of affluent customers and most importantly retain these customers. Affluence and luxury products go hand-in-hand. The question remains, Why do consumers desire luxury goods? Why are Starbucks, Ben & Jerry's, Lexus, BMW, Williams-Sonoma, Victoria's Secret, and Coach successful in reaching the affluent market?

Consumers today are more knowledgeable, selective, and discerning. More of them fall into the affluent income category so that even economic downturns hardly have an impact on buying luxury goods. The affluent take pride in their purchasing expertise; they desire value, and cross shopping is commonplace. Shopping is fun for them and allows them to realize their aspirations. The affluent market is a global phenomenon.

Targeting the affluent consumer market involves a strong customer orientation supported by research. The most effective marketing strategies are built around lifestyle market segmentation analysis and positioning, and they provide the products and services that meet the needs and wants of the affluent customer and those customers who trade up in their purchasing behavior.

Notes

CHAPTER 1

1. Marion Asnese, Andy Bornstein, and Douglas King, "The Changing Face of Affluence," *Money Magazine*, Fall 2002, pp. 42–56.

2. *The Mendelsohn Affluent Survey* (New York: Mendelsohn Media Research Inc., 2005), pp. 1–31.

3. "Survival of the Richest," *Forbes*, March 17, 2003, p. 132.

4. Alex Taylor, "Got $300,000," *Fortune*, January 20, 2003, pp. 118–124.

5. Shelly Brenchi, "For Frugal Fashionistas," *Wall Street Journal*, August 15, 2003, p. B1.

6. Marion Asnese, Andy Bornstein, and Douglas King, "The Changing Face of Affluence," *Money Magazine*, Fall 2002, pp. 42–56.

7. David Leonbordt, "Defining the Rich in the World's Wealthiest Nation," *New York Times*, January 12, 2003, sec. 4, pp. 1–4.

8. David Whelan, "Census 2000: Black Boom in the 'Burbs'," *American Demographics* 23 (July 2001): 19–20.

9. Jennifer Aaker, "The Malleable Self: The Role of Self-Expression in Persuasion," *Journal of Marketing Research* 36 (February 1999): 45–58.

CHAPTER 2

1. Tiffany Meyers, "Marketers Learn Luxury Isn't Simply for the Very Wealthy," *Advertising Age*, September 13, 2004, p. S2.

2. David Leonhardt, "Defining the Rich in the Worlds' Wealthiest Nation," *The New York Times*, sec. 4, January 12, 2003, p. 16.

3. Christina DeValle, "They Know Where You Live—and How You Buy," *Business Week*, February 7, 1994, p. 89.

4. Everett Rogers, *Diffusion of Innovations*, 4th Edition (New York: The Free Press, 1995).

5. James Lucas, "The Critical Shopping Experience," *Marketing Management* (Spring 1999): 60–62.

CHAPTER 3

1. Abraham H. Maslow, "A Theory of Human Motivation," *Psychological Review* 50 (July 1943): 370–96.

2. Rebecca Gardyn, "Live Richly," *American Demographics* 25 (April 2003): 16.

3. Edward M. Tauber, "Why Do People Shop?" *Marketing Management* 4 (Fall 1995): 58–62.

4. Thorstein Veblen, *The Theory of the Leisure Class* (New York: Macmillan, 1899).

CHAPTER 4

1. Based on the U.S. Census Bureau, *Statistical Abstract of the United States: 2000*, Section 14, *Income, Expenditures and Wealth*, pp. 447–481.

2. Miriam Jordan, "Seeking Growth, Ski Areas Target Minorities," *Wall Street Journal*, December 22, 2004, pp. B1, 8.

3. B. Johnson, "The Gay Quarterly: Advertising's Most Elusive, Yet Lucrative Target Market Proves Difficult to Measure," *Advertising Age* 64 (January 1993): 29–34.

4. Robert Frank, "U.S. Led a Resurgence Last Year Among Millionaires World-Wide," *Wall Street Journal*, June 15, 2004, pp. P1, 8.

5. Thomas J. Stanley, *The Millionaire Mind* (Kansas City, MO: Andrews McNeel Publishing, 2000), pp. 6–9.

6. Thomas J. Stanley, *The Millionaire Next Door: The Surprising Secrets of America's Wealthy* (New York: Pocket Books, a division of Simon & Schuster Inc., 1996).

CHAPTER 5

1. James P. Rubin, "Parents Scrape to Find Sports Dreams," *Wall Street Journal*, June 4, 2003, p. D2.

2. Brian Goff, and Arthur A. Fleisher III, *Spoiled Rotten: Affluence, Anxiety and Social Decay in America* (Boulder: Westview Press, 1999), pp. 1–20.

3. Marion Asnese, Andy Bornstein, and Douglas King, "The Changing Face of Affluence," *Money Magazine*, Fall 2002, pp. 42–56.

4. Richard Florida, *The Rise of the Creative Class* (New York: Basic Books, 2002).

CHAPTER 6

1. Kurt Lewin, *A Dynamic Theory of Personality* (New York: McGraw-Hill, 1935): 54.

2. David Riesman, Nathan Glazer, and Revel Denney, *The Lonely Crowd* (New Haven, CT: Yale University Press, 1950).

3. Paul M. Herr, Frank R. Kardes, and John Kim, "Effects of Word-of-Mouth and Product Attribute Information on Persuasion: An Accessibility-Diagnosity Perspective," *Journal of Consumer Research* 17 (March 1991): 454–462.

4. Jan Gertner, "What Is Wealth?" *Money* 29 (December 2000): 94–107.

5. Susan Carey, and Evan Perez, "Competition Heats up in Private Jet Rentals," *Wall Street Journal*, October 23, 2003, p. D1, 4.

6. Christina Binley, "Shooting for Stars, Hotels Add Spas, Spritzers, Umbrellas," *Wall Street Journal*, October 17, 2003, pp. P1, 6.

7. George P. Moschis, Evelyn Lee, Aril Mathur, and Jennifer Streutman, *The Maturing Marketplace: Buying Habits of Baby Boomers and Their Parents* (Westport, CT: Quorum Books, 2000).

8. Robert Frank, "Affluence Rises for Asian-Americans," *Wall Street Journal*, February 25, 2004, p. D4.

9. Deborah L. Vence, "Multicultural Marketing," *Marketing News*, September 1, 2005, p. 37.

CHAPTER 9

1. Paul H. Ray, "The Emerging Culture," *American Demographics* 19 (February 1997): 29–34, 56.

2. Annette Miller, "The Millennial Mind-Set." *American Demographics* 21 (January 1999): 60–65.

3. David Futrelle, Jan Birger, and Pat Regnier, "Getting Rich in America," *Money* (May 2005): 101–103.

4. Susan M. Graninno, "Is Populism Death for Luxury?" *Advertising Age* (October 4, 2004): 36.

5. James O. Mitchell, "Finances of the Affluent: Special Analysis of the Survey of Consumer Finances," *Journal of Financial Service Professionals* (September 2002): 64–71.

Selected Bibliography

BOOKS

Aaker, David. *Brand Portfolio Strategy*. New York: Free Press, 2004.

Abrams, Bill. *The Observational Research Handbook: Understanding How Consumers Live with your Product*. Lincolnwood, IL: NTC Business Books, 2000.

Alba, Richard, and Victor Nee. *Remaking the American Mainstream*. Boston: Harvard University Press, 2003.

Amber, Tim. *Marketing and the Bottom Line*. 2nd ed. London: FT Prentice-Hall, 2003.

Atkin, Douglas. *The Culting of Brands*. New York: Penguin, 2004.

Baldcock, Robert. *Destination Z: The History of the Future*. New York: John Wiley and Sons, 1999.

Banks, Stephen. *Multicultural Public Relations: A Social-Interpretive Approach*. 2nd ed. Ames, IA: Iowa State University Press, 2000.

Barnes, James G. *Secrets of Customer Relationship Management: It's All About How You Make Them Feel*. New York: McGraw-Hill, 2001.

Barone, Michael. *The New Americans: How the Melting Pot Can Work Again*. Washington, DC: Regency, 2001.

Berry, Christopher J. *The Idea of Luxury: A Conceptual and Historical Investigation*. New York: Cambridge University Press, 1994.

Berry, Leonard J. *Discovering the Soul of Service*. New York: Free Press, 1999.

Best, Robert J. *Market Based Management*. Upper Saddle River, NJ: Prentice-Hall, 2000.

Black Americans. Ithaca, NY: American Demographic Books, 1994.

Brooks, David *Bobos in Paradise: The New Upper Class and How They Got There*. New York: Simon & Schuster, 2000.

Cox, W. Michael, and Richard Alm. *Myths of the Rich and Poor.* New York: Basic Books, 1999.

Cram, Tony. *Customers That Count: How to Build Living Relationships with Your Most Valuable Customers.* London: Financial Times Prentice Hall, 2001.

Cross, Gary. *An All-Consuming Century: Why Commercialism Won Out in America.* New York: Columbia University Press, 2000.

Dalgic, Tevfik. *Handbook of Niche Marketing.* New York: The Haworth Press, 2006.

Davis, Scott. *Brand Asset Management.* San Francisco: Jossey-Bass, 2000.

Falk, Pasi, and Colin Campbell, eds. *The Shopping Experience.* London: Sage, 1997.

Florida, Richard C. *The Rise of the Creative Class.* New York: Basic Books, 2002.

Frank, Robert H. *Luxury Fever: Money and Happiness in an Era of Excess.* New York: Free Press, 1999.

Frank, Thomas C. *The Conquest of Cool: Business Culture, Counter Culture and the Rise of Hip Consumerism.* Chicago: University of Chicago Press, 1997.

Gabbott, Mark, and Gillian Hogg. *Consumers and Services.* New York: Wiley, 1998.

Galbraith, John Kenneth. *The Affluent Society.* Boston: Houghton-Mifflin, 1998.

Garcia, Guy. *The New Mainstream.* New York: HarperCollins, 2004.

Glazer, Nathan. *We Are All Multiculturalists Now.* Boston: Harvard University Press, 1997.

Gobe, Marc. *Emotional Branding: The New Paradigm for Connecting Brands to People.* New York: Allworth Press, 2001.

Grimshaw, David. *Bringing Geographical Information Systems into Business.* 2nd ed. New York: Wiley, 2000.

Gummesson, Evert. *Total Relationship Marketing.* Boston: Butterworth-Heinemann, 1999.

Halter, Marilyn. *Shopping for Identity: The Marketing of Ethnicity.* New York: Schocken Books, 2000.

Handy, Charles. *The Elephant and the Flea: Reflections of a Reluctant Capitalist.* Boston: Harvard Business School Press, 2002.

Hartley, Robert F. *Marketing Mistakes and Successes.* 8th ed. New York: Wiley, 2000.

Hill, Sam, and Glenn Rifkin. *Radical Marketing.* New York: HarperBusiness, 1999.

Hill, Nigel, and Jim Alexander. *Handbook of Customer Satisfaction and Loyalty Measurement.* 2nd ed. Brookfield, VT: Gower, 2000.

Holt, Douglas B. *How Brands Become Icons: The Principles of Cultural Branding.* Cambridge, MA: Harvard Business School Press, 2004.

Horner, Louise L., ed. *Hispanic Americans: A Statistical Sourcebook.* Palo Alto, CA: Information Publications, 1995.

Horowitz, Daniel. *The Anxieties of Affluence.* Amherst, MA: University of Massachusetts Press, 2005.

Hughes, Arthur M. *Strategic Database Marketing.* 2nd ed. New York: McGraw-Hill, 2000.

Iacobucci, Dawn, and Bobby Calder, eds. *Kellogg on Integrated Marketing.* New York: John Wiley & Sons, 2003.

Kardes, Frank R. *Consumer Behavior and Managerial Decision-Making.* 2nd ed. Upper Saddle River, NJ: Prentice Hall-2003.

Kates, Steven M. *Twenty Million New Customers.* New York: The Haworth Press, 1998.

Kaul, Chandrika, and Valerie Tomaselli-Moschovitis, eds. *Statistical Handbook on Consumption and Wealth in the United States.* Phoenix, AZ: Oryx Press, 1999.

Keister, Lisa. *Wealth in America: Trends in Wealth Inequality.* Cambridge: Cambridge University Press, 2000.
Keller, Kevin L. *Building, Measuring, and Managing Brand Equity.* Upper Saddle River, NJ: Prentice-Hall, 2003.
Kelly, Kelvin. *New Rules for the New Economy.* New York: Viking, 1998.
Kirk, Bradford. *Lessons from a Chief Marketing Officer.* New York: McGraw-Hill, 2003.
Kohl, Susan. *Getting Attention: Leading-Edge Lessons for Publicity and Marketing.* Boston: Butterworth-Heinemann, 2000.
Korzenny, Felipe, and Betty Ann Korzenny. *Hispanic Marketing: A Cultural Perspective.* Boston: Elsevier Butterworth-Heinemann, 2005.
Kotler, Philip. *Kotler on Marketing.* New York: The Free Press, 1999.
Kumaa, Nirmatya. *Marketing as Strategy.* Boston: Harvard Business School Press, 2004.
Lasn, Kalle. *Culture Jam: The Uncooling of America.* New York: William Morrow, 1999.
Lears, Jackson. *Fables of Abundance: A Cultural History of Advertising in America.* New York: Basic Books, 1994.
Lewis, David, and Darren Bridger. *The Soul of the New Consumer: Authenticity—What We Buy and Why in the New Economy.* London: Nicholas Brealey Publishing, 2000.
Linstrom, Martin, and Tim Frank Andersen. *Brand Building on the Internet.* London: Kogan Page, 2000.
Maklaw, Stan, and Simon Knox. *Competing on Value.* Upper Saddle River, NJ: Prentice-Hall 2000.
Marchand, Roland. *Advertising the American Dream.* Berkeley: University of California Press, 1985.
Maslow, Abraham H. *Motivation and Personality.* 3rd ed. New York: Harper & Row, 1987.
Meredith, Geoffrey, and Charles D. Schewe. *Defining Markets, Defining Moments: American's Seven Generational Cohorts: Their Shared Experiences and Why Businesses Should Care.* New York: Hungry Minds, 2002.
Michman, Ronald D., Edward M. Mazze, and Alan J. Greco. *Lifestyle Marketing: Reaching the New American Consumer.* Westport, CT: Praeger, 2003.
Miller, Daniel. *A Theory of Shopping.* Ithaca, NY: Cornell University Press, 1998.
Nevaer, Louis E.V. *The Rise of the Hispanic Market in the United States.* New York: M.C. Sharpe Inc. 2004.
Norman, Donald A. *Why We Love (or Hate) Everyday Things.* New York: Basic Books, 2004.
Nunes, Paul, and Brian Johnson. *Mass Affluence.* Boston: Harvard Business School Press, 2004.
Ohmann, Richard. *Selling Culture: Magazines, Markets and Class at the Turn of the Century.* London and New York: Verso, 1996.
Oliver, R. L. *Satisfaction: A Behavioral Perspective on the Consumer.* New York: Irwin/McGraw-Hill, 1997.
Ostroff, Jill. *Successful Marketing to the 50+.* Englewood Cliffs, NJ: Prentice-Hall, 1989.
Pine, Joseph, and James H. Gilmore. *The Experience Economy.* Boston: Harvard Business School Press, 1999.
Popcorn, Faith. *EVEolution: The Eight Truths of Marketing to Women.* New York: Hyperion, 2000.

Postrel, Virginia. *The Substance of Style.* New York: HarperCollins, 2003.
Reichheld, Frederick F. *The Loyalty Effect.* Boston: Harvard Business School Press, 1996.
Ries, Al, and Laura Ries. *The Fall of Advertising and the Rise of PR.* New York: HarperBusiness, 2002.
Ries, Al, and Jack Trout. *Positioning the Battle for Your Mind.* New York: Warner Books, 1982.
Rogers, Everett M. *Diffusion of Innovations.* 5th ed. New York: Free Press, 2003.
Rud, Olivia Parr. *Data Mining Cookbook: Modeling Data for Marketing, Risk and Customer Relationship Management.* New York: Wiley, 2001.
Rust, Roland T., Katherine N. Lemon, and Das Narayandas, *Customer Equity Management.* Upper Saddle River, NJ: Pearson Prentice-Hall, 2005.
Samuel, Larry. *The Trend Commandments: Turning Cultural Fluency into Marketing Opportunity.* New York: Bang Zoom Books, 2003.
Schiffman, L. G., and Leslie L. Kanuk. *Consumer Behavior.* 8th ed. Upper Saddle River, NJ: Pederson, 2004.
Schor, Juliet. *The Overspent American.* New York: Basic Books, 1998.
Schrieber, Alfred L. *Multicultural Marketing.* Lincolnwood, IL: NTC Business Books, 2001.
Selden, Larry, and Geoff Colvin. *Angel Customers and Demon Customers.* New York: Portfolio, 2003.
Seybold, Patricia P. *The Customer Revolution.* New York: Crown Business, 2001.
Silverstein, Michael J., and Neil Fiske. *Trading Up.* Rev. ed. New York: Portfolio, The Penguin Group, 2005.
Sirgy, M. Joseph. *Handbook of Quality-of-Life Research: An Ethical Marketing Perspective.* Boston: Kluwer Academic Publishers, 2001.
Solomon, Michael R., and Nancy J. Rabott. *Consumer Behavior in Fashion.* Upper Saddle River, NJ: Prentice-Hall, 2004.
Stanley, Thomas J., *The Millionaire Mind.* Kansas City, MO: Andrews McNeel Publishing, 2000.
Stanley, Thomas, and William Danko. *The Millionaire Next Door.* New York: Pocket Star Books, 1996.
Strasser, Susan. *Satisfaction Guaranteed: The Making of the American Mass Market.* New York: Pantheon Books, 1989.
Swaddling, David C., and Charles Miller. *Customer Power.* Dublin, OH: The Wellington Press, 2001.
Swift, Ronald S. *Accelerating Customer Relationships.* Upper Saddle River, NJ: Prentice-Hall, 2001.
Terrill, Craig, and Arthur Middlebrooks. *Market Leadership Strategies for Service.* Lincolnwood, IL: NTC Business Books, 1999.
Trout, Jack. *Differentiate or Die.* New York: Wiley, 2000.
Underhill, Paco. *Call of the Mall.* New York: Simon & Schuster, 2004.
Underhill, Paco. *Why They Buy: The Science of Shopping.* New York: Simon & Schuster, 1999.
Valdes, M. Isabel. *Marketing to American Latinos.* Ithaca, NY: Paramount Marketing Publishing, 2002.
Vandermerwe, Sandra. *Customer Capitalism: Increasing Returns in New Market Spaces.* London: Nicholas Brealey, 1999.
Veblen, Thorstein. 1899. *The Theory of the Leisure Class.* Repr. New York: Penguin Books, 1994.

Weiss, Michael J. *The Clustered World.* Boston: Little, Brown and Company, 2000.

Whybrow, Peter C. *American Mania: When More Is Not Enough.* New York: W. W. Norton & Company, 2005.

Wipperfürth, Alex. *Brand Hijack: Marketing without Marketing.* New York: Portfolio, 2005.

Wood, Marian Burk. *The Marketing Plan: A Handbook.* Upper Saddle River, NJ: Prentice-Hall, 2003.

Zaltman, Gerald. *How Customers Think.* Boston: Harvard Business School Press, 2003.

Zyman, Sergio. *The End of Marketing As We Know It.* New York: Harper-Business, 1999.

ARTICLES

Aaker, Jennifer, Anne Brumbaugh, Sonya Grier and Patti Williams: "Empathy versus Pride: The Influence of Emotional Appeals across Cultures." *Journal of Consumer Research* 25 (December 1998): 241–261.

Ainscough, Thomas L., and Carol M. Motley. "Will You Help Me Please? The Effects of Race, Gender and Manner of Dress on Race." *Marketing Letters* (May 2000): 129–136.

Alba, Joseph W., and J. Wesley Hutchinson. "Knowledge Calibrations: What Consumers Know and What They Think They Know." *The Journal of Consumer Research* 27 (September 2000): 123–156.

Albonette, J. G., and L. Dominguez. "Major Influences on Consumer-Goods Marketers' Decision to Target U.S. Hispanics." *Journal of Advertising Research* 29, no. 1 (1989): 9–21.

Arjona, L. D., R. Shah, A. Tinivelli, and A. Weiss. "Marketing to the Hispanic Consumer." *McKinsey Quarterly* 3 (1998): 106–114.

Arnold, Mark J., and Kristy E. Reynolds. "Hedonic Shopping Motivations." *Journal of Retailing* 79, no. 2 (2003): 77–95.

Asnes, Marion. "The Affluent American." *Money* 32 (December 2003): 40.

Bagozzi, Richard P., Mahesh Gopinath, and Prashanth U. Nyer. "The Role of Emotion in Marketing." *The Journal of the Academy of Marketing Science* 27 (Spring 1999): 184–206.

Bakewell, Cathy, and Vincent-Wayne Mitchell. "Generation Y Female Consumer Decision-Making Styles." *International Journal of Retail and Distribution Management* 31: 95–106.

Baumgartner, Hans. "Toward a Personology of the Consumer." *Journal of Consumer Research* 29 (September 2002): 286–292.

Bazerman, Max H. "Consumer Research for Consumers." *Journal of Consumer Research* 27 (March 2001): 499–504.

Berger, Paul D., and Nada I. Nasr. "Customer Lifetime Value: Marketing Models and Applications." *Journal of Interactive Marketing* 12 (January 1998): 17–30.

Bhatnagar, Amit, and Sanjoy Ghose. "Segmenting Consumers Based on the Benefits and Risks of Internet Shopping." *The Journal of Business Research* 57 (December 2004): 1352–1360.

Blattberg, Robert C., and John Deighton. "Manage Marketing by the Customer Equity Test." *Harvard Business Review* 74 (July–August 1996): 136–144.

Bolton, Ruth N. "A Dynamic Model of the Duration of the Customer's Relationship with a Continuous Service Provider: The Role of Satisfaction." *Marketing Science* 17 (January 1998): 45–65.

Bowen, John J. "Narrow It Down: Serve One Affluent Niche Market—and Serve It Well—and You'll Be Better Positioned to Build Your Business." *Financial Planning*, July 1, 2005,1.

Braun, Ottmar L., and Robert A. Wicklund. "Psychological Antecedent of Conspicuous Consumption." *Journal of Economic Psychology* 10 (2): 161–186.

Braverman, Beth. "Poll: Hispanic Market Ripe for Retail Jewelers." *National Jewelers* 99 (April 1, 2005): 6.

Bristol, Terry, and Tamara F. Mangleburg. "Not Telling the Whole Story: Teen Deception in Purchasing." *Journal of the Academy of Marketing Science* 33 (Winter 2005): 79–95.

Brown, Ann. "Marketing to Black Travelers." *Black Enterprise* 27 (March 1997): 97.

Brown, Stephen. "Torment Your Customers (They'll Love It)." *Harvard Business Review* 81 (October 2003): 82–88.

Burns, John. "The Retirement Housing Boom." *Professional Builder* 68 (June 2003): 67.

Bush, Victoria D., Alan J. Bush, Paul Clark, and Robert P. Bush. "Girl Power and Word-of-Mouth Behavior in the Flourishing Sports Market." *The Journal of Consumer Marketing* 22 (2005): 257–264.

Carbone, Lewis P. "What Makes Customers Tick." *Marketing Management* 12 (July–August 2003): 23–27.

Cardone, M. Mercedes. "Affluent Shoppers Like Their Luxury Goods Cheap." *Advertising Age* 74 (December 1, 2003): 6.

"Catching the Hispanic Market Wave." *PR News* 61 (March 16, 2005): 1.

Chaudhuri, A., and M. B. Holbrook. "The Chain of Effects from Brand Trust and Brand Effect to Brand Performance: The Role of Brand Loyalty." *The Journal of Marketing* 15 (April 2001): 81–94.

Chen, Haipeng, Sharon Ng, and Akshay R. Rao. "Cultural Differences in Consumer Impatience." *Journal of Marketing Research* 42 (August 2005): 291–301.

Chernev, Alexander. "Goal Orientation and Consumer Preference for the Status Quo." *The Journal of Consumer Research* 31 (December 2004): 557–565.

Clayton, Michelle. "They're Getting Old. They're Tired. They're Stressed. But They Have Money to Invest." *America's Community Banker* 8 (February 1999): 26–30.

Cooper, Lee. "Strategies Marketing Planning for Radically New Products." *Journal of Marketing* 64 (January 2000): 1–16.

Corneo, Giacoma, and Olivier Jeanne. "Conspicuous Consumption, Snobbism and Conformism." *Journal of Public Economics* 66 (October 1997): 55–71.

Cox, Anthony D., Dena Cox, and Gregory Zimet. "Understanding Consumer Responses to Product Risk Information." *Journal of Marketing*, January 2006, 79–91.

Cui, Geng. "Marketing to Ethnic Minority Consumers: A Historical Journey (1932–1997)." *Journal of Macromarketing* 21 (June 2001); 23–31.

Cui, Geng. "Marketing Strategies in a Multi-Ethnic Environment." *Journal of Marketing Theory and Practice* 5, no. 1 (Winter 1997): 122–134.

Curasi, Carolyn Folkman, Linda Price, and Eric J. Arnoud. "How Individuals' Cherished Possessions Become Families' Inalienable Wealth." *The Journal of Consumer Research* 31 (December 2004): 609–622.

Cutler, Ivan Saul. "Open the Way to Market Niches and Riches." *Upholstery Design & Management* 16 (December 2003): 44.

Davidson, Charlie. "In the Service of Baby Boomers: A Seismic Mind Shift for Financial Service Providers." *The CPA Journal* 75 (September 2005): 18–19.

Dempsey, Key. "How to Avoid Costly Mistakes in the Affluent Women's Market." *Journal of Financial Service Professionals* 59 (November 2005): 35–37.

DeSimone, Marcella. "Reaching African-American Prospects." *National Underwriter* 106 (June 10, 2002): 6.

DeVaney, Sharon A. "The Millionaire Next Door: The Surprising Secrets of America's Wealthy." *The Journal of Consumer Affairs* 34 (Summer 2000): 147–149.

Dwyer, Robert F. "Customers Lifetime Valuation to Support Marketing Decision-Making." *Journal of Direct Marketing* 11 (April 1997): 6–13.

Edlin, Mari. "Hispanic Market Momentum." *Managed Healthcare Executive* 11 (June 1, 2005): 10.

Epstein, Jeffrey H. "The Net Generation Is Changing the Marketplace." *The Futurist* 32, no. 3 (1998): 14.

Fournier, Susan. "Consumers and Their Brands: Developing Relationship Theory in Consumer Research." *The Journal of Consumer Research* 24 (March 1998): 343–373.

Frank, Robert H., "Does Growing Inequality Harm the Middle Class?." *Eastern Economic Journal* 26 (Summer 2000): 251–264.

Friedman, Hersey H. "The Impact of Jewish Values on Marketing and Business Practices." *Journal of Macromarketing* 21 (June 2001): 74–80.

Garbato, Debby. "Wal-Mart Targets Affluent Shoppers." *Retail Merchandiser* 45 (July 2005): 6–7.

Garfein, Richard T., "Cross-Cultural Perspectives on the Dynamics of Prestige." *Journal of Sciences Marketing* 3 (Summer 1989): 17–24.

Gabarino, Ellen, and Mark Johnson. "The Different Roles of Satisfaction, Trust and Commitment for Relational and Transactional Consumers." *Journal of Marketing* 63 (April 1999): 70–87.

Goodwin, Cathy, and James W. Gentry. "Life Transition as a Basis for Segmentation." *Journal of Segmentation in Marketing* 4, no. 1 (2000): 71–83.

Gotsis, Tracey. "The High-Stakes Luxury Market." *Chain Store Age* 80 (August 2004): 164.

Grayson, Kent, and Radan Martinec. "Consumer Perceptions of Iconicity and Indexicality and Their Influence on Assessments of Authentic Market Offerings." *Journal of Consumer Research* 31 (September 2004): 296–313.

Green, Barbara. "Age Group Marketing." *National Jeweler* 97 (February 1, 2003): 48–50.

Grier, Sonya A., and Anne M. Brumbaugh. "Noticing Cultural Differences: Ad Meanings Created by Target and Non-Target Markets." *Journal of Advertising* 28, no. 1 (1999): 79–93.

Guilford, Dave. "GM Beefs Up Its Quest to Reach Minorities." *Automotive News* 76 (February 4, 2002): 38.

Guiry, Michael, Anne W. Magi, and Richard Lutz. "Defining and Measuring Recreational Shopper Identity." *Journal of the Academy of Marketing Service* 34 (Winter 2006): 74–83.

Gupta, Sunil, Donald Lehmann, and Jennifer Ames Stuart. "Valuing Customers." *Journal of Marketing Research* 41, (January 2004): 1–6.

Guyette, James E. "The Loyal Hispanic Market Is Hardly a 'Niche' Market." *Aftermarket Business* 114 (November 2004): 42.

Hall, Owen P., Jr. "Mining the Store." *Journal of Business Strategy* 22 (March–April 2001): 24–27.

Harrington, Cynthia. "The Rich Truly Are Different." *Journal of Accountancy* 197 (April 2004): 32–36.

Haytko, Diana L., and Julie Baker. "It's All at the Mall: Exploring Adolescent Girls' Experiences." *The Journal of Retailing* 80, no. 1 (2004): 67–83.

Herbig, P., and R. Yelkur. "Hispanic and Anglo Differences in Consumer Behavior." *Journal of International Marketing & Marketing Research* 23, no. 1 (1998): 47–56.

Hilton, James L., and William Von Hippel. "Stereotypes." *Annual Review of Psychology* 47 (1996): 237–271.

Holt, Douglas B. "What Becomes an Icon Most?" *Harvard Business Review* 81 (March 2003): 43–49.

Holt, Douglas B., and Craig J. Thompson. "Man-of-Action Heroes: The Pursuit of Heroic Masculinity in Everyday Consumption." *The Journal of Consumer Research* 31 (September 2004): 425–440.

Honore, Babette A. "Marketing and Selling Diverse Markets." *Advisor Today* 98 (December 2003): 38.

Johnson, Bradley. "Half of Boomers Hit the 50 Mark, But Spending Not Likely to Slow Down." *Advertising Age* 76 (July 4, 2005): 18.

Johnson, Bradley. "No Haggle Pricing Climbs Higher, Finds Fans Among Affluent, Educated." *Advertising Age* 76 (August 1, 2005): 23.

Johnson, Craig R., and Don E. Schultz. "A Focus on Customers." *Marketing Management* 13 (September/October 2004): 20–26.

Kim, Youn-Kyung, and Jikyeong Kang. "The Effects of Ethnicity and Product on Purchase Decision Making." *Journal of Advertising Research* 41, no. 2 (2001): 39–48.

King, Carole Ann. "Researchers Say U.S. Is Giving Birth to First Affluent Mass Market." *National Underwriter* 104 (May 8, 2000): 7–8.

Kinley, Tammy, and Linda Sivils. "Gift-Giving Behavior of Grandmothers." *Journal of Segmentation in Marketing* 4, no. 1 (2000): 53–70.

Kleber, Steve. "Keeping Up with Generation Jones." *Kitchen and Bath Business* 52 (June 2005): 30–31.

Koslow, Scott, Prem N. Shamdasani, and Ellen E. Touchstone. "Exploring Language Effects in Ethnic Advertising: A Sociolinguistic Perspective." *Journal of Consumer Research* 20, no. 4 (1994): 575–585.

Kostrunek, Shelley. "Find Strength in Numbers: Sell to Women 50 and Over." *National Underwriter* 109 (October 31, 2005): 16–17.

Krebsbach, Karen. "Attracting Multicultural Clients: As Ethnic Groups Grow in Size and Affluence, Banks Find a Pot of Gold at End of This Rainbow." *Bank Investment Marketing* 10 (May 1, 2002): 28.

Lee, Louise, and David Kiley. "Love Those Boomers." *Business Week* no. 3956 (October 24, 2005): 25.

Lewis, Michael. "The Influence of Loyalty Programs and Short-Term Promotions in Customer Retention." *Journal of Marketing Research* 41 (August 2004): 281–292.

Linville, Jeff. "How to Sell to Hispanics." *Furniture Today* 29 (November 29, 2004): 1.

Littrell, Mary A., Ma Yoon Jin, and Halepete Jaya. "Generation X, Baby Boomers, and Swing: Marketing Fair Trade Apparel." *Journal of Fashion Marketing and Management* 9 (2005): 407–419.

"Lifestyle Marketing." *Progressive Grocer* 76 (August 1997): 107–110.

Mangleburg, Tamara F., and Patricia M. Doney, and Terry Bristol. "Shopping with Friends and Teens' Susceptibility to Peer Influence." *Journal of Retailing* 80, no. 2 (2004): 101–116.

McCarthy, Michael. "Stalking the Elusive Teenage Trendsetter." *The Wall Street Journal* 19 (November 1998): B1–B10.

McDougall, Gordon. "Customer Retention Strategies: When Do They Pay Off?" *Services Marketing Quarterly* 22, no. 1 (2001): 39–55.

McNeal, James U. "Tapping the Three Kids' Markets." *American Demographics* 20 (April 1998): 34–39.

McNeil, Kimberly R., and Edna J. Ragins. "Staying in the Spa Marketing Game: Trends, Challenges, Strategies and Techniques." *Journal of Vacation Marketing* 11 (January 2005): 31–40.

Menendez, T., and J. Yow. "The Hispanic Market: An Overview of the Major Markets." *Marketing Research* 1 (June 1989): 11–15.

Mina, Erica, and Stephen J. Hoch. "Spending Time v. Spending Money." *Journal of Consumer Research* 31 (September 2004): 313–323.

Mitchel, James O. "Finances of the Affluent: Special Analysis of the Survey of Consumer Finances." *Journal of Financial Service Professionals* 56 (September 2002): 64–71.

Morrison, Michael, and Michael Beverland. "In Search of the Right In-Store Music." *Business Horizons* 46 (November/December 2003): 77–82.

Neeklakantan, Shailaja. "Culture Class: How America's Youth Defines Luxury." *Brandweek* 40 (April 19, 1999): 66–69.

Noble, Stephanie M., and Charles D. Schewe. "Cohort Segmentation: An Exploration of Its Validity." *The Journal of Business Research* 56 (December 2003): 979–987.

Nunes, Paul F., Brian A. Johnson, and R. Timothy Breene. "Selling to the Moneyed Masses." *Harvard Business Review* 82 (July/August 2004): 94–104.

Payne, Adrian, and Pennie Frow. "A Strategic Framework for Customer Relationship Management." *Journal of Marketing* 69 (October 2005): 167–176.

Pratt, Laura. "How to Market to Millionaires." *Marketing* 110 (May 9, 2005): 12–13.

"Price, Quality Key for Hispanic Customers." *HFN: The Weekly Newspaper for the Home Furnishings Network* 79 (August 29, 2005): 18.

Price, Linda L., Eric J. Arnold, and Carolyn Folkman Curasi. "Older Consumers' Disposition of Special Possessions." *Journal of Consumer Research* 27 (September 2000): 179–201.

Ratchford, Brian T. "The Economics of Consumer Knowledge." *Journal of Consumer Research* 27 (March 2001): 397–411.

Raynor, Michael E., and Howard S. Weinberg. "Beyond Segmentation." *Marketing Management* 13 (November/December 2004): 22–28.

Reichheld, Frederick F., and Phil Schefter. "E-Loyalty: Your Secret Weapon on the Web." *Harvard Business Review* 78 (July–August 2000): 105–113.

Reid, Calvin. "New Effort to Reach Black Readers." *Publishers Weekly* 251 (July 26, 2004): 15.

Rivlin, Alice M., "The Challenges of Affluence." *Business Economics* 36 (January 2001): 6–12.

Roberts, James A., Chris Manolis, and John F. Tanner, Jr. "Family Structure, Materialism, and Compulsive Buying." *The Journal of the Academy of Marketing Science* 31 (Summer 2003): 300–311.

Rogers, Martha. "Customer Strategy: Observations from the Trenches." *Journal of Marketing* 69 (October 2005): 262–263.

Russell, Thomas. "Senior Moments." *Furniture Today* 28 (April 5, 2004): 12–13.

Rust, Roland T., Katherine N. Lemon, and Valerie A. Zeitaml. "Return to Marketing: Using Customer Equity to Focus Marketing Strategy." *Journal of Marketing* 68 (January 2004): 109–127.

Santoro, Elaine. "Direct Mail Is Top Media to Reach African-Americans." *Direct Marketing* 58 (December 1995): 10.

Seybold, Patricia B., "Get Inside the Lives of Your Customers." *Harvard Business Review* 79 (May 2001): 81–89.

Simpson, Ethel M., Thelma Snuggs, Tim Christiansen, and Kelli E. Simples. "Race, Homophily and Purchase Intentions and the Black Consumer." *Psychology and Marketing* 17 (October 2000): 877–889.

Spiegler, Marc. "Marketing Street Culture." *American Demographics* 18 (November 1996): 28–32.

Stock, Howard J. "The Gen X Factor: Why Banks Can't Afford to Ignore the Post-Boomers." *Bank Investment Consultant* 12 (January 12, 2004): 17.

Su, Chenting, Edward F. Fern, and Keying Yee. "A Temporal Dynamic Model of Spousal Family Purchase Decision Making." *The Journal of Marketing Research* 40 (August 2003): 268–281.

Suri, Rajneesh, and Kent B. Monroe. "The Effects of Time Constraints on Consumers' Judgments of Prices and Products." *The Journal of Consumer Research* 30 (June 2003): 92–104.

Taylor, Charles R., and Barbara B. Stern. "Asian-Americans: Television Advertising and the 'Model Minority' Stereotype." *Journal of Advertising* 26, no. 2 (1997): 47–61.

Thelen, Shawn, Sandra Mottner, and Barry Berman. "Data Mining: On the Trail to Marketing Gold." *Business Horizons* 47 (November/December 2004): 25–32.

Thomas, Jacqueline S. "A Methodology for Linking Customer Acquisitions to Customer Retention." *Journal of Marketing Research* 38 (February 2001): 262–268.

Urban, Glen L. "Customer Advocacy: A New Era in Marketing." *Journal of Public Policy and Marketing* 24 (May 2005): 155–159.

Urban, Glen L., and John R. Hauser. "Listening In to Find and Explore New Combinations of Customer Needs." *Journal of Marketing* 68 (April 2004): 72–87.

Wathieu, Luck. "Consumer Habituation." *Management Science* 50 (May 2004): 587–596.

Wellner, Alison Stein. "Ethnic Marketing Just Got Tougher." *Shopping Center World* 31 (March 2002): 12.

Wellner, Alison Stein. "The Forgotten Baby Boom." *American Demographics* 23 (February 2001): 46–51.

Williams, George. "Using Multi-Generational Marketing to Target Donors." *Nonprofit World* 23 (September/October 2005): 8–12.

Williams, Krissah. "Advertisers Embrace the Power That Gospel Music Has to Offer." *Washington Post* (November 27, 2005): A1.

Wyner, Gordon A. "Beyond Customer Understanding." *Marketing Management* 12 (July–August 2003): 6–7.

Wyner, Gordon A. "Segmentation of Architecture." *Marketing Management* 11 (March–April 2002): 6–7.

Zbar, Jeffrey D. "The Web Goes Multicultural." *Advertising Age* 70 (November 29, 1999): S1.

Zhang, Shi, and Bernd H. Schmitt. "Activating Sound and Meaning: The Role of Language Proficiency in Bilingual Consumer Environments." *The Journal of Consumer Research* 31 (June 2004): 220–228.

WORKING PAPERS

Carroll, Christopher D. "Why Do the Rich Have So Much." Working Paper 6549, National Bureau of Economic Research, 1998.

Dynan, Karen E., Jonathan Skinner, and Stephen P. Zeldes. "Do the Rich Have More?" Working Paper 7906, National Bureau of Economic Research, Cambridge, 2000.

Index

About the Authors

RONALD D. MICHMAN is professor emeritus of marketing at Shippensburg University in Pennsylvania. Previously, he held faculty positions at the Utica Campus of Syracuse University and at the University of New Hampshire. His articles have appeared in journals such as *Business Horizons*, *Industrial Marketing Management*, *Journal of Retailing*, and the *Journal of Business Strategy*. He served as associate editor of the abstract section of the *Journal of Marketing* and prepared bibliographies for the *American Marketing Association*. He is the author or coauthor of 10 books, including *Lifestyle Marketing: Reaching the New American Consumer* (Praeger, 2003), *Specialty Retailers: Marketing Triumphs and Blunders* (Quorum, 2001), and *The Food Wars: Marketing Triumphs and Blunders* (Quorum, 1998). He has also published books in the areas of retailing, marketing channels, and advertising.

EDWARD M. MAZZE is distinguished university professor of business administration and previously served as dean of the College of Business Administration and holder of the Alfred J. Verrecchia-Hasbro Inc. leadership chair in business at the University of Rhode Island. He consults extensively with industry executives and government officials on marketing, management, and economic development issues. He is a member of the board of directors of a number of public corporations. He is the author, coauthor, or editor of 11 books in business and over 150 articles appearing in journals such as the *Journal of Marketing*, *Journal of Retailing*, *Journal of Advertising Research*, and *Journal of Marketing Research*. He serves on the editorial board of the *Journal of Global Marketing*. He is coauthor with Ronald D. Michman of *Lifestyle Marketing: Reaching the New American Consumer* (Praeger, 2003), *Specialty Retailers: Marketing Triumphs and Blunders* (Quorum, 2001), and *The Food Wars: Marketing Triumphs and Blunders* (Quorum, 1998). He is often quoted on marketing issues in the media.